T0063092

Victorious Christian Living

DR. ALFRED EE & SANDRA EE

PARTRIDGE
A Penguin Random House Company

ISBN:	Hardcover	978-1-4828-9823-1
	Softcover	978-1-4828-9822-4
	Ebook	978-1-4828-9863-7

To order additional copies of this book, contact
Toll Free 800 101 2657 (Singapore)
Toll Free 1 800 81 7340 (Malaysia)
orders.singapore@partridgepublishing.com
www.partridgepublishing.com/singapore

Contents

Preface

This book is a formation of 38 years of ministering teaching sharing to tens of thousands from Asia to Europe and is basically dealing with the dilemma and practical daily issues of how one can live a successful life in a a world where we face so many things which many that hinder some from experiencing and enjoying an abundant life. In it are the keys, dynamics or principles if heartily in-calculated will enable us to live successfully and face the hindrances or opposition with confidence. We deal with practical issues of life and how we can breakthrough as we understand the nuema (Spirit,) psychology and dynamics of faith. The teachings lectures have been time tested by thousands bringing healing and blessings to tens of thousands You will find that as you understand and have a handle of the truths in the book your life will definitely change and you can bounce back from any setbacks in life and live in victory.

Foreword

In this book, Dr Alfred and Susan Ee cover a wide range of topics that enables a Christian to have Victorious Christian Living. The contents are not just words alone but are distillates of years of experiencing God in a blessed and miraculous way. Though Dr Ee functions primarily in the office of an Evangelist, yet he recognizes that Jesus never commanded us to make converts but disciples. Here then is a book for all disciples of Jesus Christ on how to live a victorious Christian life for the Glory of God.

Warmest regards & God bless

Ps Chew Weng Chee (MD)

SIBKL 4th Floor Bangunan Yin, Section 16/11 Jalan Damansara, 46350 Petaling Jaya, Selangor, Malaysia

Tel:603-79572701
Fax:603-79572702   website: www.sibkl.org.my

CHAPTER 1:

YOU ARE WHAT YOU THINK YOU ARE

Three thousand years ago, King Solomon wrote by the inspiration of God, "For as he thinks within himself, so he is". When Jesus Christ walked this earth, He said, "Out of the overflow of his heart, his mouth speaks" (Luke 6:45). So our minds, our thoughts are very important because they influence our speech and our actions. It is our thinking that makes us what we are. So what fills our thoughts and minds most and what influences our thoughts most? These are the questions we need to ask ourselves:

WHAT/ WHO CAN INFLUENCE OUR THINKING?

1. **The Family**
   What were our parents' attitudes towards us? Did they ever say, 'You're no good! You're a failure. You're just like your mother/father'? Often, our parents say things out of frustration, little realizing the continuing effects their words have upon us their children.

   Thanks be to God that by the power of the Holy Spirit we can be set free from the effects of these words for otherwise they can become a curse on us and we may never reach our full potential. In Christ Jesus we can do **all** things through Him that strengthens us.

2. **Unbelieving Friends**
   These friends can affect our thinking and thought patterns. They may tell us that being a Christian is okay but that we must not be too committed or too zealous for then we might become fanatical. Let's see what the Bible has to say about this.

   Revelations 3:15-16: "I know your deeds, that you are neither cold nor hot. I wish you were either one or the other! So, because you are lukewarm—neither hot nor cold—I am about to spit you out of my mouth."

3. **The World**
   The world influences our thinking through books, magazines, newspapers, music and television. Ladies, soap operas are not reality. The message they send you is that your man must be six feet tall, with a body built like Mr. Universe, he must be romantic 365 days in the year—and it's all right if he's not a Christian!

   The Bible's message is this:
   2 Corinthians 6:14-15 "Do not be yoked together with unbelievers. For what do righteousness and wickedness have in common? Or what fellowship can light have with darkness? What harmony is there between Christ and Belial?"

   What does a believer have in common with an unbeliever? The best man for you is GOD'S BEST, not the world's. Seek first the Kingdom of God and all these things will be added unto you— including the right man.

4. **Our Culture**
   Culture affects our thinking. Asian culture especially as many Asian religions contain a lot of superstitions. The result is that believers have many fears and the Word of God clearly tells us that Christians should not live in fear, they should live by faith. When we are born again by the Spirit of God, fear is replaced by faith. Thus we must cut ourselves off from superstitious fears. For example, Feng Shui should have no place in a Christian's life. Reading our horoscope is

a definite no-no. Only God knows our future. That is why we must keep ourselves in His Word.

2 Timothy 1:7 "For God hath not given us the Spirit of fear, but of power and of love and of a sound mind."

5. **Our Past Experiences**
   Our past experiences can shape and control our present and our future without our realizing it. For instance, we may have experienced a bad relationship with a man. This may cause us to fear entering into another relationship because we think all men are the same—which is far from the truth.

   We may also have made a mistake at our place of work resulting in our being embarrassed or humiliated. Then, for fear of repeating the mistake, we choose to stick to what we know. We choose to play safe and not attempt to advance in our career. We thus never achieve our highest potential.

   Philippians 3:13 & 14 "Brothers, I do not consider myself yet to have taken hold of it. But one thing I do: Forgetting what is behind and straining toward what is ahead, I press on toward the goal to win the prize for which God has called me heavenward in Christ Jesus."

   This is something we must remember:
   It is THE WORD that has to change our thinking.
   It is THE WORD that must influence our thinking daily.

WHY DO WE NEED TO CHANGE OUR THINKING?

1. **We need to do this because accordingly to Proverbs 23:7, 'We become who we think we are'.**

   Think 'failure' and we fail.
   Think 'sick' and we become sick.
   Think 'no money' and we'll get no money.
   Think 'problems' and we'll always have problems.
   Think 'fear' and 'worry' and there'll be no peace always.

And so the list goes on . . . .

We need to change our thinking because we want to be successful, victorious Christian men and women. We want to be able to rise and conquer. To do this, we need to think 'faith and 'victory'. We need to hold on to God's promise that we are more than conquerors through Christ Jesus.

2. **We need to change our thinking because the Word tells us to.**

    Romans 12:2 "Do not conform any longer to the pattern of this world, but be transformed by the renewing of your mind. Then you will be able to test and approve what God's will is—his good, pleasing and perfect will."

    'Be transformed' in the original text is in the present continuous tense. This means we must be continually transformed by the renewing of our minds. It is a daily process. The negative, old way of thinking must go and be replaced by God's Word—which are faith-filled words.

3. **We need to change our thinking so we can have minds filled with life and peace.**

    Romans 8:6 "For to be carnally minded is death, but to be spiritually minded is LIFE AND PEACE"

    What does being carnally-minded mean? It means being influenced by what we see, hear and feel instead of being influenced by the Holy Spirit through God's Word. For example, a carnally-minded person, when out of a job, will think like the world does: "I have no money, no security, no future." A spiritually-minded person, however, will ask: "What does the Word say?" It says, "Jehovah Jireh is my Provider."

    Matthew 6:25-26 "Therefore I tell you, do not worry about your life, what you will eat or drink; or about your body, what you will wear. Is not life more important than food, and the body more important than clothes? Look at the birds of the air; they do not sow or reap or store away in barns, and yet your heavenly Father feeds them. Are you not much more valuable than they?"

As we meditate on God's Word, it changes our thinking. Through God's Word we will have life and peace.

4. **We need to change our thinking so we can influence others.**

As we allow the Word of God to change our negative thoughts, our speech will change and our actions will change too. The 'I' will change and people will see the difference.

1 Peter 3:1-4 "Wives, in the same way be submissive to your husbands so that, if any of them do not believe the word, they may be won over without words by the behavior of their wives, when they see the purity and reverence of your lives. Your beauty should not come from outward adornment, such as braided hair and the wearing of gold jewelry and fine clothes. Instead, it should be that of your inner self, the unfading beauty of a gentle and quiet spirit, which is of great worth in God's sight."

We will have a gentle and quiet spirit if our thoughts are in line with the Word of God.

HOW DO WE CHANGE OUR THINKING?

1. **Have a Yielded Mind**
    Desire to do the will of God—by abiding in Christ. Every day, submit ourselves to God and this includes submitting our minds. When we are fully yielded to God, we will have the power of the Holy Spirit to think victorious thoughts and live victorious lives.

    John 15:4 "Remain in me, and I will remain in you. No branch can bear fruit by itself; it must remain in the vine. Neither can you bear fruit unless you remain in me."

2. **Have a Set Mind**

   Colossians 3:2 "Set your minds on things above, not on earthly things."

   Love heavenly things and be engrossed by them. Don't become engrossed with problems, problems, problems.

3. **Have a Renewed Mind**

   Romans 12:2 "Be ye transformed by the renewing of your mind."
   How do we renew our minds? Read, meditate, memorize and confess the Word.

   Joshua 1:8 "Do not let this Book of the Law depart from your mouth; meditate on it day and night, so that you may be careful to do everything written in it. Then you will be prosperous and successful."

   Pray in the Holy Spirit to build up our inner man and to break the curse of words over us. Praying in the Holy Spirit makes us more sensitive to God speaking to us through His Word.

4. **Have a Steadfast Mind**

   Isaiah 26: 3,4 "You will keep in perfect peace him whose mind is steadfast, because he trusts in you. Trust in the LORD forever, for the LORD, the LORD, is the Rock eternal."

   JEHOVAH (THE LORD) is the ROCK of ages, the undefeatable one, the Eternal Strong One. It is He who will keep us in perfect peace, without worry, fear or doubts.

5. **Have a Disciplined Mind**

   Philippians 4:8 "Finally, brothers, whatever is true, whatever is noble, whatever is right, whatever is pure, whatever is lovely, whatever is admirable—if anything is excellent or praiseworthy—think about such things."

A disciplined mind has the following characteristics:

True and honest thinking
Think about things that are true. The Bible is the truth. Meditate and think of His promises and faith-filled words.

Righteous thinking
Don't judge other people unfairly. First know all the facts. Stand up for righteous things. Be righteous in our business and God will bless us.

Pure/clean thinking
Don't listen to dirty jokes or yellow stories. Be careful of what you read and see.

Matthew 15:18 tells us, "Out of the abundance of the heart (mind) the mouth speaks."

Lovely thinking
Take time to appreciate the birds, animals, flowers . . . . We live in Kuala Lumpur now. I used to live in Taipei which is surrounded by hills. There, I used to quote Psalm 121:1: "I lift up my eyes to the hills—where does my help come from?"

Excellent thoughts
Don't think about gossip and slander. Don't always believe the worst of others. Think instead the best of them.

As we adhere to the above, we will develop a disciplined mind, a strong mind and consequently our speech and actions will be right.

You are what you think you are. Let our thoughts always be in line with the Word of God. Let His Word change our minds, our thinking, and we will be more than conquerors in every circumstance of our lives.

CHAPTER 2:

RENEWING OF THE MIND

God wants to do special things through us in these last days! The Israelites before they came back to rebuild the altars, had spent seventy years in exile. They had to rebuild the altars because they were too comfortable in Canaan. They had neglected their life especially their devotional life.

Once the spiritual life is neglected, the enemy will come in to kill, steal and destroy. Be alert to the enemy! The strategies he uses are:
To deceive us
To dominate us
To destroy us

The devil will tell us "Do not be too committed as Christians, go to church on Sundays but be casual on Monday to Saturday." These are the lies of the enemy and his deception.

Secondly, the enemy wants to dominate or control our thoughts, speech and actions so that we are led further away from God. Thirdly, he wants to destroy our spiritual life.

We are made of three parts—spirit, soul and body. Our spirit must be in right relationship with God, otherwise we hear other voices. We must take care of our spiritual needs or the enemy will sap our spiritual strength. Beware of being too comfortable like the Israelites. In Malaysia, we have too much e.g. food, clothes, good jobs. Let us be prepared to move on and take the land for Jesus. We must not be too comfortable—we must change our church life and not get in the same seat every Sunday. Don't' get too comfortable where you are.

In Taiwan, there was no heating in winter, I preached with a scarf around my neck and gloves on. The people were keen to hear the Word of God and would come and sit on the cold, hard wooden seats for two to three hours, singing, clapping and praising God. Would you come to church if the air-conditioners were not functioning? Or would you complain that was is too hot?

God wants to stir us up so that we will rise up like a strong army to take our land. Therefore watch our spiritual man. Stir up the gifts in us. Every one of us has gifts / talents / time. We should not neglect to build our altar. Don't work everyday till late at night which will kill your spiritual life. Men, do not be so consumed with your work otherwise like the Israelites, you will need to rebuild the altar. Parents, are your children walking with God? Do they see you praying, reading the Word or do they hear you moaning and groaning about others and for the service to finish early!
Be careful you do not neglect your spiritual man, your prayer life and the study of the Word of God.

Romans 12:2 "Do not conform to the pattern of this world."

Prayer and the Word of God can renew the mind.

Adam was the first man God created. He was a perfect person (before the fall). His spirit was in right relationship with God, he communed with God. His physical health was good and mentally, his thoughts were in line with God's thoughts. After the fall, spiritually, there was a gap between man and God; there was sickness and his thoughts were different and not in line with the Word of God.

Romans 12:20 ". . . man had a depraved mind." Before being born again, everyone of us has a depraved mind but thanks be to God, by the blood of Jesus shed for us, we are now forgiven and washed clean and filled with

His Spirit. Our thoughts can now be in line with His. The question is "Are they?" We must continuously check our thoughts. If we are in right relationship with God, we have been given power by the Holy Spirit to control them and reject bad and negative thoughts.

We must no longer have a depraved mind but we must have a mind constantly and daily renewed. The Greek word for "renew" means to renovate. For example, to renovate a house, you will take out all the old furniture and put in new furniture. If the old furniture is not completely removed, after a few months you will find that wood worm will have got into and destroyed the new furniture. There has to be a total replacement or renovation. The same way applies to the things of God. We take out the old depraved mind and by prayer and the Word of God have our mind renewed. It is important that selfish thoughts, sexual thoughts, negative thoughts are replaced with right thoughts, clean thoughts and positive thoughts. The negative thoughts come from the world and from non-Christians. These are the voices of the people who are led by the Holy Spirit e.g. This morning some people will say negative things like 'Pastor Sandra is preaching so long!' They moan about the length of the sermon or complain why the worship did not include more songs that they like to sing. Instead of moaning and groaning, they should be worshipping and seeking a touch from God. Don't let negative things come in.

We must remember that God want us to reject the negative thoughts. Even if you have read through all the books in the Bible (from Genesis to Revelation) you only have head knowledge. That is only half way to renewing your mind because head knowledge is not the same as heart knowledge. Head knowledge will kill us but heart knowledge is revelation and is life.

When we read the Word of God every day, we should know what God has spoken. We should hear the voice of God. Pray, "Lord, open my mind and help me to renew my mind by the power of your Spirit".

Illustration:
A man in Taiwan was fearful when he heard a lot of negative news of companies collapsing. He feared his company would also collapse even

though it was financially sound. These negative thoughts came to his mind and finally out of his mouth. Thank God there was no collapse but he needed renewal of the mind.

On another occasion, my husband was in the car with another person who kept on saying negative things about his church, the pastors and himself. My husband asked God "Why did you put me in this car with him?" The Lord said "to teach you patience". But what I want to point out is that all these negative words and moaning and groaning will drain up your spirit. Don't put your self down or others down.

The Word of God says that everyone is special. No matter who you are, you are special. Why? The answer is that God has redeemed us, we have been justified by the blood of Jesus and have the resurrection power in us, God has chosen us and we belong to Him. We are special and should not speak negatively. We should be positive, full of faith and full of the Word of God. This is not positive thinking or mind over matter. You must fill your mind with the Word of God. Say you can do all things—not you can't. Ah Lord God, nothing is too difficult for You.

HOW TO RENEW THE MIND?

Head knowledge is only half way to renewing the mind. We also need revelation of the Word. You do not have to go to Bible College to learn. I have been there and I have seen that some of the stuff that is taught can kill the brain and heart. Bible College may be an answer to some people but is not for everyone. In fact, I had to relearn some of the things that did not minister practically to us. I had to pray for the Holy Spirit to lead me to read the right books. You can have big discussions of the Holy Trinity; the second coming of Jesus but you I you do not see anyone healed, delivered or born again by the Holy Spirit then you know something is wrong.

Most of us will pray and ask God to change our circumstances, e.g. change our husband, change our wife—divorce and remarry. We have to be gentle here—there are some people who are divorced but it is not necessarily their fault, we have to love every one of them. The whole family—father, mother and children need to have their minds renewed by the Holy Spirit. We need to take the negative things out. For example, in Taiwan, the parents often call their children stupid. This is not the right way. We must love them. If our children do silly things, don't call them names or say negative things but stop them and discipline them.

I call both my boys Einstein I and Einstein II. Not that they are going to be extraordinarily brilliant, but we need to instill confidence in our children. Our children are wonderfully and fearfully made by God. We must speak the right things. Therefore make RIGHT CONFESSIONS. Confess the Word of God.

Colossians 3:1, 2 "You have been raised with Christ, so set your hearts on things above. Set your mind on things above not on earthly things."

Set our minds above—we must discipline our minds. Seek first the Kingdom of God and all these things will be added to you. (Matthew 6:33) Earthly things are our job, problems at home, financial difficulties, problems and difficult circumstances. Don't set your mind on these things. Renew your mind daily. Stand on the promises of God. Our minds are not fully renewed until we go to be with Jesus but do not give up trying.

Daily set our mind on heavenly things. Don't depend on the five senses that is sight, sound, smell, taste and touch. These are our soulish areas. Carnal Christians are controlled by their senses and circumstances. When I have a bad cold like today, some of you may think "Don't get near her or we will catch the cold". This is what your thoughts tell you, and because you thought so, you said it and you got it. Instead, I confess the Word of God and say: "In the Name of Jesus, I won't get a cold. I am healed by the stripes of Jesus. I am redeemed by the blood of Jesus." It works because it is in the Word of God. Stand firm on the Word of God.

Set our minds on things above and not just look at our circumstances and our feelings. For example, don't say that my marriage won't work. By your own words, you have condemned it. You must tell yourself God will restore your marriage and work a miracle for you by the power of His Spirit. Walk in the spirit. What you say, think and do is related. God showed me 5 to 6 years ago that I need to renew my mind daily and stop thinking negatively. Speak positive things and your action will not be negative. Some of you may say "you do not know our circumstances".

No matter what your circumstances, Praise God. No matter what you are going through, Praise Him. I don't know but Jesus knows everything and all that is in your heart. You are not on your own. Ladies, in your marriages—look God. God is in you, with you and for you. No matter what the enemy says, God will not destroy. He will build and restore. You are not on your own. You need to change the negative.

Joshua 24:15 "As for me and my household we will serve the Lord."

Many wives are burdened today with taking responsibility of work and to earn for the family while their husbands are smoking, drinking, etc. God has not forgotten you. God wants to touch your hearts. Be open to the touch of the Holy Spirit. Do something new this year. This is the year of new things.

Testimony:
When I was pregnant with David and staying in Taiwan, my doctor remarked that I was too old (at 36 years) and said many negative things. The outward circumstances looked like I would miscarry—I was bleeding and was bed ridden. One day, while reading the Old Testament, Exodus 21, 23, 25 and 26 the Word of God says: "You will not miscarry in this land".

By faith in the Word of God, I rejected the negative things said. I prayed: "Lord, in the Name of Jesus I am going to confess your Word and I will not miscarry." Praise God I did not miscarry. I have two boys and I had them at the ages of 36 and 38. I am 40 and not negative about reaching 40. We can live till 80 if we fear God and believe His Word. The Word of God says 70 years and if we are strong, 80 years. I always tell my husband that "you can't get rid of me that fast." We must be strong in the Lord and the might of His power. We need to be renewed by the Word.

HOW CAN WE BE RENEWED BY THE WORD OF GOD?

1. **Read the Word of God**
   Read the Bible—both the Old Testament and New Testament. Hear the voice of God speak. Hear the Holy Spirit say "This is the way, walk ye in it" Holy Spirit, you are my teacher, my guide, open my eyes to the truth in the Old Testament and New Testament. Praise God I read the Old Testament and did not miscarry. We must take hold of the Word of God.

   Read daily. We must have time. Everywhere in the world today people work very hard and long hours. When they get home late at night, they have dinner, read the newspapers, watched TV and by the time they read the Bible—they would have fallen asleep after five minutes. They could spend hours reading the newspapers and TV. What are our priorities?

2. **Meditate on the Word of God**
   It is not just reading fast to finish reading the Bible from Genesis to Revelation. We must chew on the Word of God over and over in our minds. Allow the Holy Spirit to work in our minds. Every morning take one Psalm and Proverb and meditate on it. David, despite his trials and weaknesses sang praises to God and came out of them. Meditate on the Word and we will rise above our negative circumstances. Our thoughts will change.

3. **Memorize the Word of God**
   Don't say you're getting old. What you think, you say and it shall be! Don't say I can't. But say "By the power of the Holy Spirit, the same resurrection power can restore my memory (This is a key for victory). If it is just too much stress—release the stress.

   One morning for the first time I drove on my own from Cheras to the church to Petaling Jaya. David said "Mummy if we get lost, we can pray to Jesus". I said "We will not get lost!" I only made a wrong turning once and I said "I'm not lost!"

"Trust the Lord with all your heart and do not rely on your own understanding." (Proverbs 3:5)

4. **Confess the Word of God**
    Put the Word of God in our mind and heart. There is power in what we say. At creation, God spoke "Let there be light" and there was light. We are made in the image of God and when we are born again, we are born of His image.

    Proverbs 18:21 "Life and death is in the power of the tongue."

    What you say is very important. If a person is sick, don't say pain. Say "By the blood of Jesus, I am healed." Don't look at your five senses. The outward senses tell you it is painful and the symptoms are still there but say I am healed. Just believe God. At age 19, I had rheumatism and the bones swelled up. One day after graduated from Bible College, the Holy Spirit said to me "You are healed". I heard the voice clearly and turned round and asked the woman next to me "Did you say that?" She replied "No I did not say anything." She thought I was cuckoo. When I went home, I was about to take my tablets and heard the voice of God again "You are healed". I flushed the tablets down the toilet and praise God, till now I have no sign of rheumatism and I am healed. One word of advice, do not do this unless you hear the voice of God for yourself.

The Word of God can renew our mind.
Prayer can renew our mind.
The voice of God can renew our mind.
Prepare to listen and obey His voice.
Our God is mighty.

Pray in the Holy Spirit
Pray in tongues.
Rebuild our altars.
Burnt offerings are our prayer life.

When we pray to God, are we moaning and groaning "change my husband, change my wife, change my children, and change my Pastor"?

Our prayer should be:
O Lord, change me. (This is one of the keys to breakthrough). We need our minds to be renewed. Our prayer life should be such we speak the Word of God, His promises and praise Him and the heavens will shake for us.

Pray in the Holy Spirit. Speaking in tongues is not a one time experience—we must continually be filled with the Holy Spirit. The Apostle Paul said that he spoke in tongues more than any of them. We must pray without ceasing and pray inthe Holy Spirit. Pray, Pray, Pray. When we pray in the spirit—it clears our mind and makes us stronger especially strong in the spirit, soul and five senses.

God wants our mind renewed, so that we are successful and positive and filled with the things of God.

God has not finished with anyone of us yet. He is shaking all things. Do not neglect the rebuilding of our altar (our devotional life). Jesus is the only One that can heal our hearts and set us free.

CHAPTER 3:

AS YOU SPEAK SO IT SHALL BE

What we say is so very powerful. In the book of James it tells us that our tongue is a small part of our body but it can cause so much destruction if it is not under the Lordship and control of the Holy Spirit. Likewise our tongue can be very effective as we speak the right words and as we recognize that as God spoke creation into being so we can speak things into being in our lives through confession of His Word.

1. SPEAK WORDS THAT ARE POWERFUL AND CREATIVE

    In Genesis 1:1-3, we notice that the Spirit of God was hovering over the waters. The water was there, the darkness was there and the Spirit of God was there. But nothing happened until words were spoken, until God said 'Light'. God spoke and 'Light' came into existence. God's words were and are His creative power.

    According to Genesis 1:26 we are all created in the image and likeness of God. Therefore, if God's words are powerful, so are ours.

    Many people today think of words as being unimportant. But Proverbs 18:21 says, "Thetongue has the power of life and death and those who love it will eat its fruits."

    From Genesis 1:2-3, we realize that words have the power to create. And from Proverbs 18:21, we learn that words have the power of life and death.

When we were born again by the Spirit of God, Jesus became our Savior and Lord. Therefore, the words that come out of our mouths should be in line with the Word of God. We must speak God's Words for otherwise we would be speaking like the world, that is, Satan's words.

Joshua 1:8: "Do not let this book of the Law depart from your mouth. Meditate on it day and night so that you will be successful."

Part of meditation is muttering, conversing aloud with oneself or declaring something. Confessing the Word of God helps to establish it in the heart and as we do so, we will be successful.

2. **SPEAK WORDS THAT ARE POSITIVE AND NOT NEGATIVE**

Mark 11: 22-25: "Have faith in God," Jesus answered. "I tell you the truth, if anyone says to this mountain, 'Go, throw yourself into the sea,' and does not doubt in his heart but believes that what he says will happen, it will be done for him. Therefore I tell you, whatever you ask for in prayer, believe that you have received it, and it will be yours. And when you stand praying, if you hold anything against anyone, forgive him, so that your Father in heaven may forgive you your sins."

We are to speak 'to this mountain'. 'Mountain' here means 'problems'. We are to speak to our problems, not about them.

Philippians 2:14 "Do everything without complaining or arguing."

We are therefore to speak faith-filled promises to the mountains in our lives. There is to be no complaining, moaning or groaning about our problems. For example, when we have problems with our children, we should not reprimand them by using words like 'Stupid!' We should instead say "That was a silly thing you just did, now don't do it again because you are a very clever boy/girl."

3. SPEAK WORDS THAT ARE LIFE AND NOT DEATH

We must not make negative statements about our husbands either. And when we have financial problems, our words should be the promises of God—'Jehovah Jireh is my provider'—and not the complaint 'I never seem to have enough'.

Negative words, curses always bring death. We may not physically murder someone but our words can kill! For instance, if we speak 'divorce' it will happen but if we claim it's opposite then the marriage will be successful. Likewise, if we speak illness—'I'm always sick'—and we will remain ill. Claim health and you will be healthy. Those who go about saying 'My diabetes', 'My arthritis' or 'I have cancer' are using words of ownership—'my' and 'have'. Disease becomes their property and unless and until they give up ownership of it, it will remain theirs!

I read this story about a doctor who was not a Christian but who had discovered the principle of the power of words. His prescription to his patients was this: Go home and repeat several times daily these words—'I am getting better and better every day.' He had such marvelous results that people traveled from all over the world to get his help!

Now, this is a non-believer. What about us who are Christians? We have the Word of God. I give you an illustration from my own experience. When I was pregnant with David our first son, I developed a water infection. I went to see the doctor who gave me a mild antibiotic as she did not want the baby harmed. Within one week the infection had cleared. However one week later it returned, I did not go back to the doctor as I did not want to take too much medicine— every time I urinated, I confessed the Scriptures on healing and within another week I was totally healed. The Word of God is life and can bring healing to the body.

4. SPEAK WORDS THAT ARE A BLESSING AND NOT A CURSE

Ephesians 4:29: "Do not let any unwholesome talk come out of your mouth, but only what is helpful for building others up according to their needs, that it may benefit those who listen."

As God's people, we are to bless people, not curse them. We curse if we find fault with them, if we criticize them. Our words should always be words of praise, words of gentleness, and words of encouragement.

For example in the Bible, Barnabas and Paul took Mark on a missionary journey but half-way through he deserted them. So when, they were planning the next trip Barnabas wanted to take him again but a dispute broke out between him and Paul because Paul refused to take Mark again. So eventually, Barnabas took Mark and, Paul took Silas. However, years later, Paul recognized that Barnabas, whose name means 'Son of Encouragement', was right because he says in 2 Timothy 4::11 "Get Mark and bring him with you, because he is helpful to me in my ministry."

5. SPEAK THOSE THINGS THAT ARE NOT AS THOUGH THEY ARE

Romans 4:17 "As it is written: "I have made you a father of many nations" He is our father in the sight of God, in whom he believed— the God who gives life to the dead and calls things that are not as though they were".

Examples:
Abraham and Sarah were past the age of child bearing but God enabled those things that are not as though they were and Isaac was born.

A bad marriage can become good as we speak it into being.
Children who are rebellious will be obedient to God and their parents as we speak those things that are not as though they are.

In order for us to lead victorious, spirit-filled lives, we need to change the words we use. We need to be conscious of every utterance we make. Our hearts and our tongues must be transformed. They must make that shift from the negative to the positive, from death to life and from curses to blessings. Then, what was impossible to us before becomes possible. Then, God's promises and divine plans for us will take root in our hearts and our lives and the fruit we bear will be a testimony to the power in us.

CHAPTER 4:

LIVING BY THE WORD, NOT BY FEELINGS

God created us spirit, soul and body. Our spirit is the area that has a personal relationship with God; our soul is our mind, emotions and will; and our body is the physical outer shell. Our spirit man should always be in control of our soul and body, however, as women we are too much governed by our emotions—what we feel. I don't feel like cooking today! I don't feel like praying today. I don't feel like going to the Women's Meeting tonight! Sometimes, we may even say 'I don't feel loving towards my husband—especially as he has forgotten our wedding anniversary again?!'

But what does the Word, the Bible say? God's Word has a promise and an answer for our every situation, no matter how difficult it is. The Word of God enters our spirit so that we are able to rise above our feelings and conquer what we feel. The Bible points out very clearly that we are to live by the Word of God and not our feelings.

Feelings say: "All is Lost" "No Hope" "A Lousy Day."
The Word says: "I know that my Redeemer lives.'

Let us look at Job's life and learn from his responses.

Job's trials

He lost his seven sons, three daughters, 7,000 sheep, 3,000 camels, 500 yoke of oxen, 500 donkeys but Job never once blamed God.

Job 1: 20-22 "At this, Job got up and tore his robe and shaved his head. Then he fell to the ground in worship and said: "Naked I came from my mother's womb, and naked I will depart. The LORD gave and the LORD has taken away; may the name of the LORD be praised. In all this, Job did not sin by charging God with wrongdoing."

He could have gone by his feelings but he did not. Instead, he placed his hope, trust and faith in God.

Job was then afflicted with boils from head to toe. His wife told him to curse God. What Was Job's reply?

Job 2:10 He replied, "You are talking like a foolish woman. Shall we accept good from God, and not trouble?"

Notice that in the midst of his trials, Job did not sin in what he said. Sometimes, when we feel bad, we may say bad things and this can be a sin. Job must have felt bad but he would not curse God.

Then Job's friends accused him of sin even though he was blameless. This was his response to them:

Job 19:2 "How long will you torment me and crush me with words?"

A 'feelings' response to the accusation of his friends might have been 'What friends you are!' Their words were crushing Job but he did not rely on his feelings, he still continued to see them as friends no matter what they said.

Job's faith and victory
Job 19:25 "I know that my Redeemer lives, and that in the end he will stand upon the earth."

For nine months Satan kept bringing trouble to Job but because Job did not depend on his feelings, he would not do or say the wrong thing, but the result was victory.

Job 42:10 "After Job had prayed for his friends, the LORD made him prosperous again and gave him twice as much as he had before."

Job 42:12 "The LORD blessed the latter part of Job's life more than the first. He had fourteen thousand sheep, six thousand camels, a thousand yoke of oxen and a thousand donkeys."
In studying Job's life, what is of paramount importance becomes crystal clear. We have something extra that Job did not have at that time. We have God's written Word.

2 Timothy 3:16,17 "All Scripture is God-breathed and is useful for teaching, rebuking, correcting and training in righteousness, so that the man of God may be thoroughly equipped for every good work."

Remember that God's Word is powerful. It is life and truth. We must use the Word of God to overcome our feelings.

Feelings say:
'The problem is too big, too difficult, no way out . . .'

The Word says:
"At midnight pray and praise God."

Let's turn next to Paul and Silas to find out their responses to trials and the outcome of their faith in God.

Paul and Silas's trials
Paul and Silas were at one time in Philippi. They had been brought before the magistrates and accused of causing trouble. They had been persecuted, stripped and severely flogged and then thrown into prison. There they were locked up in the inner cell and their feet fastened in the stocks.

Paul and Silas's victory

What did Paul and Silas do in a situation where there seemed to be no way out for them? This is what they did:

Acts 16: 25-26 "About midnight Paul and Silas were praying and singing hymns to God, and the other prisoners were listening to them. Suddenly there was such a violent earthquake that the foundations of the prison were shaken. At once all the prison doors flew open, and everybody's chains came loose."

'Midnight' in the Bible represents a crisis or the crises in our lives. In their hour of crisis, what did Paul and Silas do? They praised the Lord.

The result of their praise, their unwavering faith was this: The prison doors flew open, the chains that bound every prisoner, not just Paul and Silas, were loosened. Such was the response of God to the prayers and praise of his people.

Remember that as we praise the Lord, the same thing will happen. We will be set free from the yoke of oppression and depression.

Sometimes our problems or difficulties make us feel like we are in a prison because we 'feel' that our problems seem too big for us to handle however the Scriptures clearly show us that we are not to depend on feelings. We are not to think negative thoughts. We are not to speak negative words.

Proverbs 18:21 "The tongue has the power of life and death and those who love it will eat its fruit."

Hebrew 13:15 "through Jesus, therefore, let us continually offer to God a sacrifice of praise—the fruit of lips that confess his name."

Clearly we are to continually offer to God a sacrifice of praise. 'Sacrifice' pertains not to pleasant times when our 'feelings' would be good for then it would be easy to praise God and no sacrifice would be involved. Rather, it refers to trying times, to situations and circumstances that make it difficult for us to praise the Lord. When, despite our painful circumstances, we give Him praise, it is a sacrifice. The Bible says,' . . .

continually offer to God a sacrifice of praise.' The word 'continually' means we are to do it all the time.

Feelings Say:
"Why Lord, Why Me?"

The Word Says:
"May it be to me as You have said."
Finally, let us study the response of Mary, the mother of Jesus, when an angel appeared to her and said, 'You are going to have a baby.'

Luke 1: 35-37 The angel answered, "The Holy Spirit will come upon you, and the power of the Most High will overshadow you. So the holy one to be born will be called the Son of God. Even Elizabeth your relative is going to have a child in her old age, and she who was said to be barren is in her sixth month For nothing is impossible with God."

Mary was a virgin when the angel spoke to her. She had been pledged to be married to Joseph. If she had reacted to the angel's astounding statement with 'feelings', she might have said, 'Why Lord, why me?'

It would have been natural for Mary to have been afraid and dismayed with the news. To have a child out of wedlock in Jewish culture meant bringing shame to her name, to her family name and to Joseph's name. She could also have been stoned to death.

Imagine what she must have felt. And she was then not even in her twenties. Yet, this was her response to the angel's news:
Luke 1:38 "'I am the Lord's servant,' Mary answered. 'May it be to me as you have said.' Then the angel left her.'"

Mary's response was one of complete obedience to the will of God.

We need to ask ourselves what we do when we are faced with difficult situations. Do we go by our feelings and say, 'Why Lord, why me?' Or can we, like Mary, say, 'I am the Lord's servant. May it be to me as You have said.

We must let the promises in the Word of God stir us to rise in our faith. Nothing is impossible with God. Whatever our situations—at home, at the workplace or at the church—nothing is impossible with God.

We are not to live our lives by our feelings. We are to stand on the promises of God. He has given us all authority to trample on snakes and scorpions and to overcome all the power of the enemy and nothing will harm us. We are to rise and conquer the negative feelings we have in the name of Jesus.

CHAPTER 5:

DEATH TO SELF

The most significant death in all history is Jesus' death on the cross. He did not put self first. He put us first when He became the supreme sacrifice. By His act of pure love for us, He put to death sin and sickness and won the victory over death itself. Jesus is all deserving of our praise.

Psalm 103:1-3 "Praise the LORD, O my soul; all my inmost being, praise his holy name Praise the LORD, O my soul, and forget not all his benefits—who forgives all your sins and heals all your diseases."

Jesus died for us and we in turn have to die to ourselves. Self is the 'I' in our lives, our egos. The apostle Paul said, 'I die daily.' Notice that Paul said daily, not just once at salvation, once at water baptism, once more when baptized in the Holy Spirit, then once more when we become a cell leader, worship leader, overseer or pastor but every day.

Be aware that the biggest hindrance or obstacle to our dying daily is our pride. We are proud people, no matter what our race, social standing, gender or age. Pride is something that cannot always be seen; it can be subtle or deceptive. This is because asChristians we are careful about what we say or do, especially in front of our pastoral staff.

DEFINITION OF PRIDE

The Bible definition of pride is very different from the world's definition of it. The world says people have pride when they think that they are very good at something or that they are better than other people. The Bible, however, goes beyond that definition. It says that pride means an independent-from-God attitude, a dependence on our own strength, abilities and wisdom instead of a dependence on God's supernatural strength, supernatural ability and wisdom.

John 15:5 "I am the vine; you are the branches. If a man remains in me and I in him, he will bear much fruit; apart from me you can do nothing."

Truly, apart from Him, we can do nothing. I, for one, cannot lead a cell without Him. I cannot lead worship without Him. I cannot oversee without Him. I cannot lead anyone to the Lord without Him. And neither can I baptize anyone in the Holy Spirit without Him.

Why? Because it is God who does it, not us. We are just vessels, instruments to be used by Him. In ourselves we are empty.

A PROUD, INDEPENDENT-FROM-GOD ATTITUDE LEADS TO OUR DOWNFALL

Lucifer and his pride
Isaiah 14:12-16 "How you have fallen from heaven, O morning star, son of the dawn! You have been cast down to the earth, you who once laid low the nations! You said in your heart, "I will ascend to heaven; I will raise my throne above the stars of God; I will sit enthroned on the mount of assembly, on the utmost heights of the sacred mountain. I will ascend above the tops of the clouds; I will make myself like the Most High." But you are brought down to the grave, to the depths of the pit. Those who see you stare at you, they ponder your fate: Is this the man who shook the earth and made kingdoms tremble."

Notice that the words 'I will' appear five times in the above text but the words 'God's will' do not appear at all. That was how much Lucifer had changed.

We may feel that we are different, that each of us would never let our wills override God's. However, our attitudes may prove otherwise. Our attitudes may very well be the following:

I know better than God!
I know what I should do.
I know how the church should be run!
These are words of pride and they will lead to our downfall.

The verses in Isaiah clearly show us that it was the beginning of pride which changed the angel Lucifer from being an individual full of love for God to being the increasingly wicked and selfish creature called Satan.

We see that Lucifer ceased to depend on God's guidance and wisdom. He started to think and act as though he knew more than God.

When the proud, self-reliant attitude took hold of Lucifer, he no longer wanted to love and know God intimately. When we have proud, self-reliant attitudes, we also will lose our first love for God and that intimate relationship we once had with Him.

God wants a heart of obedience, a humble heart and then he will use and work through us.

1 Peter 5:5 "Young men, in the same way be submissive to those who are older. All of you, clothe yourselves with humility toward one another, because, God opposes the proud but gives grace to the humble."

Peter is not telling one person or a few to be humble. His words are "All of you . . ."
Peter and his pride
Luke 22: 31-34 "Simon, Simon, Satan has asked to sift you as wheat. But I have prayed for you, Simon that your faith may not fail. And when you have turned back, strengthen your brothers. But he replied, 'Lord, I am ready to go with you to prison and to death.' Jesus answered, 'I tell you, Peter, before the rooster crows today, you will deny three times that you know me.'"

Why did Peter deny Jesus three times? It was because he was filled with great fear. Peter was relying on his own natural strength and when the crisis occurred, Peter did not have enough of his own strength to overcome it.

Later, when Peter was less self-reliant, he became much more dependent on the Holy Spirit and on God's supernatural abilities. Peter was able to perform many miracles, even his shadow healed people.

Philippians 4:13 "I can do everything through him who gives me strength."

Pride in Nebuchadnezzar's Life
Daniel 4: 27 "Therefore, O king, be pleased to accept my advice: Renounce your sins by doing what is right, and your wickedness by being kind to the oppressed. It may be that then your prosperity will continue." This was Daniel's warning to King Nebuchadnezzar but his pride prevented him from heeding it. We know this because twelve months later, as Nebuchadnezzar was walking on the roof of the royal palace of Babylon, he said the following with utmost pride:

Daniel 4:30 "Is not this the great Babylon I have built as the royal residence, by my mighty power and for the glory of my majesty?"

Even while his words remained on his lips, the answer to pride came to him:

Daniel 4:31-32 "The words were still on his lips when a voice came from heaven: "This is what is decreed for you, King Nebuchadnezzar: Your royal authority has been taken from you. You will be driven away from people and will live with the wild animals; you will eat grass like cattle. Seven times will pass by for you until you acknowledge that the Most High is sovereign over the kingdoms of men and gives them to anyone he wishes."

At one stage in his life, Nebuchadnezzar did recognize that Jehovah God was the only true God. This was due to the influence of Daniel, Shadrach, Meshach and Abed-Nego over him. However, Nebuchadnezzar allowed pride to take control of his thoughts and speech.

Pride is very subtle. It affects our thinking first, then our attitudes, then our speech and finally our actions. What happens next is a glorification of self, not of God. The words we use and the thoughts we think reflect this state:

Is not this the great cell I have built?
Is not this the great church I have built?
Is not this the great Sunday School class I have built?

No recognition is given to God for what He has done, for His supernatural ability and power.

What was God's reaction to Nebuchadnezzar's pride? He took everything from him and Nebuchadnezzar became insane.

TO DIE TO SELF, DIE TO PRIDE

We can die to self by doing the following:

Recognize the Pride Within Ourselves
Pride in ourselves leads to a dependency on our own strength rather than God's. We may lack natural ability, skills, material possessions, power and social status and yet still be proud.

In other words, having wealth and power does not necessarily cause a person to be proud. There are those with wealth and power who do walk humbly before God. Pride is subtle and we've got to learn to recognize it!

Repent
As we recognize our problem we must humble ourselves under the mighty hand of God and repent. True repentance is not just saying 'sorry' but turning away from our proud spirit and walking in humility.

1 John 1:9 "If we confess our sins, he is faithful and just and will forgive us our sins and purify us from all unrighteousness."

Clothe ourselves with humility and walk in humility
True humility makes us see that we are really nothing without Him and His Holy Spirit's Strength, Wisdom and Love.
Stephen was one great example of this.

Acts 6:5 . . . They chose Stephen, a man full of faith and of the Holy Spirit . . .

Faith is defined as a trusting reliance on God, His Word and His Spirit's strength and guidance. We can see from *Acts 6:3-15* that Stephen allowed his own natural abilities of physical strength, human reason, common sense and human love to be filled and controlled by the Holy Spirit and to be dependent on God's strength.

When Stephen debated with men of religious and worldly intellect, he depended on the Holy Spirit to guide him. Even when they were stoning him, he remained dependent on the Holy Spirit. For he said, "Lord, do not charge them with this sin". (Acts 7:60)

The apostle Paul was another example of faith. He could not depend on his intellect or his own strength alone to be a mighty Apostle of God. To preach and move in the miraculous, he could only rely on the supernatural ability of God, and Paul knew he had to walk by faith and not by sight.

Galatians 3:4-11 "Have you suffered so much for nothing—if it really was for nothing? Does God give you his Spirit and work miracles among you because you observe the law, or because you believe what you heard? Consider Abraham: 'He believed God, and it was credited to him as righteousness.' Understand, then, that those who believe are children of Abraham. The Scripture foresaw that God would justify the Gentiles by faith, and announced the gospel in advance to Abraham: 'All nations will be blessed through you.' So those who have faith are blessed along with Abraham, the man of faith. All who rely on observing the law is under a curse, for it is written: Cursed is everyone who does not continue to do everything written in the Book of the Law. Clearly no one is justified before God by the law, because, 'The righteous will live by faith.'"

Like Paul and Stephen, we too must die to self to become more like Jesus. Our pride must go and we all must die to self. We need the Word to renew our minds and to have God's wisdom and to walk in faith, love and humility.

I DIE DAILY—that is to be our daily confession and prayer.

CHAPTER 6:

WALKING BY FAITH, NOT BY SIGHT

Hebrews 11:1 "Now faith is being sure of what we hope for and certain of what we do not see."

Hebrews 11:8-11 "By faith Abraham, when called to go to a place he would later receive as his inheritance, obeyed and went, even though he did not know where he was going. By faith he made his home in the promised land like a stranger in a foreign country; he lived in tents, as did Isaac and Jacob, who were heirs with him of the same promise. For he was looking forward to the city with foundations, whose architect and builder is God. By faith Abraham, even though he was past age-and Sarah herself was barren-was enabled to become a father because he considered him faithful who had made the promise."

By faith Abraham, even though he was past age—and Sarah herself was barren—was enabled to become a father because he considered him faithful who had made the promise.

Hebrews 11: 17-19. "By faith Abraham, when God tested him, offered Isaac as a sacrifice. He who had received the promises was about to sacrifice his one and only son, even though God had said to him, "It is through Isaac that your offspring will be reckoned." Abraham reasoned that God could raise the dead, and figuratively speaking, he did receive Isaac back from death."

When God created us, he made man of three parts that is spirit, soul and body. His Word says that the spirit man should be in control. But if the body (flesh) is in control, it controls our soul (emotions) and our spirit (right relationship with God). Like most men, they exercise their body, doing push ups to strengthen their bodies. When the body is in control it controls the soul (mind, emotions and will) and confusion sets in. It is not the body that should be in control.

If the soul (mind, emotions, will) is in control over the spirit man, a lot of fear comes in (through the soulish realm) and we cannot walk by faith because the body and soul are in control. There is fear in our mind and emotions and we cannot grow spiritually.

Ephesians 6:10 "Be strong in the Lord and in the might of His power."

If the spirit man is in control, we are in right relationship with God. The soul and body will have to submit to the spirit man. Then there will be love, joy, peace, self-control and the fruits of the Spirit will be very evident. As we have a strong relationship with God, we will walk by faith and not by sight because we are not depending on our feelings, our mind and our stubborn will but we're depending on faith in God.

FAITH OR FEELINGS

What are we depending on? Is it our feelings or faith?

Do our feelings say "Oh I have to go to church this morning!" or our faith says: "Wow! It's Sunday again. This is the day that the Lord has made. We will rejoice and be glad in it."

How did you get out of bed this morning and how did you feel?

Did you say? "Oh No! I have to get out of bed and go to church. I hope there is a parking space. I hope everything is going to be fine. I hope the worship is good" and we are all in hope, hope, hope. But faith is certain of what we do not see.

Hebrews 11:1 "Now faith is sure of what we hope for and certain of what we do not see."

Now feelings like to go on what you see. If the sun is shining, we'll say Oh it's going to be a good day today. If the sun is not shining because we can't see it with our natural eyes, we'll say Oh it's going to be a terrible day today. But it says in the Word of God that at one time Joshua actually commanded the sun to be still. We have authority in Christ Jesus and so our faith has to be exercised.

And so in the morning when we get up because we depend on our feelings, we are already predicting and saying with our mouth what our feelings are telling us that it is going to be a bad day. So at the end of the day when you come from the office, and when your wife greets you at the door or you walk in together and she asked: How was your day? And you replied, "Oh terrible"! "Now how about yours?" She replied, "Terrible, too" Now why? Because you already predicted it before you went out of the door! In England, they often say "Monday blues! Because we have to work on Monday after the weekends on Saturday and Sunday. Generally, throughout the office there will be an air of oppression and depression because everybody is confessing Monday blues and you get what you say.

But the Word of God says Faith is certain of what we do not see. That means we cannot depend on our feelings for healing. We cannot depend on our feelings for salvation of those in our household who are not saved. We cannot depend on our feelings to get a better job. We cannot depend on our feelings to get a better education. We cannot depend on our feelings to read the Word and pray but we have to move into the spirit realm of moving and living in faith. Now when we are born again by the Spirit of God, every one of us has been given a seed of faith but that faith like a natural seed has to be nurtured. It has to be watered. It has to be looked after before it can grow. That's why some of us who have been Christians for 10 years and others have only been Christians for say like 2 to 3 years and yet the 2 to 3 years old Christian is growing leaps and bounds ahead of those 10 year Christians. Because the 2 to 3 year old Christian is nurturing and watering that seed of faith more than the 10-year Christian! That's why there is a disparity between the two. So for every one of us, we need to nurture the seed.

When we moved from Taiwan to Kuching, we had a garden like a jungle and I said to my husband, "Let's grow a lawn". He just looked at me and said "What? Here?" I said "Yes, here". He was a nice husband and he got all the weeds out for me. Then he bought me the grass seeds and said "Do what you want". So I followed the instructions. I put the fertilizer down and the instructions said, 'Walk on the fertilizers and grass seed that was sprinkled'. So there was I two or three o'clock in the afternoon sun, walking across the seed and I was saying, "In the Name of Jesus you will grow. Oh yes you will and you will be a beautiful lawn." I was walking up and down like this in the hot sun. My husband came down the stairs and he looked out the windows and he said, "What are you doing?" I said, "the instructions told me to walk on the seeds and I am doing a bit extra. I am praying over it!"

He was a faithful husband and watered the seeds for me morning and night with my little boy, David. And then the little green sprouts started coming through and David wanted to pull them up and I said to him, "No, you don't pull out the green sprouts. That's the grass that's coming through." So everyday we faithfully watered again and within one to two weeks we began to see a lovely lush green lawn beginning to grow. Why? We looked after it, we nurtured it and of course I prayed over it.

Now the seed of faith that God has given us is exactly the same. We must water it with the Word of God, with prayer and fasting, with praise, and with faith-filled words coming out of our mouths, then the seed will blossom and flourish into a beautiful plant. Our faith will grow from leaps and bounds and we will be able to believe God for absolutely anything at this moment in time because we are not living by feelings, but by faith. If we don't nurture the seed of faith, given to us upon salvation, we will die spiritually and we will become weak Christians but we are going to find from the life of Abraham how to have an assurance of faith, persevering faith, and faith that is tested.

AN ASSURANCE OF FAITH

Hebrews 11:8 "By faith Abraham, when called to go to a place he would later receive as his inheritance, obeyed and went, even though he did not know where he was going."

Now to our five natural senses and to our physical mind, that does not make any sense. Why leave somewhere and go to a place you did not know where you are going to? Now Abraham had been given a promise and it is the promises of God that are written in the Word of God that creates faith within us.

Genesis 12:1-3 The LORD had said to Abram, "Leave your country, your people and your father's household and go to the land I will show you. I will make you into a great nation and I will bless you; I will bless those who bless you, and whoever curses you I will curse; and all peoples on earth will be blessed through you."

We find that because of the promises of God, that is why Abraham was able to leave. God's Word says in Hebrews, He continued to be faithful and we must recognize that our God is a faithful God. When we have been given a promise from the Word of God for salvation of our household or we have been given a promise for healing or we have been given a promise for our work situation or our many circumstances, if God had said it, the same God that was faithful to Abraham will be faithful to us. He will bless us and as He has blessed Abraham.

It is the promises that give us faith because it is God's Word and it says clearly in the Word of God that the Word of God will not return to Him void. Maybe God has called you to do a work for Him but like Abraham, you are not sure where you are going or what to do but like Abraham, we have a promise and we confess the promise until it has been fulfilled.

You know that God has called you into full-time ministry but you are not sure how, where, what, why but you just know that calling is there in your life—you cannot depend on the five senses. We have to trust in our God that we will get to Canaan and God has given him the Promised Land.

When Lot (Abraham had taken his nephew with him)—take note God never told him to take Lot but Abraham took Lot along with him, God said, "You and your household . . ." and his nephew was not part of his household. But he took Lot with him. Therefore there began to be strife and division within the family. Abraham's provision was getting many and Lot's provisions was getting many, and so Abraham said to Lot, "Let us not quarrel, let us not have strife because we know that this will bring a curse upon us." You see, Abraham was a very wise man and a man who was full of faith. So Abraham said to Lot "You choose the land that is before you" and Lot looked out and there was green lush land on one side and there was a dry barren desert on the other side. Now Lot relied on his five senses—he saw something that was good.

Finally, Lot decided and chose the green lush area and this land was near Sodom and Gomorrah. Although Lot chose what he thought was good, it ended up to be the worst! The people there were living in sin and he had a terrible time in that city. Let us understand that when we see something that is good, it may not always be the best!

As for Abraham, he looked out and there was just a desert—a barren dry land. Now if he had depended on his five senses, he could have said to God "Now look, You told me you are going to bless me, my descendants are going to be numerous and we are going into the Promised Land (Canaan) but look what I have got—wilderness! Desert! But we know that as Abraham was pondering and wondering God reminded him of His promises.

Genesis 13:14-17 The LORD said to Abram after Lot had parted from him, "Lift up your eyes from where you are and look north and south, east and west. All the land that you see I will give to you and your offspring forever. I will make your offspring like the dust of the earth, so that if anyone could count the dust, then your offspring could be counted. Go, walk through the length and breadth of the land, for I am giving it to you."

God called Abraham to get up, to look around, to lift up his eyes and we have got to do the same too. We must lift up our eyes and do not keep looking at our circumstances or conditions. Don't keep saying "Oh me! Oh my! Why am I down here? Why is it all desert? Why is it all wilderness?" Instead, the Word of God says, "Lift up your eyes" and God tells us to get our eyes off our circumstances. He wants us to look to Him who is a faithful God. We can look to a God who is a mighty God.

I remember a Sunday School song that we used to sing that goes like this: "Our God is so big, so strong and so mighty there's nothing that He cannot do!"

We forget these things when we are in difficulties and bad circumstances. But God says we are to lift up our eyes and he told this to Abraham. He said "Look North, look South, look East and look West. "It is all yours", He told Abraham to walk through the land. Similarly, God is telling you to walk through the land. You walk through every room in your house (every child's room) and when they are not in, you lay hands on their beds and items and say "You spirit of rebellion and disobedience, you will leave our children in the Name of the Lord Jesus Christ." You go through every room in the house and claim these promises of God for you and your family.

You walk through the land and if you need healing, with every step you take you say "By the stripes of Jesus, I am healed." At the age of nineteen I was healed of rheumatism but at one time, it came back and the pain was really strong. I had terrible pain and I thought that I would snap into two each time I moved. But I stood on the Word of God and the enemy had to go. I confessed that "By the stripes of Jesus, I am healed".

You have to walk your land and make your stand. You have to claim the land that is rightfully yours because you have all authority in the Name of the Lord Jesus Christ. Amen.

Luke 10:19 "Behold, I give you the authority to trample on serpents and scorpions, and over all the power of the enemy, and nothing shall by any means hurt you."

The devil will lie to you in your mind. He will stir up those emotions and tell you lies. But our God never lies! It says in the Word of God He never changes. He is the same yesterday, today and forever. Hallelujah. We need to stand on the promises of God. Abraham has been given those promises that of his own flesh, his wife Sarah would bear a child.

Genesis 15:1-6 "After this, the word of the LORD came to Abram in a vision: 'Do not be afraid, Abram. I am your shield, your very great reward.' But Abram said, 'O Sovereign LORD, what can you give me since I remain childless and the one who will inherit my estate is Eliezer of Damascus?' And Abram said, 'You have given me no children; so a servant in my household will be my heir.' Then the word of the LORD came to him: 'This man will not be your heir, but a son coming from your own body will be your heir.' He took him outside and said, 'Look up at the heavens and count the stars—if indeed you can count them.' Then he said to him, 'So shall your offspring be.' Abram believed the LORD, and he credited it to him as righteousness."

God kept telling Abraham to look up. To lift up his eyes and see. Look up and count the stars and Abraham's faith continued to grow every day because God kept coming back and reminded him of the promises. Similarly for us, we should stop looking down but to look up, and the Bible says "For our redemption draws nigh". God is able to fulfill His promises for you.

PERSEVERING FAITH

But one day, the five senses came in. The soulish area began to dominate the spirit man. As Abraham and Sarah had waited many years and they had not son or even a daughter, both of them began to wonder what was going on. Sarah said to her husband, "See now, the LORD has restrained me from bearing children. Please go in to my maid; perhaps I shall obtain children by her. And Abraham heeded the voice of his wife."

Sarah actually thought her way was good; it sounded logical to the human mind and that this was the answer but, God's ways are higher than our ways, His thoughts are above our thoughts and His ways are always better! We find that Sarah allowed Hagar, her maid, to sleep with her husband. Yes, they had a son called Ishmael and they thought they knew how to manipulate the situation but God's Word will never return to Him void. They found that in the end the logic of letting Hagar conceive and bear a child gave them more trouble because Sarah ended up being more jealous and bitter towards Hagar and Ishmael. She later turned both mother and son out of the house! Jealousy and bitterness got hold of Sarah and she ended up in a worse situation than her barrenness because the attitude of her heart was wrong as well!

As a result, God had to deal with them. He came again and reminded them that Sarah would have a child.

Genesis 17:1-2 "When Abram was ninety-nine years old, the LORD appeared to him and said, "I am God Almighty; walk before me and be blameless."

I will confirm my covenant between me and you and will greatly increase your numbers."

Genesis 17:19 "Then God said, 'Yes, but your wife Sarah will bear you a son, and you will call him Isaac. I will establish my covenant with him as an everlasting covenant for his descendants after him'"

Genesis 17:21 "But my covenant I will establish with Isaac, whom Sarah will bear to you by this time next year."

There was a definite confirmation of the promise that Abraham will have a son. God specifically pinpointed the time. Now why? I believe it was because Sarah laughed, "Ha! Ha! How can I bear a child? I am too old and barren." But, exactly one year later, they had that son called Isaac. We must wait for the promises of God to be fulfilled in our life. God's timing is a perfect timing. God's timing is not too slow, not too late but just on time.

We often go by our five senses and say "It has to be now, otherwise it's going to be too late" or "I want a husband now, not later". We need to understand the scriptural principles that are in the Word of God, God's timing is not our timing but it does not mean to say that the promises of God will not be fulfilled. It will be fulfilled as we stand on the Word of God and trust Him.

TESTED FAITH

Why does it take time for the Word of God to be fulfilled in our lives?

Like Abraham, our faith has to be tested. God wants to make us strong. If everything is going nice and smooth, it is very likely that our faith will not get that strong. We must learn to exercise and strengthen our faith muscles! The Israelites walked through the wilderness for forty years and every step of the way, God tested them to see what was in their hearts. All through the forty years and throughout the journey, they kept murmuring and complaining and that was the reason they did not enter into Canaan, the Promised Land, except for those below 20 years of age and Joshua and Caleb.

We find that we are so dependent on our feelings and emotions that we are up and down all the time. If we have got the Word of God in our heart, no matter what comes our way we will not let go. I remember when I was preparing to come out to Asia as a missionary, my Missions Director said to me "Sandra, you must raise $$$$(a certain sum) before you can go." Another girl who was also coming out had already started raising her funds and was leaving in April. It was already January and I had hardly raised any amount at all after having gone around the churches for six months. I said to God "Lord, this cannot be. You have called me andyou have a purpose and plan for me. You will provide for me. Thank you Lord."

My thoughts were also telling me, "Many people have gone round—some even for two years and have not been able to raise the sum required." But I refused to go by my thoughts and feelings and I faithfully confessed that Jesus is my provider every morning and every church that I went to. Suddenly by the end of January the amount had been raised as one church said they would support me and it was quite a large sum for that time. I was so excited. I remember calling my office all the way from Bristol, right up to the North of England, to inform them that I had got every pound and I could go out to Singapore. My Missions Director was not convinced and asked me to get letters to confirm what I was saying. So I wrote letters and requested for the confirmation of amount to be sent in. In April of that year I went to Singapore with my friend.

Stand on the promises of God. Our feelings will say, "It is impossible" but our faith will be tested. We will have to put our trust in God. When I was in Taiwan for ten years, my faith was tested too. I had no money and I would believe for finances to come in. God is faithful as the amount of money would come in. Remember that each test we go through makes us stronger. Don't believe that you are going to come through this test and there is no more. There are more tests coming. The more we have to face the stronger we will be in our faith.

Abraham was tested. How? God asked him to sacrifice his only son Isaac whose name means laughter. When Isaac was born, Abraham and Sarah must have laughed every day and were very happy, especially as he was the son that God promised. Can you imagine how they must felt when God told Abraham that he has to sacrifice Isaac? This is the truth, not a story.

Genesis 22:1-3 "Some time later God tested Abraham. He said to him, 'Abraham!' 'Here I am,' he replied. Then God said, "Take your son, your only son, Isaac, whom you love, and go to the region of Moriah. Sacrifice him there as a burnt offering on one of the mountains I will tell you about." Early the next morning Abraham got up and saddled his donkey. He took with him two of his servants and his son Isaac. When he had cut enough wood for the burnt offering, he set out for the place God had told him about."

Abraham obeyed God's command without any hesitation. He got the donkey saddled and the wood ready and as they were going up, I am sure Isaac like my four year son David, who would never miss a thing would have asked his father "Where is the animal sacrifice?" Abraham did not worry or panic or wonder "What am I a going to tell my son?"

Instead he replied, "My son, God will provide for Himself the lamb for a burnt offering."

Genesis 22:9-12 "When they reached the place God had told him about, Abraham built an altar there and arranged the wood on it. He bound his son Isaac and laid him on the altar, on top of the wood. 10 Then he reached out his hand and took the knife to slay his son. 11 But the angel of the LORD called out to him from heaven, 'Abraham! Abraham!' 'Here I am,' he replied. 'Do not lay a hand on the boy,' he said. 'Do not do anything to him. Now I know that you fear God, because you have not withheld from me your son, your only son.'"

Hallelujah! God did provide!

Genesis 22:13 "Abraham looked up and there in a thicket he saw a ram caught by its horns. He went over and took the ram and sacrificed it as a burnt offering instead of his son.

Abraham did not even have to chase after the ram to catch it. The ram was presented to him, caught by its horns in the bushes. God is able to provide and also at the right time i.e. His timing is perfect. In the times we are going through testing and trials, remember that God will provide. He is Jehovah Jireh our Provider. Abraham's worst time was the time he had to obey God and sacrifice his son Isaac but he trusted God and believed the Lord would provide.

Trust God and believe that He is able to provide for all our needs, whether physical, emotional, healing, financial or spiritual. Be strong in the Lord and in the might of His power and let us walk by faith and not by sight.

CHAPTER 7:

LIVING A LIFE OF FAITH

Everything we receive from God comes through faith. Why faith? What is faith and what are the dynamics of faith? The Bible defines faith as: Hebrews 11:1 "Now faith is being sure of what we hope for and certain of what we do not see."

1. Faith is now
2. Faith is substance
3. Faith is endurance
4. Faith is related to hope
5. Faith is in the unseen
6. Faith is hearing from God, for example, Peter walking on water
7. Faith is supernatural sight—faith sees. For example, the woman with issue of blood, David sees victory
8. Faith is knowing from the heart.
9. Faith is speaking and saying what God says and seeing results. It is not presumption. (A presumption is based on a good idea or intention but it does not produce results.)
10. Faith is a spirit.
11. Faith acts and makes the devil tremble.
12. Faith is the eye of the spirit.
13. Faith is needed in spiritual warfare and we have to put on the whole armor of God.
14. Faith is the door to the supernatural and the miraculous. Faith is needed to take off the limitations we place on God.
15. Faith is victory. Worry is sin.

16. Faith is the only thing, including love and hope, that will last for eternity.

Everyone has a measure of faith but not everyone develops or uses it. Use your faith and do not say, "I have no faith" or "I have little faith" Fight your fight of faith which has already been fought for you. We can be strong in God, in faith and in our spirit man. When we hear God speak, we are bold to step out in faith and not doubt or fear. God is looking for men and women of faith. Without faith, we cannot please God.

Learn to release your faith to God. As you do, act on what God's Word says. Believe as if it were already done. Believe that you have received. For example (e.g. salvation for your household, healing . . .) even before you see any evidence (James 1: 6-8). You can release your faith through faith-filled words. For example, David, Paul and Silas; through the point of contact and understanding divine seasons and timing in God; through abiding in His presence and His anointing and power.

Psalm 101:1 "I will sing of your love and justice; to you, O LORD, I will sing praise . . ."
Psalm 103:1 "Praise the LORD, O my soul; all my inmost being praise his holy name."

Acts 16:25-26 "About midnight Paul and Silas were praying and singing hymns to God, and the other prisoners were listening to them. Suddenly there was such a violent earthquake that the foundations of the prison were shaken. At once all the prison doors flew open, and everybody's chains came loose."

Romans 4:18-21 "Against all hope, Abraham in hope believed and so became the father of many nations, just as it had been said to him, "So shall your offspring be." Without weakening in his faith, he faced the fact that his body was as good as dead—since he was about a hundred years old—and that Sarah's womb was also dead. Yet he did not waver through unbelief regarding the promise of God, but was strengthened in his faith and gave glory to God, being fully persuaded that God had power to do what he had promised.

Faith without works is dead

James 2:21-22 "Was not Abraham justified by works when he offered Isaac his son on the altar? Faith was working together with his works, and by works faith was made perfect"

How does faith come?
1. Through dreams and visions
2. Through the Word of God getting into your heart
3. Through the renewal of your mind
4. Through trusting/fellowship with the Holy Spirit—growth (spiritually) and godliness
5. Through your heart not head knowledge of God—Have a pure heart and a humble spirit
6. Through seeking and knowing the will of God—His plans, time and place
7. Through walking in love/forgiveness and not living in fear or offences
8. Through obedience—seeking God with our whole heart

Faith is based on God's nature, God's presence, God's promises and God's purposes.

Faith is obtaining what God has purposed for you, agreeing with what God says and not with the voices of the devil and people in the world.

Faith relies totally on God who does not lie. His Word is the truth.

Why believe, you ask? Be wise. It pays!

Romans 15:13 "May the God of all hope fill you with all joy and peace in believing so that you may abound in hope by the presence of the Holy Spirit."

Faith will transform the natural into the supernatural and cause you to soar like an eagle and see into the supernatural. Be an eagle. Do not live like a turkey or chicken. See things from God's perspective.

Faith makes the devil tremble and flee in defeat.
Great men of faith persist in spite of the obstacles and hindrances. They overcome overwhelming odds and exchange their weakness for God's ability and faith in God. Faith transforms them into giants to overcome and be triumphant over adversities and problems. The story of the Bible is the story of weak men with tremendous problems who, through faith, were changed, who turned to God and went on to gain great victories, turn tragedies, trials and casualties into conquests all through God's love and power.

Men of faith persist with bulldog faith and will not quit or give up. For example, Lister, despite the sneers of others, discovered antiseptic (carbolic) and the whole course of medicine was changed because of his faith and persistence. He patiently worked, researched and dared to believe there is a cure. We need to catch hold of the spirit of faith in the lives of great men. See how they operate in faith and stop believing the lies of the enemy that says "You are of no use, no good, no value, just a member with no significance and an underachiever at best, it is of no use to try". Stop being negative. But you may say, "You don't understand my circumstances, dilemma, etc." God knows what we are going through. Start believing what God says in the Word about you. Believe that His promises are true and for us.

Hebrews 11:30 "By faith the walls of Jericho fell down after they were encircled for seven days."

Hebrews11:33-35 ". . . Gideon, Barak, Samson . . . . who through faith subdued kingdoms, worked righteousness, obtained promises, stopped the mouths of lions, quenched the violence of fire, escaped the edge of the sword, out of weakness were made strong, became valiant in battle, turned to light the armies of the aliens. Women received their dead raised to life again. Others were tortured, not accepting deliverance, that they might obtain a better resurrection."

"Let us run the Race of Faith with endurance, looking unto Jesus, the author and finisher of our faith . . ." Hebrews 12:2. The Word of God says that Jesus is the source of our faith and He will bring our faith to maturity (i.e. to become 'full grown'). In Him and through Him we have conquering faith to believe God for miracles in our lives.

It was said of Abraham Lincoln that at seven he was forced out of his house and home and had to find work to help support his family. It was a tender age to fend for work. He lost his mother at nine—a great misfortune. Lost his job at twenty-three and his partner in business left him a huge debt and ran away. He had to repay the whole debt himself. The women he had hoped to marry refused to marry him. His sweetheart broke his heart and finally he collapsed under a nervous breakdown. At forty-one, his son died.

He failed in the Senate electoral, was misunderstood, despised, laughed at, scorned, ignored, yet he become one of America's greatest statesmen. What was the secret and how did he overcome discouragement? At fifty-six he was gunned down, yet he is known as one of the greatest presidents of the United States of America.

Two things why he is remembered in the natural:
1. He saved the nation from Civil War, and
2. He was responsible for the abolishment of slavery.

How did he overcome depression, nervous breakdown, discouragement and crises? He prayed to God for wisdom and put his faith in God for a miracle.

John Wesley, on one of his first missionary trips, saw the faith of the Moravian brothers. John Wesley, at that point of time, was unsaved and he saw the reality of the faith of these brethren. They were full of zeal, love and faith, dedication, had no fear of the storms, winds and were filled with joy. They sang and did not panic and were calm. He asked 'How can I have faith like that?' The reply was "Say you have it and act like it because God says so you have victory. Jesus calms the storm and is master of the storms." Do you believe? If so, why fret and fuss?

The Bible says that the apostle Paul impacted the world because of his faith in the Gospel to save, heal and deliver.

Galatians 2:20 "I have been crucified with Christ; it is no longer I who live, but Christ lives in me; and the life I, which I now live in the flesh I live by faith in the Son of God, who loved me and gave Himself for me."

Real faith is tested faith and lasts!
Romans 1:17 "For in the gospel a righteousness from God is revealed, a righteousness that is by faith from first to last, just as it is written: The righteous will live by faith."

Romans 15:13 "May the God of hope fill you with all joy and peace as you trust in him, so that you may overflow with hope by the power of the Holy Spirit."

God promises us in His Word that we who believe in faith will have joy, peace and hope.

CHAPTER 8:

SPIRITUAL LAW OF IMAGINATION

John 14:12 I "Tell you the truth, anyone who has faith in me will do what I have been doing. He will do even greater things than these, because I am going to the Father."

Galatians 3:3-6 "Are you so foolish! After beginning with the Spirit, are you now trying to attain your goal by human effort? Have you suffered so much for nothing—if it really was for nothing? Does God give you his Spirit and work miracles among you because you observe the law, or because you believe what you heard? Consider Abraham: 'He believed God, and it was credited to him as righteousness.'"

How to work the works of God?
A work of God is a miracle. How do miracles operate?

God speaks the end from the beginning. He speaks forth the results. (That is how faith operates). Many people destroy their faith with their praying. They repeat their problem, pray their problem but they forget to pray the result. Mark 11:23

People have more faith in their problems than their answers. Do not pray the problem. The Bible teaches us to pray the answer.

This principle is used in the Old Testament.
2 Kings 4:8-11, 14,18,19,23,26,32
In this story we see:
The raising of the dead in Elisha's ministry
God is a God of life
It was not God who took the child. It was the devil who did it.

The Shumanite woman would not even tell the prophet what her problem was. She called what was not as if they were. She called the things well when it was not so in the natural. The Shumanite woman held to her confession of faith.

Jesus used this principle in His ministry.

1. **The miracle of changing water into wine (John 2:1-10).**
   Jesus told the servants to "fill the pots with water" and "they filled them to the brim". There was no wine in the pots but Jesus was calling it wine and as they went it became wine.

   Was Jesus playing make believe?
   These people who name it and claim it are they deluded? No, they operate according to the spiritual principle of calling forth that which is not into existence.

2. **The healing of the ten lepers (Luke 17:12-19).**
   Jesus called them clean when He said, "Go and show yourself to the priest." But the manifestation of healing only took place as they went on their way.

This is God's method and principle of faith and miracles.

The problem with most believers is that they insist on saying "I believe in saying it like it is." So they never receive their miracle because they are always confessing the symptoms of their sickness.

What you believe is what you receive.

Do what Jesus tells you to do and you will receive your miracles, call it done.

3. **The healing at the pool (John 5).**
   Jesus asked him, "Do you want to get well?" Jesus did not say "can you".

   The man then talked about his problem. "Sir, I have no one to put me in the pool when the water is stirred up; while I am trying to get in, somebody else gets there first." He had no idea who he was talking to.

   Jesus said: "Rise, take up your bed and walk."

   Jesus spoke faith and exercised authority.

   What was Jesus doing: playing make belief—a cripple man can walk? No, He was calling the man well.

   Verse 8—Jesus said, "You are well, rise up". He called forth healing before the man picked up his mat.

4. **Jesus heals a crippled woman (Luke 13:10-17).**
   Jesus said to her, "woman, you are free from your illness." Jesus spoke it before she was healed but she was not better until He laid His hands on her. She believed in the laying of hands. Some release faith in the word, others by laying on of hands. What you believe is vital.

The Spiritual Law or Principle of Imagination

John 5:19 Jesus gave them this answer: "I tell you the truth, the Son can do nothing by himself; he can do only what he sees his Father doing, because whatever the Father does the Son also does."

We see the spiritual law of Imagination or Self Image in Genesis 11:6 The LORD said, "If as one people speaking the same language they have begun to do this, then nothing they plan to do will be impossible for them."

Speaking the word is not enough to call something into being; it first has to become an image on the inside of you.

What is in your consciousness? Is it failure, doubt, sickness, lack of faith, or success, healing and victory?

Mark 11:23 ". . . shalt not doubt in his heart . . ." this means that in his spirit man, he sees.

We see things in our imaginations continually and it plays a very important part in our faith.

Satan engineered the fall of man through the law of imaging. How do we fall into sin? Satan plays with the mind of man.

Genesis 13:10, "Lot looked up and saw that the whole plain of the Jordan was well watered, like the garden of the LORD, like the land of Egypt, toward Zoar. (This was before the LORD destroyed Sodom and Gomorrah.)" Lot got into trouble because of what he saw.

Joshua 7:21 is the story of Achan. He sinned by stealing the forbidden objects and caused Israel to be defeated. How was he defeated or what caused him to sin?

". . . When I saw . . ."

Begin to see what God says. Let God's Word point a picture on the inside of you.

Before your family comes together the way you want them, you have to see it happen on the inside of you. This is a spiritual law, the Law of Imagination.

You can confess, pray, speak the Word of God until your lips are numb but unless you see it on the inside of you, you are just blowing hot air.

If Jesus could do nothing unless He saw it first, certainly we are limited by the same Law.

All through Jesus' life and ministry, Jesus saw things in the spiritual, and then He acted on what He saw. Luke 4:18 'The Spirit of the Lord is on me, because he has anointed me to preach good news to the poor. He has sent me to proclaim freedom for the prisoners and recovery of sight for the blind, to release the oppressed . . .''

You can have anything that you see in the Word of God but you must paint it into your imagination or spirit.

Abraham was a great man of faith but he also had to learn this principle of faith. God tried to get Abraham to see what God had promised him but he failed. Genesis 13:14-16 says, "I am going to give you and your descendants all the land that you see . . ."

Abraham did not have the revelation yet until in Genesis 15:1-6.

What did Abraham see?
He did not see his seed as dust of the earth. "Seeing I go childless"

According to God's Word unless you see it first, it will not come into being.

God had already given him the promise but he still did not see or have the picture inside.

Verses 4-5 God further helped him—"Look, see"
God gave him a picture of a natural visual aid.

If you are believing God for something and it has not come to past, what do you see?
See your body healed.
See your family back together.
See yourself in financial prosperity.
See your relationships as good.
See yourself as a success.

There has not been a thing in this earth from the beginning of creation until now that did not start out as an image. Even God used this principle when He created the world. Genesis 1:26-27 says, ". . . And now we will make human beings, they will be like us and resemble us . . ."

God had on the inside of Him an image of the man He wanted to create and He put into words what He desired. Such is the Law of Imagination.

CHAPTER 9:

KNOWING GOD

". . . the people who know their God shall be strong and carry out great exploits." Daniel 11:32

One of the most important foundations for our faith is to know God. Daniel was a prophet and he was speaking prophetically to our times and our day. The people who know their God shall be strong and do great exploits.

HOW DO WE KNOW GOD?

1. **Know God through His Name**
   We know God through His Name. His Name reveals His nature and character. Daniel called God, Elohim—the God of might and power who is sovereign in our lives.

   Look at the life of Joseph. He was rejected and suffered much anguish and pain; sold as a slave by his own brothers into Egypt, betrayed, misunderstood and finally thrown into prison. Joseph could be bitter about this, but he knew Elohim God, the God of might and power who was sovereign in his circumstances and situations, no matter how hard and difficult it was. He knew His God.

   God has His timing! The Psalmist says, ". . . Joseph—who was sold as a slave; they hurt his feet with chains . . . Until the time that his word came to pass, the word of the Lord tested him." (Psalm 150:

17-19). Joseph knew his God and believed God and his faith in the Word was tested. People let him down, disappointed him, rejected him, hurt him. But he was not affected by them. The key to Joseph's success was that he knew God and he has a right spirit. He knew Elohim God was sovereign in his life, and nothing could harm him. He had the right spirit and when the time came, he was delivered, exalted and promoted to Pharaoh's palace.

In these last days, God wants a people who know Him and be like Him. God wants a people who have renewed minds, who think like He thinks, who see like He sees, a people who are conformed to be like His Son Jesus, so that we can inherit the promises of God in the year of 'exceeding abundant expansion'. Unless we become like Him, we cannot receive the blessings of God. If we want to contain all the blessings of God and expand, we must expand inside first!

We cannot fulfill God's plan in our own strength and understanding, like Moses or like King Saul! But when we know God and walk in His ways, God will bring His plans to pass in our lives!

2. **Know God through His Word**
   In the beginning is the Word, and the Word is with God, and the Word is God. We must know and understand the Word of God. We must have the light of God's Word, for only in His light we see light. The Word of God is living and powerful that sharply divides the spirit and the soul. To know God, we must know His Word. When you know the Word, the Word will speak to you. The Bible tells us that when we lie down, the Word will keep us; when we awake, the Word will speak with us. (Proverbs 6:22)

3. **Know God through the lives of people of faith**
   We can know God through the lives and experiences of people of faith. One of the things that have greatly helped me in my Christian life is by studying the lives and biographies of men like Martin Luther, John G. Lake, Smith Wigglesworth and Alexander Dowie. There is still such an anointing in their books and tapes. They have revelations and truths that they had experienced firsthand. They are not what we call arm-chair theologians but they have written out of

their experience. And anything that is in the Word can be and should be experienced in our lives!

4. **Know God through love**

We know God by loving God. He who does not love, does not know God, for God is love (1 John 4:8). The Apostle Paul speaks of a more excellent way—the way of love. In the famous love chapter, 1 Corinthians 13, we have the source of love, the force of love and the cause of love. When you know the source of love, you will not run dry. When you know the force of love, you will not be intimidated and will walk with God. When you know the cause of love, you can be the channel and the instrument that God wants you to be. When you walk in love, you know your God, and you can do great exploits.

5. **Know God through the spirit**

Man is created in the image and likeness of God. God is Spirit and man is a spirit being. That is why we can know God. Man can worship God in spirit and in truth. We serve God in our spirits (Romans 1:9). God reveals Himself and His plans and purposes to us through His Spirit. "Eye has not seen, nor ear heard, nor have entered into the heart of man, the things which God has prepared for those who love Him. But He has revealed them to us by His Spirit. (1 Corinthians 2: 8,9)

The love of God is in the Spirit (Colossians 1:8) and the love of God has been poured out in our hearts by the Holy Spirit (Romans 5:5).

The prophet Malachi says, "Take heed to your spirit, that we do not deal treacherously . . ." (Malachi 2:15). One of the spirits released to the church in these last days is the spirit of unfaithfulness anddisloyalty, causing much strife and division. Unfaithfulness is spiritual adultery.

We must know what manner of spirit we have. The disciples wanted to command fire to come down from heaven just like Elijah did but Jesus rebuked them and said, "You do not know what manner of spirit you are of." (Luke 9:55) They quoted the right scriptures but their spirit was wrong!

Do you want to know why Samson was killed? It was not because of Delilah, not because he cut his hair but because in his heart there was a spirit of revenge. He did what he did out of revenge against the Philistines. He had the anointing and the gifts, but he operated out of a wrong spirit and that destroyed him. In these last days, God is looking for people who are holy. You may have the anointing and all the gifts, but if your spirit is not right, you will destroy yourself in the end. But if we are holy and have the right spirit, we will not make the same mistake like Samson did, and we can take the cities and the Philistines are going to bow down!

It is so important for us to have the right spirit. "Above all else, keep your heart with all diligence, for out of it spring the issues of life." (Proverbs 4:23)

2 Corinthians 7:1 "Therefore, having these promises, beloved, let us cleanse ourselves from all filthiness of the flesh and spirit, perfecting holiness in the fear of God."

We have to cleanse ourselves from all filthiness of the flesh and spirit. There are many ways our spirit can be defiled:

Bitterness
"Looking carefully lest anyone fall short of the grace of God; lest any root of bitterness springing up cause trouble, and by this many become defiled." (Hebrews 12:15)

Sexual immorality
1 Corinthians 6:18

Tongue
"But those things which proceed out of the mouth come from the heart, and they defile a man (Matthews 15:18)

Sadness
"A merry heart does good, like medicine, but a broken spirit dries the bones . . ."
(Proverbs 17:22)

". . . but who can bear a broken spirit."
(Proverbs 18:14)

Anger
"But he who is slow to anger is better than the mighty, and he who rules his spirit than he who takes a city"
(Proverbs 16:32)
A critical and fault-finding spirit

Familiar spirits
"Give no regard to mediums and familiar spirits; do not seek after them to be defiled by them." (Leviticus. 19:31).

Five Ways We Can Refresh Our Spirits

i) **Praying in the Spirit**
"For with stammering lips and another tongue . . . This is the rest with which you may cause the weary to rest . . . this is the refreshing . . ." (Isaiah 28: 11,12)

ii) **Experiencing God's goodness and love**
"The blessing of the Lord makes one rich, and He adds no sorrow with it." (Proverbs 10:22)

iii) **Fellowship with spirit-filled saints**
The Apostle Paul was refreshed in his spirit by his friends and supporters" . . . they refreshed my spirit . . ." (1 Corinthians 16:18)

iv) **Anointed music**
". . . David would take a harp and play it . . . then Saul would become refreshed and well, and the distressing spirit would depart from him." (1 Samuel 16:23)

v) **Abiding in God's presence**
". . . times of refreshing come from the presence of the Lord."(Acts 3:19)

6. **Know God through a holy life**

Blessed are the pure in heart for they shall see God (Matthew 5:8). God reveals Himself as Jehovah M'Kaddesh (Leviticus 20:8). He is the Lord that sanctifies us. We are to consecrate ourselves and be holy. Our spirit, souls and bodies must be sanctified so that we can come into His inheritance and into the year of exceeding abundant expansion.

They that know their God shall do great exploits. Like the Apostle Paul, let our prayer be,
". . . that I may know God . . ." (Philippians 3:10)

CHAPTER 10:

MONEY WITH A MISSION

We all get excited to hear preachers preach about faith, healing, praise and worship, deliverance, etc but the moment MONEY is preached about we all groan on the inside and we have a very negative response. It is alright outside in the world to talk about it, go to seminars and learn about money making ways. But in church it is taboo. I, as a Pastor, will naturally ask the question why?

Broken trust—we live in a very distrustful age. Back in the mid 1960's, three out of four Americans said they trusted the federal government to do what is right all or most of the time. Ten years ago the figure dropped to forty-four percent. Today, 2004, only nineteen percent have in government.

People will also warn you to "believe only half of what you hear and be sure it's the right half"!

The common ground that connects a person to another intimately is mutual trust. But that trust is so easily broken—even amongst us Christians—especially when some preachers have abused and extorted God's people and all in the "name of raising money for God".

Trust is also broken when so called Christians go into a business deal with you and the deal goes sour and they take off with your money!

Or a Christian brother or sister say they have a need, you believe them and you give and give to them and then they take off for a holiday in Switzerland!

You need to forgive that person—and ask God to heal your heart of the broken trust that has come in—not every pastor or Christian is like that—so false expectancy also needs to be broken—well it happened to me once so I must watch out for every pastor or Christian businessman—they are all the same. They are not!

But when you really get down to it broken trust is not the only reason why people don't like their pastor to talk about money. The primary reason why people don't like money to be preached about is because it address a heart issue—Matthew 6:21 says, "For where your treasure is, there your heart will be also."

Money has a way of revealing a person's true nature. It is easy to determine your past, your present and your future by taking a look at your cheque book. It will tell about your lifestyle, your priorities, your values and your relationship with God. Because if you really want to know where your heart is, all you need to do is find out where your treasure is. For example, if a lot of your money goes into buying golf equipment and paying membership fees at local golf clubs—that is where your heart is.

If you write a lot of cheques to the computer software store, the clothes store, the book store, the shoe store, or dare I even say the pornography store that is where your heart is.

Your heart will always be found where your money goes!

Money is one of the biggest competitors with God in people's lives. That is why you don't like sermons on it. The truth hurts and you would rather have a nice sermon that tickles your ears and leaves you in your comfort zone.

Jesus said, in Luke 16:13 "No one can serve two masters for he will hate the one and love the other, or else he will be loyal to the one and despise the other. You cannot serve God and Mammon."!

Take note: Jesus drew a parallel between two master and He called them both "masters"—God is your "master" or mammon (meaning money) is your "master". And our allegiance to one automatically means we are disloyal to the other. We cannot give our heart to both at the same time. Money has the power to take God's place in our life. How can you tell if money is your master? Ask yourselves these questions?

Do you think and worry about money frequently?

Do you give up doing what you should do or would like to do in order to make more money?

Do you spend a great deal of your time caring for your possessions?

Is it hard for you to give money away?

Are you in debt?

Having money can be deceptive—we think of comfort, power, and control and it is all to gratify SELF, and to look good in front of others. No amount of money can provide health, happiness or eternal life. How much better it is to let GOD be your master.

The Bible is not saying we cannot have money or be rich but where is your heart? Is money your slaves or are you slave to your money?

The Pharisees were "lovers of money" (Luke 16: 14) and when they heard Jesus teach on money they "derided Him". Do we laugh when we heart preaching about money? Do you go out for lunch now and criticize your pastor's sermon on money and tear it apart point by point? Or do you say "I won't go to that church again." Because you don't like to hear the truth or the truth hurts?
We live in an age that measure's people worth by how much money they make. But it doesn't matter how much money or how little money you make—the most important thing is your heart. Do you love Jesus more than your money? "For where your treasure is, there your heart will be also.

The third reason why we don't like to hear about money is exactly what the devil wants. He wants the church poor so we cannot impact our world with the gospel. So he (Satan) convinces Christians that talking about money in church is wrong. He wants us to have a wrong attitude about money so that church will walk in lack and insufficiency and will not get the world's attention. It costs to run a church. It cost to have miracle services. It costs to go on mission trips. And the longer the devil can keep the church poor and its members poor the great commission of preaching the gospel to all nations will not be fulfilled.

Many churches in the world today carry a strong anointing and a powerful message but they are making a very little impact. Why? Because they lack the financial resources to get their message out.

The church is poor because its members are poor. The members are poor because they will not face up with their wrong attitudes concerning money. They have a spirit of poverty mentality. Do not play into the devil's hands—if you are not free in your giving that is exactly where he wants you!
Brothers and sisters in Christ, allow the Holy Spirit to reveal to you your heart attitude—if you have been hurt because of broken trust allow God to heal your heart—don't stay in bitterness and unforgiveness—and start to release those finances again.

If you know that money is your master repent, say sorry to God and make Him Lord of your life and release those finances.

Don't give the devil a foothold over your life by keeping you poor because of wrong thinking—break the stronghold of poverty mentality and rise up and release your finances.

Does God want to bless you? Yes, He does. It is God's will for you to prosper.

CHAPTER 11:

THE KEYS TO A DIVINE RELEASE

Why do I give and nothing happens?
2 Corinthians 9:7 Each man should give what he has decided in his heart to give, not reluctantly or under compulsion, for God loves a cheerful giver.

Are you giving with joy in your heart?
Some people say give till it hurts. But we really should continue giving until it doesn't hurt then there is joy in our giving and it will be blessed; if it still hurts we are not dead yet.

In Mark 4 and Matthews 13 we see God guarantee returns of 30, 60, or 100 fold of our investment of money, time, energy, love, kindness and prayer.

Why are there no returns?
Is your giving on the wayside giving?
Shallow or stony ground represents wrong motives or motivation, competition, control, reputation, pride, guilt, obligation, lose face, etc. This kind of giving does not bring a harvest and there are no returns.

The thorns and thistles are symbolic of the pressures of the world. It also speaks of carnality.

We must understand divine timing and the law of sowing and reaping.

If what you have at hand is not enough to spend it is meant for you as a seed to sow, so don't eat the seed or there will be no harvest.

Any unforgiveness and hurts not released can hinder your harvest and don't give out of duty, fear or hurt but give liberally from a generous joyful spirit. Be like Naaman's maid—give up your right to be hurt and release others.

Unbelief, doubt and double-mindedness hold back our harvest.
Don't you expect a return? What are you expecting?

Be quick to respond. Don't miss the opportunities and privileges to sow and reap.

Did you plant and sow in faith?
Who is your source? Are you walking in the spirit? If you want to receive your harvest you must give out of faith, not out of doubt or unbelief.

Malachi 3:10-11 "Bring the whole tithe into the storehouse, that there may be food in my house. Test me in this," says the LORD Almighty, "and see if I will not throw open the floodgates of heaven and pour out so much blessing that you will not have room enough for it."

Following God's leading, hearing and obeying God's voice is a key to effective giving. Does the devil ask you to give or God? The devil doesn't want you to give and get God's blessings.

Le Truream was the originator of earth moving caterpillars and due to his commitment; God gave him ideas, concepts and creative inventions. How do you know it's God? The moment he stopped giving, the creative ideas also stopped flowing.

We must live under God's blessings and not curses.
When you identify the thief who had stolen from you, he must return seven-fold. If you have been robbed, cheated—claim back.

What are you saying?
Out of the abundance of the heart the mouth speaks.

He is El Shaddai and not El Cheapo!
He is more than enough for your every need and not a God of lack.

Is your bad-mouthing or negativity causing your own seed to die or are you sowing blessings and thanksgiving with praise to God?

It is not the sum of your giving but the spirit of your giving that determines the outflow (release) from God.

We see in Luke chapter five eight characteristics of the last day prophetic church which are:-

- Great hunger for the Word and emphasis of the Word.
- People who are not quitters but breakthrough like sons of Perez.
- People who wholly follow God or are committed.
- People who are bold, courageous and have persistent faith.
- People who repent quickly and are holy.
- People who breakthrough in miracles. There is a great anointing and outpouring of the Holy Spirit and sign, wonders and miracles are common with a large harvest in these last days.
- A church that is united and shares in love.
- A church of abundance and that shares and gives to others.

WHAT IS THE KEY?

We see in the Scriptures that many people had boats but Peter allowed Jesus to use his boat; he gave Jesus permission.

Giving releases the key to the miraculous and releases divine revelation of the nature of the last day prophetic church.

How I give inevitably impacts how I live and how I view and relate to people. These are times to give generously and willingly, not in despair or resignation but in surrender of self-will and self-righteous. Let us give up blaming, judgment, negativism, and give faith, praise and thanksgiving.

These are times to forgive, to release grudges, anger, pain and hurt; to give up real or perceived injustice.

These are times to give over into God's hands matters that only He can handle.

These are times to give to provide for others in need. We must not back away from God's laws of reciprocal giving because giving is God's law of a release of God's Spirit and open heavens.

CHAPTER 12:

OVERCOMING FEAR

There are five Hebrew words which can be translated into one English word meaning fear. From the book of Genesis through to Revelation fear is mentioned six hundred times. For example, Abraham, Moses, Gideon, David, Daniel, Mary the mother of Jesus, Peter and John when he was on the island of Patmos were all commanded "fear not". There are three hundred and sixty-five days in a year and so there are promises not to fear for every day. In fact, there are nearly two for every day!

We will either conquer fear or fear will conquer us. So we must distinguish between the emotion of fear and the spirit of fear. One helps us whereas the other can harm us. For example, when we hear a gunshot we jump and run and hide. Here the emotion of fear helps us as it is God given for our well being. When fear attacks our minds, clouds our reason and perception and steals our peace—that is a spirit of fear and it is very unhealthy and harms us.

Where did fear come from? It entered into the Garden of Eden when Adam and Eve sinned. Then throughout the Bible we can see many great men of God influenced by fear. Elijah ran in fear because of Queen Jezebel's threat to kill him. David ran in fear of his son Absalom. King Saul lost his ministry anointing because fear of the people. Peter in hisdenial of Jesus, lied out of fear and Judas Iscariot betrayed Jesus because of fear that his personal agenda would be terminated.

Fear is contagious. There is the story of a man from a mid-western American town who started to run down the street and scream, "The dam is broken! The dam is broken!" Women who were shopping in the supermarket heard him and so left all their shopping to join the crowd in the street. They ran past a barber's shop and people in the barber's shop also joined them. They ran past a police station and the police also came out and started to run with them. By this time there was a chaotic mob and they ran all the way to the bridge leading out of the town. On the bridge, a crippled man with a walking stick, slowly stood to his feet and held his stick in the air. The mob came to a standstill as he said to them, "Why are you all running? This town has no dam!" Fear spreads its wings of doubt and it spreads like a plague. When fear knocks we should send faith to the door.

Fear can also be a self-fulfilling prophecy. There was a man called Nick who worked with refrigeration containers. He was a good man but he had a deep fear that one day he would be locked in the refrigerator container and die. One day, by accident, he was locked in. He banged on the doors but nobody heard him. Nick believed that the temperature in the container was zero degrees and he would certainly die. So he managed to find a piece of cardboard and write his last words to his family and wrote that if he didn't get out he would certainly freeze to death. The next day, he was found frozen to death and the autopsy recorded that he died of freezing. However, the refrigerator container was a damaged one and had broken down. So the actual temperature in the container was sixty one degrees and not zero. His mind allowed him to believe the deep rooted fear that he had had. That fear came to be a self-fulfilling prophecy.

The spirit of fear can rob us of our inheritance. In Numbers chapter thirteen, the Israelites saw the descendants of Anak, who were giants but they also saw themselves as grasshoppers. So they refused to go into the land of Canaan, a land flowing with milk and honey. Fear hindered them from receiving the blessings of the Lord.

Revelation 21:8 tells us that "the cowardly (fearful) unbelieving, abominable, murderers, sexually immoral, sorcerers, idolaters and all liars shall have their part in the lake which burns with fire and brimstone, which is the second death." There are different types of fear. There is fear of the unknown, fear of death, fear of sickness, fear of failure, fear or rejection, fear of lack, fear of man, fear of betrayal etc. Let us take a look at the fear of death. Death takes no holiday and it is no respecter of persons. Only those who are prepared to die are truly prepared to live. Hebrews 9:27 tells us that "it is appointed for men to be once, but after this the judgment." Life is not permanent it is transitory. Death is not termination or cessation but transition, a changing from one dimension to another.

James describes death as a vapor and life as grass. Ecclesiastes also says that there is a "time to live and a time to die." Death is when the spirit leaves the body. In Psalm 23, death is called a shadow. The shadow of a lion or a sword cannot cut me. Jesus has keys of life and death. Revelation 1:17,18 says, ". . . Do not be afraid; I am the First and the Last, I am He who lives and was dead and behold I am alive for evermore. Amen. And I have the keys of Hades and Death."

Fear can knock us down but not knock us out. Jesus was betrayed by Judas, David by Absalom, Paul by Demas but those betrayed became better and not bitter. They refused to allow a bad experience to become a fear in their lives.

We have a choice for fear to conquer us or to trust Jesus to help us overcome our fears. We can be victorious as we surrender our lives to Him and live a life of obedience to His Word. As Luke 1:74 says, "To grant us that we being delivered from the hand of our enemies, might serve Him without fear."

CHAPTER 13:

HOW TO BE VICTORIOUS IN SPIRITUAL WARFARE

When we are born again by the Spirit of God, everyone of us immediately enters into spiritual warfare. So in our lives, there are four strategic battlegrounds; the mind, the heart, the mouth and the body. In the Bible, we see that four persons had direct confrontation and encounter with Satan. They were Adam and Eve, Job, Nebuchadnezzar and David. They fought their battles in the four areas mentioned above and from these men, we can learn how to be victorious in spiritual warfare.

FOUR PERSONS			
	Adam & Eve	Job	Nebuchadnezzar	David
Satan's Target	The mind	The body	The mouth	The heart
Satan's weapon	Lies Deception	Suffering	Pride	Accusation Confusion Regret Remorse Repression
Satan's purpose	Ignorance of God's will	Impatience with God's will	Independence of God's will	Independence of God's will

Your weapon of Defense	Word of God	Imparted grace of God	Yielding to the indwelling Holy Spirit	Intercession of Jesus, God's son

THE MIND

Every thought that enters the mind comes from four possible sources: self, Satan, people of the world or God.

According to John 8:44, Satan is the father of lies and so his weapons are deception, pressures, persecution, cares and worries. So we must protect our minds from the lies of Satan as a mind that is unrenewed is dangerous, for our mind is part of the image of God, where God communes with us and reveals Himself.

For example, Satan asked Eve, "Has God said?" He thereby questioning God's Word. Then he denied God's Word by telling her, "You will not surely die?" Finally, he substituted God's Word by saying, "You will be like God?" It was all lies and deception.

Satan also tempts people through obsession, vexation, harassment, suppression, oppression and depression. So again, we need to discern the actual source of our thinking, is it argumentative, self-glorying, critical of leaders, negative, fault-finding, greedy, selfish, accusing, suspicious, doubtful, fearful or always worrying?

Proverbs 23:7 says:
"As he thinks within himself so he is."

THE BODY

Satan attacked Job through his circumstances around him, his children, his wealth, his loss of friends, his wife and neighbors and then his body with a terrible disease. This suffering was not from God but He allowed it to happen so that Job would be tested and come forth as gold (*Job 23:10*).

Satan wants to attack and destroy our body because it is God's temple of the Holy Spirit. God wants to use our body as a vehicle for revealing

Himself to a lost world, so Satan knows He can hinder God's work by attacking God's workers and putting their tools out of commission. The members of our body are tools in the Holy Spirit's hand to help build the church on earth.

I Corinthians 6:19 "Do you not know that your body is the temple of the Holy Spirit who is in you . . ."

Satan attacks our body because it is God's testing ground. As God's children we must take care of the body and use it for God's glory.

THE MOUTH
Proverbs 18:21 "Death and life are in the power of the tongue and those who love it will eat its fruit."

The mouth can defile us as it blames and speaks negatively. If it is full of pride, it can lead to our downfall as in the case of King Nebuchadnezzar.

Daniel 4:30-33 "The king spoke, saying, 'Is not this great Babylon that I have built for a royal dwelling by my mighty power and for the honor of my majesty?' While the word was still in the king's mouth, a voice fell from heaven: 'ing Nebuchadnezzar, to you it is spoken: the kingdom has departed from you! And they shall drive you from men, and your dwelling shall be with the beasts of the field. They shall make you eat grass like oxen; and seven times shall pass over you, until you know that the Most High rules in the kingdom of men, and gives it to whoever He chooses.' That very hour the word was fulfilled concerning Nebuchadnezzar; he was driven from men and ate grass like oxen; his body was wet with the dew of heaven till his hair had grown like eagles' feathers and his nails like birds' claws."

Job never sinned with his lips despite of all that happened to him (Job 2:10). How about us? What would come from our lips if we were in Job's situation?

James 3:8-10 "But no man can tame the tongue. It is an unruly evil, full of deadly poison. With it we bless our God and Father, and with it we curse men, who have been made in the similitude of God. Outof the same mouth proceed blessing and cursing. My brethren, these things ought not to be so.

THE HEART

Satan's aim is to get our hearts and control it, for the heart is the seat of our emotions.

In 1 Chronicles 21, David's mind was not deceived but his heart motive was under attack. He himself was not suffering, his kingdom was in great shape and he had won a number of notable victories and so he was enjoying a height of success and popularity. However, because of the sin of self-importance and self-glory, it resulted in the loss of 70,000 lives.

The mind, body, mouth and heart are constantly under attack by Satan, so how do we overcome? The devil is a defeated foe but many of us are still living defeated lives because we have not recognized our authority in Christ, our authority in His Word and the importance of the armour of God.

OVERCOMING OUR ENEMY

Who We are in Christ

As born again believers we must recognize who we are in Christ and what He has done for us. First, we have been chosen by Him (Ephesians 1:4). Secondly, we have been redeemed by His blood (Ephesians 1:7). He has forgiven and forgotten our sins and we are a new creation in Him. Thirdly, we belong to God and have been sealed with the Holy Spirit. So when Satan comes along, he sees that we are marked, we belong to God so he cannot hurt us (Ephesians 1:13).

We have Christ's Authority

God has given us all authority to trample over the power of the enemy and nothing can harm us when we walk in the Spirit and obey His Word.

Luke 10:19 "I have given you authority to trample on snakes and scorpions and to overcome all the power of the enemy; nothing will harm you."

The Word of God
Every time Jesus was tempted in the wilderness, He said to Satan "It is written . . ."

We all must know the Word of God so that we too are able to ward off the attacks of the enemy. We need to memorize the Word, meditate on God's Word and apply God's Word which means obey and do it. It is the Word which will renew our minds and keep us strong in our spirit man.

The Armour of God
Ephesians 6:13 "Therefore put on the full armor of God, so that when the day of evil comes, you may be able to stand your ground, and after you have done everything, to stand."

The belt of truth—Jesus is the truth so we must believe in the truth and speak the truth.

The breastplate of righteousness—so that we are able to do that which is right.

Feet shod with the gospel of peace—Jesus is our peace. Let us tell others about it and be peace makers when there is turmoil around us.

The shield of faith to quench all the fiery darts of the evil one.

The helmet of salvation to protect the mind.

The sword of the Spirit which is the Word of God to overcome the lies and deception of Satan.

Prayer and Fasting
Prayer and fasting should be a regular exercise for every Christian. From the Old Testament to the New, believers would regularly pray and fast. According to Isaiah 58:6-9, it will loose the cords, of wickedness, undo the heavy burdens, let the oppressed go free, break every yoke and healing shall come quickly.

Praying in the Holy Spirit
Ephesians 6:18 "And pray in the Spirit on all occasions with all kinds of prayers and requests. With this in mind, be alert and always keep on praying for all the saints."

Colossians 3:16 "Let the word of Christ dwell in you richly as you teach and admonish one another with all wisdom, and as you sing psalms, hymns and spiritual songs with gratitude in your hearts to God."

Praying in tongues will strengthen our inner man and give us extra power in spiritual warfare praying. I know that during intense spiritual warfare in Taiwan, praying in the Holy Spirit was the key to victory over strongholds personally, in the church and in the city where I lived.

Praise
Hebrews 13:15 ". . . therefore, let us continually offer to God a sacrifice of praise-the fruit of lips that confess his name."

Paul and Silas prayed and sang praises to God at midnight in prison after having been severely flogged. An earthquake came, the prison doors were opened and when we praise God during our difficult circumstances, God will open our prison doors and we will have victory over the enemy. It will be a sacrifice of praise but one that will enable us to overcome.

Adam and Eve, Job, Nebuchadnezzar and David were attacked in the mind, body, mouth and heart. Let us learn from their mistakes and as Romans 8:37 says: "Yet in all these things we are more than conquerors through Him who loved us."

CHAPTER 14:

A LIFE OF HOLINESS

Holiness is not external dressing but inward moral attitudes and heart condition.

2 Peter 1:4 "Through these he has given us his very great and precious promises so that through them you may participate in the divine nature and escape the corruption in the world caused by evil desires."

Some people find it hard to believe that God wants us to be holy. They think that it's only when they die and go to heaven that they will and can be holy. What God wants, is that you be HOLY NOW. The Christian will miss the heart of God's purposes for him if he doesn't want to be holy. If you truly want God's holiness, you must be prepared to face your unholiness, painful though it may be.

1 Peter 1:15, 16 "But just as he who called you is holy, so be holy in all you do; for it is written 'Be holy, because I am holy.'"

God is calling us to Holiness:

Chosen   —What a privilege!
Royal   —Kingship, to rule, and be victorious.
Holy   —Character of the people.
Peculiar   —Unique, special.
                Isaiah 8:18; Mark 16:18
For God's Praises —To glorify God is the highest honor God gives to man.

What type of vessels do you choose to be? Vessels for honor or dishonor? (Hebrews 10:10). 2 Timothy 2:21 says that "We should choose to be vessels of gold and silver, sanctified and useful for the Master, prepared for every good work . . ."

Paul says in Hebrews 12:10 that we "we share or are partakers of His holiness . . ." but sin, unbelief, disobedience, compromise, lies, deceit, doubts, complaints or fear, will prevent us from seeing God's glory or Holiness.

It is the recognition of God's Holiness that brings true worship and praise, for Holiness is related to God's Glory, His presence, His power and His goodness. (Exodus 15:11). Therefore we need to pursue Holiness to see God's glory and to experience His goodness, blessings and power. God's will is our sanctification (1 Thessalonians 5: 23)

GOD IS A HOLY GOD
"For the Lord, our God is Holy." (Psalms 99:9) If God is Holy, how can we worship Him if we are unholy? It's not only His power that is evidence or proof that Jesus is the Son of God, but His Holiness of life that is also a characteristic.

WHY BE HOLY?
1 Corinthians 6:9-11 "Do you not know that the wicked will not inherit the kingdom of God? Do not be deceived: Neither the sexually immoral or idolaters nor adulterers nor male prostitutes nor homosexual offenders nor thieves nor the greedy nor drunkards nor slanderers nor swindlers will inherit the kingdom of God. And that is what some of you were. But you were washed, you were sanctified, you were justified in the name of the Lord Jesus Christ and by the Spirit of our God."

It is God's will that we be holy: 1 Thessalonians 4:1-4

We belong to God; we are born of His Holy Spirit to live a holy life, to be like our Father: Genesis 1:26, 1 John 4:17, 2 Peter 1:4, Ephesians 1:4, Hebrews 2:11.

We are the Temple of the Holy Spirit or the habitation of God: Ephesians 2:22, 1 Corinthians 6:9-11, 1 Corinthians 3: 16, 17.

Without holiness, we cannot have a revelation of God: Hebrews 12:14 "The pure in heart shall see God" Jesus says.

God is seeking for and will come for a Holy Church: Ephesians 5:26, 27

A holy life is a life of power: Romans 1:4

It is the recognition of God's Holiness that brings true worship and praise. Holiness is related to God's Glory: Exodus 15:11, Revelations 15:4

Through a Holy life we reveal God to the world.
1 Corinthians 3:16-17 "Do you not know that you are the temple of God and that the Spirit of God dwells in you? If anyone defiles the temple of God, God will destroy him. For the temple of God is holy, which temple you are."

As we study the Scriptures we see that God expects us to live a holy life and no life is pure and holy unless it is Christ like. It is my belief that God is calling us, His people, to Holiness.

PUT ON THE NEW MAN
Colossians 3:8-10 "But now you yourselves are to put off all these: anger, wrath, malice, blasphemy, filthy language out of your mouth. Do not lie to one another since you have put off the old man with his deeds, and have put on the new man who is renewed in knowledge according to the image of Him who created him."

1 Corinthians 6:9-11 tells us what we were and what we are now.
1 Corinthians 1:30, 2 Thessalonians 2:13,14, Hebrews 2:11, Ephesians 4:22. We are called to put on the new man. Colossians 3:8-10.

Romans 6 speaks of the glory of Holiness. The Bible speaks of the glory of righteousness and the glory of the Holy Spirit's ministry. It also speaks of the glory of Holiness.

HOLINESS CAN BE VIEWED FROM TWO POINTS OR PERSPECTIVES

Positional, which is legal, conferred, imputed to us.

Progressive, which is the outworking and requires our decisions, will, participation and co-operation and testings or trials.

DEFINITION OF HOLINESS

Holiness really means a separation unto God from carnal to, or, for sacred or spiritual purposes, or for walking in the Spirit. e.g. in the life of Abraham, Jacob and Joseph.

Sanctification is instantaneous when one accepts Christ but it is also progressive: Romans 1:11, Philippians 2:12.

HOW ARE WE SANCTIFIED AND HOW DO WE LIVE A HOLY LIFE?

2 Corinthians 7:1 "Therefore, having these promises, beloved, let us cleanse ourselves from all filthiness of the flesh and spirit, perfecting holiness in the fear of God." This verse is saying that we perfect love or Holiness in the fear of God.

What is the fear of God?
1 Peter 1:17, Proverbs 9:10, Proverbs 8:13 define the fear or God as: To live for Him and to stay away from sin and what displeases Him to do His will.

Ephesians 4:23, put on the new man. It is a deliberate act of choice. Asking God to make us Holy, Hebrews 2:11.

Walk in the Spirit or Love: Romans 8, Galatians 5:6-16, 22-25.

Walk and live in the awareness of our union with Christ and yielding ourselves to God, Romans 6.

Renewing our minds by the Word and surrendering to God, Romans 12:1.

Romans 12:1 ". . . to offer your bodies as living sacrifices, holy and pleasing to God—this is your spiritual act of worship."

Galatians 5:16-17 ". . . Walk in the Spirit, and you shall not fulfill the lust of the flesh. For the flesh lusts against the Spirit, and the Spirit against the flesh; and these are contrary to one another, so that you do not do the things that you wish."

Galatians 5:22-23 "But the fruit of the Spirit is love, joy, peace, patience, kindness, goodness, faithfulness, gentleness and self-control."

Progressive sanctification is the putting off of the old self and putting on of the new man: Ephesians 4:17-32.

Holiness is the development of a Christ like nature. What is sanctification? It is turning to Light and it is the receiving of our inheritance, Acts 26:1.

Romans 6:22 "But now that you have been set free from sin and have become slaves to God, the benefit you reap leads to holiness, and the result is eternal life."

The fruit of God's servants is Holiness. We have been made free from sin to live a Holy Life and the Feast of Unleavened Bread points us to a Holy Life.

Ephesians 5:26-27 says that Jesus is coming back to a glorious church, not having spot or wrinkle or any such, but that she should be holy and without blemish.

Praise God, we have been redeemed by the blood of Jesus. Our faith and hope are in God. We are born again of the Holy Spirit and by faith in the power of God, we can overcome sin and lead a holy and victorious Christian life. In accordance to God's purpose and plan, He has created us in His own image who would reflect His righteousness and holiness.

Revelations 15:4 "Who shall not fear you, O Lord, and glorify Your name? For You alone are holy. For all nations shall come and worship You . . ."

CHAPTER 15:

VICTORY IN PRAYER

We have schools of every nature and counsel offered in every area except in Prayer and Faith. With Christ is the School of Prayer. God wants us to be successful and we can only be so through prayer. Things in the spiritual must be birthed through prayers.

Psalm 34:17-19 ". . . God promises that He hears us and His assurances are that He answers our prayers and wants us to succeed . . ."

John 6:35 Then Jesus declared "I am the bread of life. He who comes to me will never be hungry and he who believes in Me will never be thirsty".

GOD WANTS TO MEET ALL OUR NEEDS!

Jesus is our model / example: Jesus lived a life of prayer.

What is God calling the church to do? Pause to listen, pray, proclaim and to wait on God.

Why do we fail when God wants us to succeed and the key is our prayer life?

Luke 3:21 "When all the people were being baptized, Jesus was baptized too. And as he was praying, the heaven was opened."

JESUS BEGAN HIS MINISTRY WITH PRAYER (Matthew 3:13-17)

While Jesus was praying, the heavens opened and the Holy Spirit anointed Him, thus, prayer will open the windows of heaven and God will pour out His blessings on us.

What is the secret of Jesus' power?
Luke 5: 15-16 "Yet the news about him spread all the more, so that crowds of people came to hear him and to be healed of their sicknesses. But Jesus often withdrew to lonely places and prayed."

Luke 6:12-13 "One of those days Jesus went out to a mountainside to pray, and spent the night praying to God. When morning came, He called His disciples to Him and chose twelve of them, whom He also designated apostles:" He continued all night in prayer to God.

This reveals the secret behind Jesus' power and miracles. He even prayed after a great meeting so there was no let down or complacency. The early church had an hour of prayer and the things of God's kingdom are birthed through prayer.

Every minister of God is to learn a lesson that all who take upon themselves the ministry of the Word are destined to draw upon themselves the most intense fire of the enemy. We are called into spiritual warfare, not one with flesh and blood. Everyone called of God would do well after he had prepared himself for the ministry to set aside a period for special waiting before God. The early church prayed before they sent out their first missionaries, (Acts 13: 2-4). Jesus prayed before launching out into active ministry. He withdrew himself into the wilderness for prayer in a final strengthening of Himself for combat with Satan. (Acts 4:1-2).

JESUS STARTED THE DAY WITH PRAYER

Mark 1:35-37 "And in the morning, He went out and departed into a solitary place and there prayed. All men seek for thee."

No matter how powerful an anointing we may have, it is necessary that it be sustained by daily prayer.

Jesus began His day with prayer.
Luke 5:16 "But Jesus often withdrew to lonely places and prayed."

Praise and thanksgiving is an essential part of prayer. There were periods in His praying when Jesus gave thanks and praise to God.

Matthew 11:25 "At that time Jesus said, 'I praise you, Father, Lord of heaven and earth, because you have hidden these things from the wise and learned, and revealed them to little children'".

Matthew 15:36 "When Jesus feeds the 4000, then He took the seven loaves and the fish, and when He had given thanks, He broke them and gave them to the disciples, and they in turn to the people."

Jesus consulted the Father in prayer before He performed the miracle of Lazarus rising from the dead.

John 11:41-44 "Father, I thank you that You have heard Me. I knew that You always hear Me, but I said this for the benefit of the people standing here, that they may believe that You sent Me." When He had said this, Jesus called in a loud voice, "Lazarus, come out!"

Jesus knew the voice of the Father and lived in intimacy with the Father and out of the fellowship (a life of Prayer) talking with the Father a release of divine power and miracles are manifested.

Misfortune and trouble often drive people to their knees in prayer. History shows that leaders have fallen in with the word of the crowd. But Jesus was not deceived by people who were ready to crown Him King today and crucify Him tomorrow. Instead He perceived the danger was ahead and to avoid it He had to escape and pray. He saw plans that were being made to take Him by force and make Him King.

Matthew 14:23 "After He had dismissed them, He went up on a mountain side by Himself to pray."

John 6:70-71 "Then Jesus replied, 'Have I not chosen you the Twelve? Yet one of you is a devil!'" (He meant Judas, the son of Simon Iscariot, who, though one of the Twelve, was later to betray Him). He discerned that an evil spirit had already gotten into one of His disciples.

Jesus perceived there was no real heart change in the multitude. They wanted to make Him King because He fed them, John 6:26-31, 66.

If the people took Him by force and made Him King, it would completely defeat God's plan of redemption.

WE MUST PRAY BEFORE MAKING MAJOR DECISIONS

Luke 6:11-12 "But they were furious and began to discuss with one another what they might do to Jesus. One of those days Jesus went out to a mountain side to pray, and spent the night praying to God."

Before every crucial decision Jesus sought the face of the Father in prayer. Let us learn from Christ's example that when we have vital decisions to make we pray.

Luke 9:18-21 "Once when Jesus was praying in private and his disciples were with Him, he asked them, 'Who do the crowds say I am?' They replied, 'Some say John the Baptist; others Elijah; and still others, that one of the prophets of long ago has come back to life.' 'But what about you?' He asked. 'Who do you say I am?' Peter answered, 'The Christ of God.' Jesus strictly warned them not to tell this to anyone."

In Acts 9:17 God sent Annaias because of Paul's prayers and God healed and baptized him with the Holy Spirit as a result.

Prayer results in revelation and guidance.

PRAYING THAT OTHERS MIGHT RECEIVE REVELATION FROM GOD.

Paul changed the church through his prayers, Ephesians 1:18-23

Luke 9:28-29 "About eight days after Jesus said this, he took Peter, John and James with Him and went up onto a mountain to pray. As He was praying, the appearance of His face changed, and His clothes became as bright as a flash of lightning."

PRAYER CHANGES THINGS IN LIFE

2 Corinthians 3:18 "And we, who with unveiled faces all reflect the Lord's glory, are being transformed into his likeness with ever-increasing glory, which comes from the Lord, who is the Spirit."

Prayer brings the glory of God and revelation from God.

We all with open face (transparency) beholding as in a mirror the glory of the Lord are changed into the same image from glory to glory by the Spirit of God.

PRAYER INFLUENCES PEOPLE FOR GOD

We can do more on our knees than talk sometimes!

Luke 11:1 "One day Jesus was praying in a certain place. When He finished, one of his disciples said to Him, 'Lord, teach us to pray, just as John taught his disciples.'"

Prayer is the key to winning souls: John 6:44, Mark 16:10, 17. Peter had received the revelation that Jesus was the Christ but before that confession, we see Jesus alone in prayer that God would reveal His identity and mission to Peter as well as the others.

Prayer prepares you for the future
John 17:15 "My prayer is not that you take them out of the world but that you protect them from the evil one."

Luke 22:31-32 "Simon, Simon, Satan has asked to sift you as wheat. But I have prayed for you Simon, that your faith may not fail. And when you have turned back, strengthen your brothers."

A TRUE LEADER MUST SET THE EXAMPLE

Do you pray? How much time do we spend in prayer? What is our priority?
Methods may vary but the principle of prayer remains top priority.

PERSISTENCY IS VITAL IN PRAYER

Luke 18:1 "Then Jesus told His disciples a parable to show them that they should always pray and not give up."

Luke 18:8 "I tell you, he will see that they get justice, and quickly. However, when the Son of Man comes, will he find faith on the earth?"

This kind of faith never gives up on prayer. If a person doesn't pray, he is seduced by discouragement and will be despondent (depressed).

Matthew 14:12-14 "John's disciples came and took his body and buried it. Then they went and told Jesus. When Jesus heard what had happened, he withdrew by boat privately to a solitary place. Hearing of this, the crowds followed Him on foot from the towns. When Jesus landed and saw a large crowd, He had compassion on them and healed their sick."

PRAYER IS A SUPERNATURAL ACTIVITY AND RELEASES SUPERNATURAL POWER

Deliverance, miracles, healing, divine guidance and revelation come through prayer. Victory was won through prayer. The Bible tells us that:

Elijah prays for the widow's son who had stopped breathing. The Lord heard Elijah's cry, and the boy's life returned to him; and he lived, 1 Kings 17:20-23.

. . . enemies were overcome by prayers . . .
(Exodus 14:15-16)

Revival and restoration came through prayer, 1 Kings 18.

Hezekiah's prayer caused a plague of death to wipe out 185,000 men who were their enemies, 2 Kings 19:15-35.

What did Jesus do in a crisis? How did He respond?

Matthew 14:32, 39, 42 ". . . And when they climbed into the boat, the wind died down.

Jesus had already prayed ahead of time for the situation and was ready for the trial they faced.

Prayer is not escaping but Reinforcement to attack the devil's work.

In suffering Jesus prayed. Jesus prayed against evil and temptation. Jesus prayed for God's will to be accomplished. Prayer is battling spiritual forces. For example the spirit of slumber as seen in Matthew 26.

Jesus constantly sought the guidance of the Holy Spirit in prayer. His miracles were the results of His prayer. His prayer changed the destiny of the world.
His prayer prophetically influenced us.

DIFFERENT TYPES OF PRAYER:

The laying of hands in Prayer
The doctrine of laying on of hands is a scriptural one: Matthew 19:13-15, Mark 16:18.

Prayer for Healing
To every consecrated prayer warrior, there usually comes at some time or other a personal Gethsemane. Through it may exact agony yet he who meets it like Jesus in prevailing prayer will find that victory is assured.

Matthew 26:36 & 39 "Then Jesus went with his disciples to a place called Gethsemane, and he said to them, 'Sit here while I go over there and pray . . .' v.39 . . . going a little father, he fell with his face to the ground and prayed."

Praying for God's will in our life
Matthew 26:42 "He went away a second time and prayed. 'My Father, if it is not possible for this cup to be taken away unless I drink it, may your will be done.'"

Prayer of Forgiveness
Luke 23:34 "Jesus said, 'Father, forgive them, for they do not know what they are doing.' And they divided up His clothes by casting lots." (The final prayer of Jesus)

Prayer of Agreement
Matthew 18:20 ". . . For where two or three come together in My name, there am I with them."

Praying in the Spirit
Ephesians 6:18 ". . . And pray in the Spirit on all occasions with all kinds of prayer and requests . . ."

Praying and interceding for all saints
Ephesians 6:18 ". . . With this in mind, be alert and always keep on praying for all the saints."

Jesus prays for Himself (John 17: 1-5)
Jesus prays for His disciples (John 17:6-19)
Jesus prays for all believers (John 17: 20-26)

THE PRESENCE OF GOD AND PRAYER

Hebrews 13:5 "Keep your lives free from the love of money and be content with what you have, because God has said, 'Never will I leave you; never will I forsake you.'"

Matthew 28:20 "and teaching them to obey everything I have commanded you. And surely I am with you always to the very end of the age."

Psalm 139:7 "Where can I go from your Spirit? Where can I flee from your presence?"

Exodus 33:15 "Then Moses said to Him, 'If Your Presence does not go with us, do not send us up from here.'"

HOW IS JESUS PRESENT WITH US?

John 14:16-17 "And I will ask the Father, and He will give you another Counselor to be with you forever—the Spirit of truth. The world cannot accept him because it neither sees him nor knows him. But you will know him, for he lives with you and will be in you."

The New Testament celebrated three things: God for us, God with us and God in us. That is how near God is—He is Here: John 14:23, Exodus 33:14.

You and God make the majority Psalm 46:1. God is our refuge and strength, an ever-present help in trouble.

Psalm 73:17 "until I entered the sanctuary of God; then I understood their final destiny."

When David entered into the presence of God, he began to get things into perspective.

The truth is that God's presence is always with us though we may not consciously sense His Presence. By faith in His Word, He is always with us. He says that He will never leave us or forsake us. Matthew 6:5-6 "And when you pray, do not be like the hypocrites, for they love to pray standing in the synagogues and on the street corners to be seen by men. I tell you the truth, they have received their reward in full. But when you pray, go into your room, close the door and pray to your Father, who is unseen. Then your Father, who sees what is done in secret, will reward you."

Why must men get alone to pray? In the act of prayer, they are entering into the presence of God.

God is everywhere. He doesn't come and He doesn't go. The recognition of the presence of God makes it easy to pray and to have faith.

James 5:16 tells us: ". . . The effective, fervent prayer of a righteous man avails much."

Let us believe God to be effective in our prayer life, to follow the example of Jesus and so miracles and deliverance come through our prayers of intercession for ourselves and for others.

CHAPTER 16:

PRAY WITHOUT CEASING

Prayer should be both enjoyable and effective if we expect to be devoted to prayer unceasingly as the New Testament believers were. The idea that prayer is a boring ineffective task for times when nothing else can be said or done is completely false. I would like to give us three faith statements about prayer which when understood will inspire you to believe and will help prayer become a vital enjoyable unceasing part of your Christian life.

Something good will happen or things will be different because we pray, James 5:16.

The word fervent in the RSV implies continuation. Therefore, I believe that the prayer of James 5:16 is earnest, continual heartfelt fervent prayer of a godly man or woman releases mighty power and effects. Prayer causes things to happen in your marriage, your church or your Vicar's or Lay Reader's sermon. Things will be different on Sunday morning than they would have been because you, or your wife prayed a continual heartfelt fervent prayer: Luke 18:7-8 and Acts 10:3.

We are called to affect the destiny of our children, our marriages, our churches and our nations. You can affect nations. Moscow is not going to rule this world God is. The Church is going to rule this world through intercession rather than domination.

In Colossians 4:12-13 we are introduced to a man called Epaphras, who is certainly not as well known as Paul, Timothy or Titus but why was he mentioned? Paul mentions him because of his zeal, because Epaphras prayed continually that believers would stand perfect and complete in all the will of God. Epaphras devoted himself to pray for others continually. God delights in people who devote themselves continually to prayer. We see the word devoted is found several times in the Book of Acts. Prayer involved devotion—something you continue to do and are consistently doing, Acts 1:14 resulted in Pentecost. A prayer meeting established the first Pentecost Acts 2:42. The early Church established herself in four areas:

i) Devotion to Scriptures
ii) Fellowship
iii) Communion
iv) Prayer

We often want the power of God without seeking Him Acts 4:23-24, 31 are the results of seeking God in prayer. The early Church was devoted to prayer and every time they prayed the Spirit started moving. Their prayers were continual, heartfeltfervent prayers that released mighty power and effects. Ours can be the same.

The Throne of Grace is wide open to us

Paul's epistle to Titus tells us specifically what God's grace will do for us: Titus 2:11-15, Hebrews 12:15. This passage concerns holiness. The grace of God is given not as a license to sin but it shows us how to get out of sin to have victory to forgive, to be kind, to have a pure and holy mind, to have right motives and to be a man of integrity. Does grace teach us to deny ungodliness and worldly lust when we die? No, it says we should live soberly, righteously and godly in the present age.

When we talk about grace and prayer, we are talking about victory. We are talking about praying through the problems in your life until they cease to exist. The grace of God brings salvation and deliverance teaching us to deny ungodliness and worldly lust. God gives us grace to forgive but the grace moves from theory into our hearts by prayer. People fall short of the grace of God by retaining bitterness instead of praying for Jesus to take it away. We receive grace by getting down on our knees and praying Zechariah 4:6-7. Do you have a mountain you want to move in your life (a mountain of depression, fear, unclean thoughts, anger, and bad habits)? You must shout grace to that mountain. The great mountain can be overcome flat by thegrace of God. God is on your side and His grace or ability enablement is sufficient if you will continue in prayer: Hebrews 4:16, Isaiah 30:18, Isaiah 33:2, 2 Corinthians 12:9.

The will of God is done and His Kingdom is established through unceasing prayer.

Mark 1:40-41—We see here the grace of God touching a leper because it is God's will he be cleansed and be free. Jesus wants to touch you today and to manage His Kingdom in your life on earth here now today.

You are never too old, too busy or too sinful to change; you can change and prayer makes the difference. Keep on praying even if you have prayed, till you pray through, your lack of victory is never due to God's reluctance but hindrances (for example, a man smoked for years and he prayed but had not overcome, why? What blocked the victory? Rebellion to his parents caused the smoking. He dealt with rebellion, and then the smoking, and the problem was solved).

Nothing can be accomplished without intercession or unceasing prayer. The person, whom you are concerned about, will not go to Heaven unless Jesus touches him through you or somebody. The alcoholic or drug addict will not become free unless Jesus touches him through somebody or through you. No healing occurs without intercession, Isaiah 66:7-9. Although an entire congregation worships and signs every Sunday only part of them maybe touched by Jesus. Through unceasing prayer, Jesus touches us: Mark 5:27-20, 1 Kings 18:41-46.

Let us not be weary in prayer but let us be valiant men and women who pray unceasingly till we break through and see God's Kingdom come on earth and His will done to all His children. Elijah prayed seven times James 5:17-18 before it rained. Let us pursue God as Elijah did relentlessly in faith, praying for the break through and the victory you need. Pray until you know victory is on the way.

CHAPTER 17:

THE VOICE OF GOD

Since critics argue that God does not speak today through the Bible: Let's turn there first and see what Scripture reveals about the voice of God. To do so is to immediately wonder why anyone would resist the idea that God reveals Himself to humankind in many ways, including speaking directly to individuals and groups. From history's beginning, God has been and still is speaking in at least seven ways:

1. **Creation.**
   God speaks through creation's glory, artistry and majesty with such clarity that the Bible says all humankind is held accountable to believe in the Creator on these grounds alone, see Psalm. 19:1-6; Romans 1:20.

2. **Human conscience.**
   God speaks through the moral sense placed in the human conscience. A fundamental sense of right and wrong is innately present, and on these grounds God may exercise judgment, see Romans 2:14, 15.

3. **Divine providence**
   God speaks through the evidences of divine providence. These evidences affect our lives and speak to our souls, often causing humans to respond with wonder, wisdom, gratitude or repentance, see Genesis. 28:10-17; Acts 16:7.

4. **Signs, wonders and prophecies.**

   God speaks through signs, wonders and prophecies prompted by the Holy Spirit including tongues with interpretation, by these means edifying believers and convincing unbelievers of His power and presence: see 2 Kings 2:15, Acts 13:12, 1 Corinthians 14:5, 22-26.

5. **Still, small voice**

   God speaks by His "still, small voice," addressing people within their hearts with personal assurance, correction, insight or guidance by His own express choice to do so, see Isaiah. 30:21, Acts 10:9-12.

6. **Scripture**

   God speaks through His authoritative Word, the inspired and inerrant Holy Scriptures, see 2 Timothy 3:14-17, which He has given through His prophets and apostles by the Holy Spirit in the Old and the New Testaments, see 2 Peter1:19-21.

The evidence of God's Word is that He is always reaching and speaking, always seeking to touch and embrace, as well as to teach and correct. Seeing these several means, however, only reminds us again of the Bible's authority in every facet of our judgment in this issue.

First, we only know that we may believe God speaks to people in these ways, and that they are spiritually valid, because the Bible says so.

Second, we only measure what we may perceive God says in these ways by the Bible's full teaching and authority.

In other words, what God says by any means must be judged in the light of an absolute means—that absolute, of course, is the whole Bible.

These principles should settle the issue. The fear of exaggerating the relative importance of "what God said to me," or of falling into deception via any word or spirit, is dispensed as each believer resolutely avoids, and indeed rejects, any ideas of "continuing revelation." Those words address the fallacious idea that the Bible isn't the final authority concerning God's revealed will and truth.

The Bible is the final authority on all of life's foundational and ultimate issues. Anyone arguing otherwise should not be regarded; any Christian leader arguing otherwise should be confronted.
But with those points of control, nothing in the Bible justifies the position of anyone who denies the Biblical grounds for God speaking to people today. Nor is there any Biblical justification for anyone who declares that those of us who say things God has spoken to us are thereby embracers of error.

Two well-known anti-charismatic writers (both of whom call me a friend, for which I'm thankful) categorize everyone who says, "God spoke to me" as a person who believes in the fallacy of continuing revelation, or extra biblical revelation (they name me as one of these too). Of course, they are wrong about me and wrong about most Charismatics I know.

And "while we're talking extra Biblical," we might assert that it's extra Biblical to teach that God doesn't speak to His people today, since the Bible is full of instances of God speaking to people!

Further, the Bible uses the word "revelation" in a dual sense, which we must clearly understand. Let the nit-picking over the use of the word revelation be stopped. In Ephesians 1:17-18, the apostle's prayer for "the spirit of wisdom and revelation" to enlighten the hearts of believers indicates that God does reveal things to His children today. Such revelation is never to be equated with the closed canon of the Scriptures. We clearly understand that the Bible is a closed, or finished, book. But such revelation ought to be welcomed as the Holy Spirit brings the truths of His Word alive and ignites faith to embrace the Father's purpose for us.

Daniel 11:32 talks about knowing God which is intimacy with God. What is your deepest desire in life?

All that you accomplish and achieve in ministry is related to how well you know or how intimate you are with Him. Success is dependent on it. What is your desire in life? Success, favor, importance or know God what is your pursuit?

John 15:5 How far you are in God is dependent on your capacity to desire. Your desire to know God and spend time in His presence determines how far you are going in God.

If you look at the lives of great men of God there is one factor that makes them different from others not that they were articulate, famous, had charisma or education or abilities but they had an intimacy hunger or fervent desire for the knowledge of God that caused God to use them greatly. Form of outward religion verses reality and fellowship.

Deuteronomy 6:5, Mark 12:30 . . . If we love God with our whole being than it will be very difficult to sin, worry, doubt, be fearful or have wrong attitudes and not obey God. We must not put the work of God above God Himself. For example Mary versus Martha, a positional, ritualistic or routine doing and placing it above 'knowing' God. What is church? It is the vehicle to lead us to know God.

Revelation 2:1 . . . Describes the church of Ephesus' condition. Ministry life can make life so busy that we spend little time in intimate communion and fellowship with God. If our desire for God is weak then the desire of other things will be stronger and can lead us into trouble, 1 John 2:15.

Our affections and desires will lead us in this life or determine the destiny direction of our life, Psalm 27:4, was David's cry. He was focused. One thing have I desired of the Lord and that is to dwell in the house of the Lord to live in His presence. The best program cannot substitute for God Himself and His presence. Psalm 91 is the key to fulfillment is in His presence (verses 1, 9,14) All that David did arose out of His desire for God. Psalm 34:10 "Those who seek God will lack in no good thing."

Why should we know God? All our problems with issues like healing, faith, prayer, the Holy Spirit, family or other things will not be so if we only know God. We are as close to God right now andwill be in the future as we choose to be. As you draw near to God He will draw near to you.

FOUR LEVELS OF INTIMACY WITH GOD IN THE OLD TESTAMENT

The Outer Circle
Exodus 19:11-12 . . . God tells Moses His desires and intentions.

Exodus 20:18-21 . . . The people stand afar because of fear. As God descends what happens? They remained at a distance, verse 21.

They didn't want to talk to God. God was testing their hearts. But they stood afar. Only Moses drew near. We can stand before man and not judge our hearts but not before God and some people like it that way.

The Second Circle
Exodus 24:9-12,15 . . . Here Moses and the elders have a buffet with God. We see Moses and the elders went further up the mountain to speak with God. Here is leadership, we must go a bit further to get instructions. An experience like that definitely will change your life. Eating and drinking with God. However Moses and Joshua were going to go even further. Verse12 reveals the quality of a good leader. Are you more comfortable with pleasing man? In waiting than wanting on God. Exodus 32 Moses waited 6 days before God spoke.

The Third Circle
Exodus 24:14-18 . . . We see Moses and Joshua going up to the top of Sinai, further than the rest. Joshua was chosen for leadership because he drew near to God. God is looking in these last days for men who choose to abide in God's presence. Moses and Joshua were 40 days and nights on the mountain. The elders should be there but they couldn't wait.

The Inner Circle
Exodus 33:11 . . . We see Moses had intimacy, he talked with God face to face as a friend. This is also God's desire for us. The glory reflected from Moses because he spent time in God's presence.

FIVE LEVELS OF INTIMACY IN THE NEW TESTAMENT

We see five different levels of closeness to Jesus in the New Testament.

The multitudes
The largest group (spirituality versus size of a church) Always there to receive and be taught but rarely giving. A mature Christian life can only come from a life of giving and receiving and we must come out of the multitude.

The Seventy
Luke 10:17 . . . Out of the multitudes come the seventy. They were giving, feeding and teaching. They were closer to Jesus than the multitudes.

The Twelve were even closer than the seventy, Mark 3:14. Their purpose was to be with Jesus.

Many times Jesus would teach the disciples but they couldn't understand and he would later explain it to them when they were alone with Him.

The Three—Peter, James and John.
Luke 8:51 . . . On the way to Jairus's house only these three were inside the house with Jesus.

Matthew 17:1 . . . Jesus on the mount of transfiguration speaking with Moses and Elijah only these three were with him. *Mark13:3* . . . Jesus is on the Mountain of Olives and discussing about the signs of the times and the end of the age. Matthew 26:36 . . . He took the three further and left the nine at the entrance of the Garden of Gethsemane.

Peter, James and John were closer because they desired to be so not because they were super saints or perfect. Peter was constantly saying things that he had to be corrected for.

The choice is ours. Is it your desire to pursue God? God will use and bless if you will make the choice. Leadership should arise from those who walk with God. We cannot lead the church in the direction it should go if we do not spend time with God. Your strength before men depends on your time with God.

John The Beloved

John 18:15—Jesus was already betrayed. Everyone ran except Peter and John.

In John 13:22, only John knew the secret who was the traitor the others didn't hear.

Do you want to know and hear things from God your closeness to Him is a key. You will be strong and do great exploits, men of faith, courageous, sensitive to the leading of the Holy Spirit and successful.

CHAPTER 18:

DEDICATION

The Temple was dedicated to God and Solomon and the people prepared to worship Him.

Dedication means setting apart a place, an object or a person for an exclusive purpose.

The purpose of the dedication of the temple was to set apart the temple or a place to worship God.

But you and I know, it's good to have a place to worship Him together—but the church is you and I—in fact, the Bible tells us that today our bodies are God's temple—2 Corinthians 6:16 says, "For you are the temple of the living God. As God has said, "I will dwell in them and walk among them. I will be their God and they should be My people."

WE MUST DEDICATE OURSELVES.

Set ourselves apart for God. 1 Corinthians 6:19 says "Do you not know that your body is the temple of the Holy Spirit who is in you, whom you have from God and you are not your own?"

So what is expected of us when we dedicate ourselves?

1. DEDICATE TO WORSHIP
    This is you and God. Worship is not just singing choruses and hymns to God, but it is our daily relationship with Him, Mark 12:30 "Love the Lord your God with all you heart and with all your soul and with all you mind and with all your strength."

    God doesn't just want a part of our life. He asks for all our heart—but we get pulled in so many directions, by family, work, friend and money.

    But God is not interested in halfhearted commitment, partial obedience or the leftovers of our time and money. He desires our full devotion.

    Romans 6:13 (TEV) says, "Give yourselves to God . . ." Surrender your whole being to Him to be used for righteous purposes.

    The heart of worship is surrender and surrender is an unpopular word—"I surrender" in the English language today implies loosing or admitting defeat in battle or forfeiting a game or yielding to stronger opponent.

    We would rather talk about winning, succeeding, overcoming and conquering rather than yielding, submitting, obeying and surrendering.
    But surrendering to God simply means consecration, making Jesus your Lord, talking up your cross, dying to self and yielding to the Holy Spirit.

    God wants all of our life not just 95%—two things that block our total surrender to God; Fear and Pride.

    i) Fear keeps us from surrendering but love cast out all fear. The more we realize how much God loves us, the easier surrender becomes. God loves us so much He cares about every detail of our life and He has good plan for our lives.

When we completely surrender ourselves to Jesus, we discover that He is not a tyrant, but a Savior, not a boss, but a brother, not a dictator, but a friend.

ii) A second barrier to total surrender is our pride. We do not like to admit that we are created being and not in charge of everything. The oldest desire in the world is "to have complete control"—that desire means "we want to be God of everything in our lives"

But we are not God and we never will be. We are mere humans.

Surrendering to God simply means to live a life of obedience and trust.

How do we know if we are truly surrendered to Him? Because we rely on God to work things out instead of trying to manipulate others, force our agenda and control the situation. We let go of our demanding ways and let God work.

A surrendered heart will also trust more instead of trying harder—for example, we will not react to criticism and rush to defend ourselves.

In relationship with others, we will not edge others out or demand our rights and we will not self-service but surrendered.

Dedicated to worship means a total surrendered heart.

William Booth, founder of Salvation Army said, "The greatness of a man's power is in the measure of his surrender."

Surrendered people are the ones God uses. God choose Mary, the mother of Jesus, not because she was talented, wealthy or beautiful but because she was totally surrendered to Him. That is why she was able to say, "let it be to me according to Your word." (Luke 1:38)

Dedication of ourselves is not just our worship which is surrendered heart but also dedicated to serve.

2. DEDICATED TO SERVE—You and the Church
Groan "Oh no, Pastor."—let me come to church, enjoy the worship, enjoy the preaching or the word and go home until next Sunday. "But service, no, no, no, too busy, work, work, work family demands, what about my friends?"

Then, there are others who want to serve—but they will not do the "dirty" jobs, let somebody else do that. Again acting like a servant is not a popular concept.

The world defines greatness in terms of power, possession, prestige and position. If you can demand service from others you have arrived.

Jesus, however, measured greatness in terms of service not status.

GOD DETERMINES OUR GREATNESS BY HOW MANY PEOPLE WE SERVE, NOT HOW MANY PEOPLE SERVE US.

How do we know if we are dedicated to serve and are real servants?

i) REAL SERVANTS WOULD BE AVAILABLE WHEN CALLED ON.

If we only serve when it's convenient for us, we are not real servants.

ii) REAL SERVANTS WOULD PAY ATTENTION TO NEEDS

Servants are always on the lookout for ways to help others.

iii) REAL SERVANTS DO THE BEST WITH WHAT WE HAVE

Servant don't make excuses, procrastination or wait for better time. Servants never say "One of these days" or "When the time is right." They just do what needs to be done.

If we wait for perfect condition we will never get anything done.

iv) REAL SERVANTS DO EVERY TASK WITH EQUAL DEDICATION

Whatever they do servants "do it with all their hearts". The size of the task is irrelevant. God will never exempt any of us from the mundane, menial tasks, it's a vital part of our character training.

The great Apostle Paul gathered brushwood for a fire to warm everyone after a shipwreck. He was just as exhausted as everyone else but he did what everyone needed. No task is beneath us when we have a servant's heart.

v) REAL SERVANT FAITHFUL TO THEIR MINISTRY

Servants finish their task, fulfill their responsibilities keep their promises and complete their commitment. They don't leave a job half undone and they don't quit when they get discouraged. Real servants are trustworthy and dependable.

Faithfulness has always been a rare quality as most people do not understand the meaning of commitment. They make commitment casually, then break them for the slightest reason without any hesitation, remorse or regret.

Are there promises you need to keep, vows you need to fulfill or commitment you need to honor?

This is a test and God is testing your faithfulness.

vi) REAL SERVANT MAINTAIN A LOW PROFILE

They don't promote or call attention to themselves. Self promotion and servanthood don't mix. Real servants don't serve for the approval or applause of others. They live for an audience of One—God Almighty.

Don't be discouraged when your service is unnoticed or take for granted—keep on serving God.

Listen to this story—Dedication to serve means with all your heart and a servant's heart.

"A great and wise man once called one of his workmen to him saying, 'Go into the far country and build for me a house. The decisions of planning and of actual construction will be yours, but remember, I shall come to accept your work for a very special friend of mine.'"

And so the workman departed with a light heart for his field of labor. Material of all kinds was plentiful here, but the workman had a mind of his own. 'Surely,' he thought, 'I know mybusiness. I can use a bit of inferior materials here and cheat on my workmanship a little there, and still make the finished work look good. Only I will know that what I have built has weaknesses.'

And so, at last the work was completed and the workman reported back to the great and wise man. 'Very good,' he said. 'Now remember that I wanted you to use only the finest materials and craftsmanship in this house because I wanted to make present of it? My friend, you are the one I had you build it for. It is all yours.'"

God wants the best from us all.

Dedicated to worship means Surrender
Dedicated to serve means Servanthood.

3. DEDICATED TO REACH—You and the non-believer.

Matthew 28:19 "Go therefore and make disciples of all the nations baptizing them in the name of the Father and the Son and of the Holy Spirit."

We must think big! Not just locally but internationally. We must be a missions-minded church.

Think of others and not just be self-centered.
Think globally and not just locally.
Think of creative ways to fulfill the great commission and shift from thinking of excuses:

For example, "I only speak English"—may want to learn English or local dialect. You learn another language.

"I don't have anything to offer."—Yes, you do—we all have abilities and talents.

"I'm too old" or "I'm too young"—Nonsense! Have a friend missionary to Taiwan many years at over 40 year old married an English man who was about 50—he went back to Taiwan with her for twenty years and learn to speak fluent Mandarin.

Dedicated to reach—yes it cost us—yes its hard work—but fulfilling the Great Commission is the greatest and most satisfying events of our lives.

Jesus said "Go"—Go first to your family and friends, your community, your nation and then the world. No, not all of us will go overseas—but God will use you right where you are if you let Him.

Ten Little Christians

Ten Little Christians came to church all the time;
One fell out with the preacher, then there were nine.

Nine Little Christians stayed up late;
One overslept on Sunday, then there were eight.

Eight Little Christians on their way to Heaven;
One took the low road, then there were seven.

Seven Little Christians, chirping like chicks;
One didn't like the singing, then there were six.

Six Little Christians seemed very much alive;
One took a vacation, then there were five.

Five Little Christians pulling for Heaven's shore;
One stopped to take a rest, then there were four.

Four Little Christians each as busy as a bee;
One had his feelings hurt, then there were three.

Three Little Christians couldn't decide what to do;
One couldn't have his way, then there were two.

Two Little Christians each want one more;
Now don't you see, two plus two equal four.

Four Little Christians worked early and late;
Each brought one, now there were eight.

Eight Little Christians if they double as before;
In just seven Sundays, we have one thousand twenty four.

In this jingles there is a lesson true;
You belong either to the building, or to the wrecking crew.

Author Unknown
   Are you reaching or wrecking?

Conclusion
Let us all dedicate, not just the building but ourselves to the Lord:

   Dedicated to Worship—Surrender
   Dedicated to Serve—Servanthood
   Dedicated to Reach—Spreading the gospel

CHAPTER 19:

ANOINTING (PART ONE)

1 Samuel 10:1, 16:1, 1 Kings 1:29, Isaiah 61:4,
Acts 4:27, 10:38

The anointing is deeply rooted in the Old Testament.

A priest would anoint kings, priests and prophets by pouring oil all over their heads.

It is not just ceremonial but setting oneself apart for service to God and giving him divine enablement to carry out the mission.

Costly sweets and bitter spices were blended into the oil and symbolize the sweet and bitter experiences God's followers go through to receive the true power of the Holy Spirit.

The oil (anointing) was holy and not to be poured on anything unclean. It was not for strangers or anyone who was not already separated into service for the Lord. If a person substituted or imitated the anointing (holy oil) he is cut off from the priesthood and from leadership of Israel.

The anointing bestows God's divine enablement (strength) to take dominion over the enemy. It empowers you to exercise authority to establish God's rule. The anointing causes you to face challenges and opportunities beyond your talent, training, skill and education and it also imparts strength to accomplish the task.

Hebrew words for anointing:

balal—means to over flow with oil
dashern—means to be fed—symbolically healthy, satisfied
yistar—a noun for oil used to produce light (enlighten, revelation) or anointing salve eyes.
mimshach—means to apply or to rub with oil especially in medicinal applications (healing properties)
masah—means to apply oil by pouring or spreading
aleipho—a literal rubbing of oil upon the body
chrisma—a metaphor for the oil itself and the unction it imparts
Greek word chrio—means special appointment to set a person apart

The anointing is the power and influence of the Holy Spirit saturating and permeating a person. The anointing makes ministry effective.

What are the properties of oil?
It softens
Heals bruises etc.
Cannot dry under the sun
It restores/ renews
Fragrance
Used for light (revelation, guidance)
Lubricates (effectiveness)
Has value commercially and is lighter than water (lifts up); rises above water

Luke 3:21 and 4:1,14,18 is a record of the basis and foundation of Jesus' anointing and ministry, also see Acts 2:39.

Luke 3:21,22—Ten ideas and keys to the anointing.
Obedience/repentance/Jesus' submission to the will of the Father.
Humility
Purity/separation/holiness
Surrender death to self
Prayer life
Righteousness
Father's affirmation/approval

Faith/love
Open heavens
Going through testing/preparation (wilderness experience)

In the baptism of Jesus the lesser baptizes the greater. John has a revelation of Jesus and John's baptism was a baptism of repentance

The dove symbolizes the Holy Spirit (John 1:32,33)
The dove speaks of three things:
Purity/meekness/gentleness
Grace/love
Focus—faith (faithfulness)

Jesus shared His obedience through the incarnation and thirty quiet years of submission to his earthly parents waiting for the time to show Himself. Jesus' active ministry began in Galilee. His temptation took place near the Jordan River. The enemy tried to derail Christ's budding ministry.

Wilderness experience or testing always leads to fresh anointing.

New oil (anointing) is from God upon our lives and ministries after you have passed through temptations/ trials or testing. Testing and temptations come to holiest saints, 1 Corinthians 10:13.

What power are we talking about? Intellectual, social, political, economical or to win souls and work miracles (convictions, change) which enhances/vitalizes our faculties with unction to function by divine enablement/gifting. It is the victorious, abounding, abundant gift of God's wisdom, resources, strength and power, for example, Luke 1:7 and Luke 1:41. The anointing is not a fitful emotion, a wayward impulse or excitement but it saturates the recipient with a calm, constant, settled assurance or unction and the character of Jesus is formed, reflected through the vessel not mere talent or natural ability, religious knowledge (articulation), training or human emotions (personality, charm) etc.
Charisma does not give anyone power over the devil or over sin or power miracles and deliverance etc. We would see less exultation of self when these are real for true anointing will cause deliverance and extend God's kingdom.

Four proofs or impact of the anointing
1 Samuel 10:1-7, John 14:12, Luke 16:10, Colossians 1:27. Sin is anti-anointing, 1 John 2:15-17:

Restoration
Supernatural progress—go forward
Favor from God—divinely God arranges things for you
Change of status; transformation; you cannot remain the same.

Pride causes things or position to define a person's identity. The size of house, the number of degrees, job salary, experience, how many books you have written, size of church can all be a cause of pride. Self centered living, applause of men, independent outlook of life and God has its roots in pride. Pride is anti-anointing and is the work of flesh or reliance on self more than God.

1 John 2:18, 19, "Dear children, this is the last hour; as you have heard that the antichrist is coming, even now many antichrist have come. This is how we know it is the last hour. They went out from us, but they did not really belong to us. For if they had belonged to us, they would have remained with us; but their going showed that none of them belonged to us."

1 John 2: 20-26 "But you have an anointing from the Holy One, and all of you know the truth. I do not write to you because you do not know the truth, but because you do know it and because no lie comes from the truth. Who is the liar? It is the man who denies that Jesus is the Christ. Such a man is the antichrist—he denies the Father and the Son. No one who denies the Son has the Father; whoever acknowledges the Son has the Father also. See that what you have heard from the beginning remains in you. If it does, you also will remain in the Son and in the Father. And this is what he promised us—even eternal life. I am writing these things to you about those who are trying to lead you astray."

Anti-Christ, why? He is anti-anointing or false or against the anointing.

How do we know and discern it?

Independent, proud attitudes rather than depending on God. The Gnostics claimed superior knowledge revelations. The anointing causes us to love truth. Truth is simple not complex.

Psalm 68:6 "God sets the lonely in families; he leads forth the prisoners with singing; but the rebellious live in a sun-scorched land."

God sets the solitary in families. He brings out those who are bound into prosperity but the rebellious dwell in a dry land. The Spirit of God will teach the believer and help him distinguish between truth from error. A person who is stubborn, rebellious, reactionary or disobedient to the Word is not living and moving in the anointing of God. The anointing causes one to be teachable to receive correction, not proud, 1 John 3:16-5:8.

A man with the anointing has zeal, fervency, passion and enthusiasm. For example, Jesus as in Isaiah 59:1 and John 2:17.

Zeal is passionate intensity versus lukewarmness or carnality, indifferences, complacency, idleness, reluctance to sacrifice, burdenless, passionless, neglect of supernatural things, Revelation 3:16.

The anointing of the Lord encourages zeal for God's house and the things of God, God's people etc:

A zeal of loving God's house and family. See Psalm 28:6 & 132:13-18, 2 Corinthians 4:7-12 & 6:1-10, Ephesians 5:25.

A zeal in giving to God's house. See Psalm 4:24, 55:14, 122:1, 12& 127:4, Isaiah 2:1-4. Hebrews 10:25.

A zeal to and not tear down God's house, see Psalm 127:1,12, Proverbs 14:1 & 24:3, 2 Corinthians 11:1-4.

A zeal in finding satisfaction in God's house. See Psalm 36:8, 42:1-2 & 87:7, Ezekiel 47:3-6.

A zeal in being planted and rooted in God's house. See Psalm 1:1-3, 84:10, & 92:10,13, Ephesians 2:20-22.

A zeal in keeping unity in the house, see Psalm 133:1-3, Acts 1:14,21, 2:46, 4:32 & 5:12.

Negative thinking and speaking kills zeal and weakens under an independent spirit which lacks commitment to the church of Jesus Christ. Anyone who does not serve or sacrifice cannot be anointed with Christ's anointing: Mark 10:35, Philippians 2:3.

The Greeks teach:
    Be wise, know yourself.
The Romans says:
    Be strong, discipline yourself.
The Epicureans says:
    Be sensuous, enjoy yourself.
Education today says:
    Be resourceful, expand yourself.
Psychology says:
    Be confident, assert yourself.
Materialism says:
    Be satisfied, please yourself.
Humanism says:
    Be capable, believe in yourself.

But Jesus says:
    Be a servant, give yourself, deny yourself, don't live for yourself, give your life away:
    Philippians 2:21, Matthew 16:24.

The Cross speaks of death of our own will and choosing God's purpose. If you want to move and abide in the anointing, you need to heed these teachings. How much of God do you want?

A leader sacrifices his image so he can take on the image of Christ who did not come to be served but to serve, Matthew 20:28. He sacrifices his time, money, resources to become a recipient of divine resources.

For example: David in 2 Samuel 24:24 replied to Araunah, 'No, I insist on paying you for it. I will not sacrifice to the LORD my God burnt offerings that cost me nothing.' So David bought the threshing floor and the oxen and paid fifty shekels of silver for them.

The anointing of God abides upon those who abide in Christ and allow serving and sacrifice to be their way of life. God does not anoint a selfish, egoistic, sin-ridden leader. Let us seek the real anointing.

HOW TO RECEIVE DOUBLE ANOINTING OF THE HOLY SPIRIT

The Call of Elisha
The call of Elisha in 1 Kings 19:19-21 reveals that the call of God came when he left a rich family (six oxen was a sign of wealth).

He highly respected his parents (verse *20*) and he burnt everything (verse *21*). This burning of everything represents a total leaving of his former life. There is no going back, See Philippians 3:13. It was a complete commitment.

He was willing to be a prophet's servant. He could learn from Elijah by following him and hearing and him seeing. He washed Elijah's hands for over ten years. There is one version of the Bible says, ". . . he poured water on the hands of Elijah" (2 Kings 3:11). That literally means he was Elijah's personal servant.

The key to greatness is humility and submission.

There are four steps to receiving a double anointing of the Holy Spirit, see 2 Kings 2:1-14.

1. GILGAL (Joshua 5:6-9)
Joshua lead the second generation of Israelites across the Jordan to a place called Gilgal—which means 'rolling' and they were circumcised. Gilgal was the starting point to enter into Canaan.

Elisha and Elijah were at Gilgal. Gilgal represents a forgetting of the old life. It is a place where we say 'I am a new person in Christ Jesus—born again, baptized in water, baptized in Holy Spirit'. It is a place where we are comfortable but there is more. Double anointing, can be ours but we have to move on.

2. **BETHEL See 2 Kings 2:2, Genesis 28:10-22**
Bethel means House of God because Jacob said after his dream in Genesis 28, God is here.

When God is in a place it can be so comfortable again. Therefore we must make a decision to remain or keep moving.

For Elisha, Bethel was a place of decision. Elijah said to him, stay here and wait the Lord has sent me to Jericho. But Elisha was determined to go on no matter what.

3. **JERICHO**
This is a place of warfare. It was in the vicinity of Jericho that Jesus faced Satan and was tempted for forty days.

At Jericho, Joshua met the Commander of the Army of the Lord who told him what to do and how to conquer the city.

Jericho is also a place of victory because that's where the walls fell.

As we move from the place of the past and death to self to a place of decision Satan will oppose our calling, our family, our finances, our bodies, our mind and he will try to deter us. But remember we are in warfare, it means that miracle is near. Victory is ours. The walls will come down. But it is still not yet the place of double anointing.

4. **JORDAN**
This is where John the Baptist saw the Holy Spirit descend on Jesus like a dove.

At Jordan, Elisha began to see supernatural things, 2 Kings 2:6-11 and he received double anointing.

Let us pray that our eyes will be open to the supernatural and let us learn to keep oureyes focused on God and not on the things of this world and of man.

Every one of these places has the anointing but are we willing to pay the price for double anointing. That means leaving the place of comfort and dying to self, leaving the place of decision and making the decision to move on. Leaving the place of warfare because we have the victory and moving to Jordan which is a place of the supernatural and double anointing.

After thirteen years of being Elijah's servant he received a double anointing. Elijah did seven miracles, Elisha did fourteen. This is not a competition but just a desire for more. Desire more of the anointing and move on to great and awesome things in God.

CHAPTER 20:

ANOINTING (PART TWO)

THE JOSEPH ANOINTING

Joseph is a type of Christ. He is a man who thrives and overcomes in the midst of sufferings and adverse trials. He is a man with prophetic destiny and purpose of God, in his life. He is a man with an unusual anointing. God also wants to release to us the Joseph anointing in these last days.

There were mantles in Joseph's life.
A mantle is the degree of spiritual authority that has been given to you by God.

1. **The mantle of immaturity**
   Joseph was daddy's pet/ favorite son. He had a coat of many colors. Culturally during Joseph's time it symbolizes authority. The authority of favor should have been given to Reuben, the eldest son. Yet it was handed to Joseph because Jacob knew that Joseph had the authority of God's anointing on him.

   Joseph made the mistake of talking too much (loud mouth) Genesis 37:2 tells us that as a seventeen year old kid he reported / told tales to his dad on his brother which caused animosity (hatred) from the brothers. He didn't learn his lesson after the first dream he broadcast, because he also disclosed his second dream prematurely. Here is an important principle. There are times in our lives when God reveals things to us and does not expect us to reveal them prematurely but to guard it till a disclosed time. For example: Mary—when the angel appeared to her and told her of her mission she pondered these things in her heart (wise).

Joseph was the thrown into the pit (prophet in training).

PIT means Prophet *still* In Training
The pits in our lives are really God's training ground for us, which are vital for maturity and growth.

2. The mantle of favor *(Genesis 37:36)* / human authority

We must stay occupied (busy, hard work) in the things of God no matter what our circumstances in life are. One would discover that most times when God wants to get something done, He usually searches for someone who is busy. For example, Elisha had twelve oxen ploughing when Elijah found him.
Peter was busy fishing when Jesus found him.
(Allow God always to change your plans unless He says no).

We see that as a result of God's favor in Joseph's life (adversity), Joseph was appointed as Pharaoh's chief steward or manager.

The Joseph anointing is an anointing which God places on your life, empowering you to thrive and prosper in difficult times.

We see Pharaoh's house was blessed because of Joseph.

The Joseph anointing attracts two kinds of attacks from the devil: sexual temptation (Genesis 39) and persecution (Mark 10:30).

When God puts the Joseph anointing on you, be assured the enemy attacks your life to cause abortion and delay to deny you of your inheritance. Joseph's brothers mocked him because of the anointing: "Here comes the dreamer!"

3. The mantle of exultation (Genesis 41:40) / divine favor

When you have the Joseph anointing, you will gain political favor. That is you will stand bold before kings, you will prophesy and minister to kings and princes.

In one day, Joseph's situation was transformed from a prisoner to be prime minister next to Pharaoh. (The pit and prison before the palace, this is God's way of promotion). God can promote you within a day from wherever you are to a position as a spiritual prime minister.

There are seven characteristics of Joseph anointing:
1. The favor of God was on him (Genesis 39:44)

2. Joseph had good administrative skills (Genesis 39:4) and a prophetic mantle.
He foresaw the seven years of plenty and lack in advance prophetically and was thus able to prepare adequately for the future of the nation. He was an astute businessman too, Genesis 47:13-26. End time preaching of the gospel needs millions for the harvest and we need to prepare.

3. Joseph dream big dreams.
God's dreams are always bigger than us and we will not be able to do it or fulfill it on our own strength, so God alone gets all the glory.

4. Joseph had the ability /tenancy to persevere.
"Never, never give up" famous words of Woodrow Wilson. Joseph persevered in spite of sufferings. The dream took seventeen years to be fulfilled (seventeen in the Bible is the number representing victory). You are destined for victory, not defeat but in his immaturity, Joseph's victory was in the flesh. Fifteen years later at age of thirty-two, Joseph was reunited with his father. Fifteen in the Bible is the number representing rest. (The rest of faith had been developed. He was ill-treated before he was reunited with his father.) When we suffer with a purpose, our suffering becomes meaningful, Genesis 45:5. Whatever you are experiencing at this moment, understand God's

purpose for your life. Then it will help you endure what you are going through. Purpose is the end for which a beginning is created. As a prophetic people we should have the foresight to make adequate preparation so when unexpected situations arise we can survive through them confidently in the knowledge that God has a definite purpose in mind.

5. Joseph had humility.

As a young boy, he was forward and arrogant. But as he stood before Pharaoh his humility is evident. Joseph humbly tells Pharoah, "I cannot interpret the dream myself but God will give you the interpretation". We see a dependency and maturity of faith in God: Genesis 37:5-9, 41:16. In his own suffering he was able to minister to the cupbearer and the butler even though he had nothing to gain and was himself in great dire need.

God is searching for people like Joseph who, although experiencing difficulties themselves, for example, the widow with the last barrel of oil and bread, are still able to minister to others. These kind of people will get breakthrough at the end.

6. Joseph had a burning desire to provide for his brothers and family.

God used Joseph at the end to provide for a whole nation, Genesis 50:20. Whatever the devil meant for evil, God will turn around for your good. People with the Joseph anointing will create successful businesses and provide sufficiently for others.

7. Joseph had a great heart to forgive.

When great forgiveness exists, great provision will be released. Why was Joseph able to forgive his brothers in spite of the ugliness of their deeds?

The answer lies in the names of his two sons:
Manasseh means 'the Lord causes me to forget.'
Ephraim means 'the Lord repays.'

Joseph moved on with God and in life refused to be held back by his past experiences, tragedies, self-pity, remorse, despair, anger, hurt, resentment or jealousy and envy.

If in our hearts we harbor grudges, the flow of blessings is hindered but when you forgive you will experience miracles in your life.

People with a Joseph anointing are mostly likely to be misunderstood and cause jealousy and envy to surface. We must determine within ourselves to continue to release forgiveness and be humble, 1 Peter 5:6.

God wants these seven characteristics of the Joseph anointing to be in His church, Proverbs 13:22.

CHAPTER 21:

GARMENTS OF MINISTRY

In the Old Testament times people did not approach God directly. A priest acted as an intermediary between God and man.

With Jesus' victory on the cross that pattern changed. Now we can come directly into God's presence without fear, Hebrews 4:16 and we are given the responsibility of bringing others to Him, 2 Corinthians 5:18-21.

So once we are born again, we are in Christ Jesus and according to 1 Peter 2: 1-10 we are chosen by God and precious.

So like the priest of the Old Testament we need to put on our garments of ministry to reach out to others. Exodus 39:1 says, ". . . of the blue, purple and scarlet thread they made garments of ministry." Each color has a meaning and represents what kind of characteristic we should have in ministry.

The ministry is not only the five fold ministry of apostle, prophet, evangelist, pastor and teacher but also the ministry of the lay people (marketplace people/ not full time in the church). You all have a ministry to reach, the lost for Jesus. Weall have a responsibility to witness and win others for the Lord Jesus Christ.

We are going to take a look at the three colors—blue, purple and scarlet, and see what we can learn.

BLUE
The color blue is the color of the sky and represents heaven. Blue also speaks of someone who is heavenly minded.

We see the loveliness of blue in the life of our Lord Jesus Christ. He was not only heavenly in His origin but He was heavenly in His very nature and ways.

Blue speaks of heavenly mindedness.
If we are heavenly minded it will influence our thoughts, attitudes, speech and actions.

Jesus was heavenly minded He was always sensitive to the Father's voice and the Father's ways.

John 5:19 ". . . the Son can do nothing of Himself, but what He sees the Father do; for whatever He does, the Son also does in like manner."

John 5:30 He says, "I can of myself do nothing. As I hear, I judge; and my judgment is righteous because I do not seek My own will but the will the Father who sent Me."

John 12:50 ". . . whatever I speak, just as the Father has told me, so I speak."

We are in Christ Jesus and because of our identification with Him we must honor Him and live the way He wants us to live.

In order to do that we must constantly ask ourselves two questions that would help us to be heavenly minded:
What would Jesus do?
What would Jesus have me to do?

As we ask these questions, they will influence our thinking, attitudes, speech and our actions. I have mentioned before the baptism in the Holy Spirit experience is not just to make one feel good and declare to everyone that one can speak in tongues. The Holy Spirit also expects us to live and walk in His way not in carnality which is the way of flesh. For example, hatred, contentions, jealousies, outburst of wrath, selfish ambitions, envy and so on.

Ministering to others with heavenly mindedness means we must first deal with our self life if we want to be effective. It starts with our thoughts and attitudes.
Many of us say that life is unfair. We ask, "Why did this happen to me?" However, Life is ten percent of "What happens to me?" and ninety percent of "How I react to it?" Our attitudes determine what we see and how we handle our feelings. These two factors greatly determine our success in life.

Norman Vincent Peale relates this story in his book *"Power of the Plus Factor*:
"Once walking through the twisted little streets of Kowloon in Hong Kong, I came upon a tattoo studio. In the window were displayed samples of the tattoos available. On the chest or arms you could have tattooed an anchor or flag or mermaid or whatever. But what struck me with force were three words that could be tattooed on one's flesh, *Born to lose.* I entered the shop in astonishment and, pointing to those words, asked the Chinese tattoo artist, 'Does anyone really have that terrible phrase, *Born to lose,* tattooed on his body?' He replied, 'Yes, sometimes.' Once our minds are 'tattooed' with negative thinking, our chances for long term success diminish. We cannot continue to function in a manner that we do not truly believe about ourselves. Often I see people sabotage themselves because of wrong thinking."

Negative thinking/thoughts of hatred and anger are not heavenly minded thoughts and they will come out in our speech and our actions.

Jesus was also heavenly in His nature and ways; see Galatians 5:22, 23.

In ministry to others, whether in witnessing, counseling or visitation, we must all learn to have love, joy, peace, longsuffering, kindness, faithfulness, gentleness and self-control.

Jesus was never judgmental. We can see it in the examples of His encounter with the woman at the well, with Mary and Martha. He always ministers in love—love that is not sloppy or soft but can be done in firmness without hurting others.

How to be heavenly minded?

First identify your problem thoughts, feelings and behavior and then repent.

Don't keep justifying yourself that you are right and everyone else is wrong. Get right with God and if necessary get right with others.

Romans 12:2 tells us to "be transformed by the renewing of our minds". Daily renew your mind with the Word in prayer.
The Greek word for 'renew' means to renovate. For example, to renovate a house, we will take out all the old furniture and put in new furniture. If the old is not taken out and it has wood worm it will eventually destroy the new.

So it should be with our thought life—we take out the old carnal worldly way of thinking such as selfish, sexual thoughts or negative thoughts and replace them with right, clean and positive thoughts.

Psalm 119:9, 11:
"How can a man cleanse his way, by taking heed according to your word."
"Your word I have hidden in my heart, that I might not sin against You."

Colossians 3:1,2 "If then you were raised with Christ, seek those things which are above, where Christ is, sitting at the right hand of God the Father. Set your mind on things above not on things on the earth"

Seek those things which are above, set your minds on things above— double emphasize means God is trying to get our attention. It is a daily practice and a daily discipline.

Be doers of the Word and not just hearers only.

SCARLET

It speaks of sacrifice. In the times of the Bible, the color scarlet was derived from an Eastern insect (worm) that infests certain trees. It was gathered, crushed, dried and ground to powder that produced a brilliant crimson hue.

Jesus was our sacrifice.

In order to leave heaven and come to this earth He sacrificed much. The Son of God became the Son of man. Therefore, we have to sacrifice ourselves for others in ministry. Why? That is because Jesus did and He is our example in serving others.

The story of Adam and Eve reveals the origins of self-awareness, self-concern and selfishness; the emphasis of I, Me, Mine, Myself, Genesis 3:9-10.

"As God probed deeper, Adam and Eve became increasingly more defensive. They hurled accusations at each other and then at God.

'The woman . . . !'
'The woman *you* gave me . . . !'
'The serpent . . .'

The pattern hasn't changed, has it? Since the original scene down through the centuries, the history of humanity is smeared with ugly marks of selfishness.

How to live a life of sacrifice for others?

1. **Repent of selfishness.**

2. **Be different from the world.**
   "Do nothing from selfishness or empty conceit but with humility of mind let each of you regard one another as more important than himself; do not merely look out for your own personal interests but also for the interests of others. Have this attitude in yourselves which was also in Christ Jesus" (Philippians 2:3-5)

The world's attitude is completely different:
Happy are the 'pushers' for they get on in the world.
Happy are the hard-boiled for they never let life hurt them.
Happy are the blasé for they never worry over their sins.
Happy are the slave-drivers for they get results
Happy are the knowledgeable men of the world; for they know their way around
Happy are the trouble makers for they make people take notice of them.

3. **Put on the garment of ministry and sacrifice**
   The garments of ministry must be put on and the garment of sacrifice is a necessity for ministering to others.
   We are to be givers and not getters.
   We are to be forgivers not people who keep score.
   We are to be servants and not superstars.

PURPLE
It comes from mixing of blue and scarlet. It is a color of royalty.

Our kingship is in Jesus Christ
Jesus is King of kings and Lord of lords. Yes, Jesus was the Son of man. Yes, He submitted to the Father and was heavenly minded. Yes, He lived a life of sacrifice. But, He knew who He was. Do we know who we are in Christ Jesus? Are we walking in that authority or do we go around living a life of defeat?

He is a conqueror so we are conquerors. He lived a life of victory so we can live a life of victory. He has authority so we can live a life of authority. Is Jesus King in our lives?

We must put on the garments of kingship and authority in ministering to others.

Jesus spoke with authority. For example, He calmed the storm, and even the wind and waves obeyed Him. Jesus acted with authority as seen in the many miracles that place. He taught with authority—even at age of twelve, in the temple the people were amazed at how much He knew.

It has all got to do with words—"Death and life are in the power of the tongue" (Proverbs 18:21)

Why did Jesus have such authority?

You may say He was the Son of God. But remember, He gave up His divinity to become the Son of Man He was fully human like you and I.

Blue and scarlet produces purple—His heavenly mindedness and ways mixed with sacrifice or the suffering servant enabled Him to live in authority.

As we do the same—be heavenly minded in our thinking, attitudes, speech and actions, plus live a life of servanthood in sacrifice to others, we will be able to rule and reign in the Kingdom of God with such authority like Jesus and miracles will flow from our lives as we:

Speak with authority
Act with authority
Teach with authority.

Friends, this is available to all believers, for you are the royal priesthood, so rise up in authority that God has given you rise up as the victor and not the victim.

The garments of ministry are yours.

Blue—heavenly mindedness
Scarlet—sacrifice in servanthood
Purple—authority in living

It's yours but you have not because you ask not.

A man bought a ticket to go on a cruise, every night he would eat the food he took with him for his journey while others would be eating a five course meal in the restaurant. At the end of the cruise, some one asked, why he hadn't joined them and he said, 'I don't have the money so I bought my own food.' That person said, 'Don't you know it is all included in the price of your ticket.' He had been eating second best.

Many of us Christians do not realize that these garments of ministry are available to all—it is inclusive in your salvation ticket, claim what is yours.

But always remember to act and serve in humility and all authority are yours.

CHAPTER 22:

SUPERNATURAL EMPOWERMENT FOR THE CHURCH

We will consider the scriptural basis of supernatural empowerment for the church.

Church growth seems to be a buzz word for those who are attempting to find out how the church can grow and what are the latest methods, programs, plans, strategies or some new method that we can inculcate to enable the church to grow.

Have we forgotten in our pursuit and dedication that Jesus promised that He is the one who would build the church? Thus we must not substitute methods, models, and marketing strategies and put the cart before the horse, so to say, while missing the most vital element.

The supernatural empowerment of God is replaced by programs without divine supernatural unction of God. We must lay a correct foundation, that is, we must first build the character of the church. If we first depend on methods to grow our church, we run the risk of making an idol of church growth methods and suggest that we can grow the church.

In some arenas, church growth has degenerated into our feeble attempts to do in a mechanical way what God intends to do so in the supernatural manner and through Divine empowerment or energy and strength only.

The sin of carnality is nothing more than our human effort to do a supernatural work through human ability.

If programs and formulas only are the answer and are able to produce growth, we would depend on them and move towards self-sufficiency rather than entire dependence and faith in the supernatural sovereign God who is the one who causes growth we see in the Bible. Many times we see men seeking to help God do His work but human effort and the work of the flesh are not a substitute for divine empowerment.

We have the example of Abraham who sought to help God fulfill the supernatural promise in producing an heir through the flesh by resorting to adopt his slave and also by having a child through Haggai, Sarah's handmaiden as seen in Genesis 15-16. We see that the result in attempting to help God fulfill the promise through human endeavor and methodology, strategies and plans which were of the flesh rather than of divine empowerment, were predictably disastrous. We see these also in the life of King David where on two occasions the people of Israel were numbered.

In the first instance as recorded in Numbers 1, the census was at God's direct command intended for the care and the protection for people. However, in the second instance, the plan was David's idea and it aroused out of his pride and desire or plan to exhibit the military strength of Israel, 1 Chronicles 12. This second action of numbering Israel was condemned by God because God wanted Israel to remember that He alone was responsible for the victory not a plan, man, program or human work.

Church growth should come through the supernatural work of the Spirit, then the glory will always go to Christ and not to the person whether the Bishop or pastor nor method but God alone.

Why are church growth methods and models not working for a vast majority of churches in spite of success for some?

I believe we have made secondary issues primary ones. We have to focus on supernatural empowerment. I would like to suggest five things that churches seem to overlook and the fact that models and methods have certain limitations. (Quotation from Hemphill)

1. **We must understand different context.**

   You can't transfer context. What works on the west coast has little relevance in the rural village or the city. When we seek to transfer a seemingly successful model without looking into the context it will prove to be a failure.

2. **You can't transfer gifts and personality.**

   What works for one leader might not work well for you. This does not mean you are less gifted, it just means that you are different. If you seek to impersonate leadership style, like some people impersonate Elvis you may be entertaining for a song or two but little of true Elvis comes out.

3. **You can't transfer spirituality.**

   Only God can do it and it takes time because character development and spirituality involve growth.

   Just attempting to copy a working model or a program can easily neglect the more vital issue of spiritual character and spiritual empowerment. This is God's divine promise to you and spiritual development of the church.

   Spiritual development or maturity is an encounter with God that individuals or the congregation must themselves develop and experience. It doesn't come through methods or programs but from a divine touch from God.

4. **You can't transfer unique gift-mix of a congregation.**

   It is not only the pastor of the church we seek to model after is unique but so also are the congregation of the church unique. Every pastor must discover the unique gift for his particular church.

   There are seven churches the Book of Revelation. Each church received its divine promise, divine empowerment and divine calling from God for that particular church.

5. **We can't transfer time and maturity level.**
We must realize that it has taken the model church through many years of diligent seeking and program development in order for it to arise to the dynamic ministry we see today. It would be utter presumptuous and foolish to thinking you can duplicate that ministry overnight.

SPIRITUAL EMPOWERMENT IS A SUPERNATURAL EVENT AND ENCOUNTER WITH GOD.

We must be careful not to presume that we can grow a church devoid of supernatural power. I am not suggesting that we must not study to learn the effective model in growing churches or effective mission strategies. God is not a God of confusion. He often chooses to work through structures and organization but what I am saying is that church growth is a supernatural event with a supernatural encounter with God. The first priority is to develop a deep relationship with God. Church growth is not something we do by human effort but it's a byproduct of a proper relationship with God and the head of the church, which is Christ. And when the church falls deeply in love with Christ it result in empowerment. And out of this deep love relationship, spontaneously and naturally the passion and desire to win the lost, to serve one another and to share graciously arises. However at anytime we seek to force church growth methods upon the people we will realize that the result will be of the flesh.

Many pastors are excited when they return from the spiritual growth conferences or retreats and often face casual hostility or downright rejection.

PAYING THE PRICE FOR SPIRITUAL EMPOWERMENT

What do we love more than anything else?
(John 21:15-19)
Are we willing to pay the price to change if we want to see growth to be supernatural empowerment no matter what?

Every church that grows has a divine vision, divine empowerment and is willing to change as God instructs and leads them further. It will be strange to talk about church growth without first considering what Jesus himself, the founder of the church has to say.

In Matthew 16, we are ushered into the critical moment, into the ministry of the Lord. If you look into the context, you will see Jesus has been on an extended mission in which many miracles occurred. There is a speculation about his identity. The Pharisees approached Jesus, testing him and seeking a sign from heaven.

The disciples themselves at this point of time were still struggling to believe Jesus to meet their needs, see Matthew 16:5-12. Their spiritual development was not impressive at this point of time. Jesus has asked his disciples in regard to the current speculation concerning His identity. Some say John the Baptist; other say Elijah; and still others, Jeremiah or one of the prophets. Peter, who was always the spokesman for the twelve, received divine revelation, impartation empowerment inside when he said, "You are Christ, the Son of the Living God." (Matthew 16:16) It is so easy to become accustomed to what Peter just vocalized and grow indifferent to the radical nature of Peter's confession.

This confession seems sacrilegious to many. What was Peter saying when he said, "You are the Christ—Messiah, the One who brings Redemption to the world, the Anointed One, God's Son"? Christ, means the supernaturally empowered One, anointed by God to build the church by the anointing. If we really believe, that the church is to be supernaturally empowered, anointed, then supernatural empowerment must forever control our thinking about the nature of the church. A few short years later, a few men literally died for this confession. This is not a confession or idea of the man but this is a teaching of the founder, Jesus, that the church should be built with supernatural empowerment and anointing by God to grow. Jesus praised Peter for receiving the divine revelation. Jesus said that upon this revelation he would build the church. Peter's apostolic confession is that Jesus is Christ, the Rock which the church is built and the gates of hell shall not prevail against it. Authentic church growth is a promised divine activity for the church rightly related to Christ (divine empowerment and anointing.)

The first step to all church growth is supernatural empowerment. It is our privilege to live in holiness and obedience so that we are vessels to which His power flows to the building of a proper understanding of the church. Its nature will enhance authentic church growth. Church growth is supernatural and natural at the same time. God designs the church to grow. He desires it to grow and He has empowered it to grow. For this very reason, church growth is natural. It is supernatural because only God can cause it to grow, not methods. Therefore, when we see the authentic church grow He receives the glory. We have the privilege in joining Him in these activities because of His grace. Man cannot engineer true growth; it is God's sovereign activity.

We will now consider an example from the Book of Acts in our attempt to discover supernatural empowerment from the church at Antioch. In Acts 11:21 we are told that the hand of the Lord was with them. This phrase clearly points to supernatural empowerment and resulting in a large number believing turning to the Lord. Whenever the Scripture mentions that the hand of the Lord is on someone throughout the Bible, the activities of that someone will be successful; when the Lord removes His hands or replaces His hands on someone else the results will be disastrous. For example, King Saul. When God removed his hand or anointing or empowerment, the result was immediate and catastrophe for him and Israel. The question we must ask is whether God's hand is on our church and our ministries? What evidence leads us to this conclusion?

Without the supernatural empowerment of the Lord nothing will be accomplished but works of the flesh manufactured out of man's good ideas. It is interesting to know that the Antioch church was founded by a layperson that was scattered by persecution, see Acts 8. There was not one Bishop, Pastor and Apostle among them.

They (the lay people) were uprooted from their homeland and began preaching and God's supernatural empowerment overcame their weakness because they were in right proper obedience and relationship with their HEAD (God). The Antioch church was founded by laypeople; their first priority was to walk in obedience to God (Christ's anointing the divine empowerment). Out of that obedience, arose churches, witnessing and passion for the lost.

Now let us look at the second significant phrase in *Acts 11:23*. The Bible said that when Barnabas had seen the grace of God. We know we can experience the grace of God but how to see it? What did Barnabas see that convinced him that he saw the evidence of the grace of God?

There are several meanings for the word 'grace'. In Greek, the word 'grace' means supernatural empowerment and enablement. Several things come to mind immediately when we read this text.

Barnabas saw GREAT numbers of people turning to the Lord. God's divine supernatural enablement will cause an increase of numbers in church growth.

He saw serious dedicated PRAYER and FASTING, see Acts 13:1-3. When the people of God truly have encounter with Him, they will develop a hunger for regular intimacy and communication with God through prayer and fasting. Every church that experiences supernatural empowerment is a church that develops an intimacy appetite for prayer and fasting.

Barnabas witnessed SACRIFICIAL AND SPONTANEOUS GIVING. A church will expand and grow or increase according to his generosity. In Acts 11:27-30, we see that the Antioch church immediately responded to the message of the Apostle Agabus about the great famine that affected Judea. They are people who had a determination to give to others generously and liberally without any limitation.

The most visible witness to the grace of God was the FELLOWSHIP established in the church in Antioch between the Jews and Gentiles, see Galatians 2:11-12. This may not impress us significantly, but Jews and Gentiles together was unheard of. There were many barriers that divided them, not only culturally, racially or traditionally but also their religion. Apparently from the inferences of the scripture, they were having the Lord's Supper together. This meant that the barriers between the Jews and Gentiles were dissolved in a moment of time by the grace of God.
Barnabas saw the GRACE of GOD in Antioch church because it was a church with a world vision and mission. An Antioch church was a church without walls. It reached to the borders beyond itself and supported

missionary global mission. It was at the Antioch church Paul began his missions. It was a church with an outward vision and not inward looking. They had a big heart with a global vision and believed in a big God.

You will see healing of relationships, love, unity, sharing, joy, peace and supernatural kingdom living or co-existence. The grace of God dissolves all pride and competition. We should see evidences of God's grace just like the church in Antioch. If the God of the universe dwells with people, there shall be fruits and evidences of grace in our lives. If we do not see this in our homes, churches, families and relationships with others we need to ask why not and are we surrendered to the Lord and divinely empowered by His grace?

We now finally conclude in this verse what it means to be a supernatural empowered church by looking at the verse found in Acts 11:26 which said the disciples were first called Christians in Antioch. The word Christian is first mentioned here in Antioch though it was a term of scorn given to the disciples by some secular community; the actual meaning of 'Christians' is 'imitators of Christ or little Christ'.
I pray that the secular world and our friends would accuse us of being like Jesus. He is the One that builds the church, empowers the church and He says your church can grow because God himself promised it and He desires to cause His people to grow.

According to Matthew 16, a supernatural encounter (revelation, empowerment, grace) with the resurrected Lord must precede the implementation of methodology. When we have supernatural empowerment and grace, we will be awakened to the holiness of God. His anointing will lead us to deep repentance and awareness of human sinfulness that causes us to have passion to witness to the lost and to live like Jesus.

<u>As an evidence of spiritual awakening in our life, five things happen like it happened in Antioch:</u>

1. A new desire for serious prayer and fasting.

2. A renewed passion to win the lost. We cannot encounter a holy God without desiring the heart of God.

3. If we have experienced God's grace it will result a healing in relationship.

4. When the church experiences God's grace, it will create an attitude and atmosphere of spontaneous giving and sacrifice which is essential to all church growth.

5. When the church experiences God's grace, it will lead to the development of God's divine strategy or method to fulfill the great commission to the world and global mission that sends out missionaries.

You will see that I am not against methods but if we attempt to introduce methods to an unprepared church or an unrevived church (character undeveloped) you will face carnal confusion. Church growth is supernatural. Prayer is the key of all authentic church growth and divine empowerment as a church. If we desire to see our church grow, impacting our society, you and I must humble ourselves and be a person of prayer and fasting and fall deeply in love with God so He can empower us and enable us to experience His grace, 2 Chronicles 7:14.

These are three levels of change or development in a church:

1. **Minor change**

2. **Major change**
   People develop a new perspective and act in new ways. Newcomers are viewed as honored guests rather than transient visitors; instead of inward looking, focus on the outward towards the lost.

3. **Transformational change**
   There are times in a congregation's life when a unique openness arrives that allows transformational change to take place, Galatians 6:10. We must seize it or may pass us by if we do not act.

Five opportunities for change:

1. **A time of crisis**
   This is a time where something has to be done. Crisis enlarges a congregation's openness to change.

2. **A time of pastoral change**
   This is a time where a new pastor raises questions of the future of the church. It opens the door to the purposed vision, missions and goals of the church.

3. **A time of budget preparation**
   We rethink priorities and direction.

4. **A time of revival**
   It is in special times of refreshing, the doors open up to new opportunities and new approaches to ministry.

5. **A time of planning**
   Development of long range plans for the future. It is also a time of renewing and envisioning a better future.

   The purpose of our church is to glorify God by reaching the lost, disciplining and building people. (Evangelization, assimilation and maturation).

The process of transformation—seven steps:

1. Opportunities and teachable moments of life.
2. Envision a preferable future for the church.
3. Vision and purpose—the biblical reason a church exists.
4. Ownership of vision and hot to actualize vision—short, medium and long.
5. Paradigm shift in perspective.
6. Mobilization.
7. Initiation of change—evaluate results.

Five things that the enemy uses to cause low morale:

1. Leaders set up the church for failure when leaders achieve failure.
2. We make the mistakes of not celebrating the victory by having negative thoughts.
3. Leaders lose trust on the congregation through misunderstanding.
4. Manipulating church wide decision with low morale.
5. Promises unfulfilled.

Ten signs of positive self-esteem:

1. Members talk good about their church to others.
2. Members want others to experience what they experienced.
3. Members get actively involved.
4. Members look to the future, not the past.
5. Members willing to take risk.
6. Members have pride in maintaining facilities.
7. Members think special of everyone.
8. Members constantly affirm their leaders and so does the leaders (vise versa)
9. Members have high standard for excellence.
10. Member have vision for the future and dare to step out in faith.

第一章

你所想的成為了你

三千年前，所羅門王在神的默示下寫著：「因著他心裡面所想的，他就成為那樣。」當耶穌在世上時，祂說：「因為心裏所充滿的，口裏就說出來。」(路加福音6：45) 因此我們的心思意念、我們的思想很重要，因為它們影響我們的言語和行為。我們的想法塑造了我們。那麼我們的思想和心思意念充滿最多的是甚麼呢?又甚麼最能影響我們的思想?這些問題我們必須自己捫心自問：

有甚麼／有誰能夠影響我們的思想?

1. **家庭**

   我們的父母對我們有怎樣的態度? 他們是否曾對你說：「你真沒用!你是個失敗者。你就是你媽／你爸的翻版?」。許多時候，我們的父母因為遭遇挫折而出口傷人，卻不知他們所說的對孩子們所帶來的後遺影響。

   感謝神的是，我們能夠透過聖靈被釋放，而不被這些負面話語所影響。要不然，這些話變成我們生命的咒詛，而使我們可能無法發揮出我們潛能的極致。在耶穌基督裏，我們靠著那加給我們力量的，凡事都能做。

2. **非信徒的朋友**

   這些朋友會影響我們的想法和思想模式。他們可能告訴我們：「成為基督徒是可以的，但我們不要過度委身或太過火熱，不然我們可能變成極端。」讓我們來看聖經對此有何說法。

「我知道你的行為，你也不冷也不熱；我巴不得你或冷或熱。你既如溫水，也不冷也不熱，所以我必從我口中把你吐出去。」(啟示錄3：15-16)

3. 世界

這世界透過書本、雜誌、報紙、音樂，和電視影響我們的想法。女士們，電視連續劇並非現實。它所要帶給你的訊息是：「你的男人必須身高六呎，擁有如健美先生般的體型，還要一年365天，天天都浪漫—如果他不是基督徒倒也無所謂！」但聖經的所說的卻是：

「你們和不信的原不相配，不要同負一軛。義和不義有甚麼相交呢?光明和黑暗有甚麼相通呢?基督和彼列有甚麼相和呢?信主的和不信主的有甚麼相干呢?」(哥林多後書 6：14-15)
你最好的男人是**神為你選的最好**，不是這世界的。你們要先求祂的國和祂的義。這些東西都要加給你們了—包括那對的男人。

4. 我們的文化

文化影響我們的思想。特別是亞洲的文化，因為亞洲的宗教涵蓋了許多迷信。造成信徒們心生恐懼，但神的話語告訴我們基督徒不該生活在恐懼中，而應憑信心而生活。當我們透過聖靈重生，信心取代了恐懼。因此我們必須破除迷信帶來的恐懼。例如，基督徒的生活中不該迷信風水。看星座更是絕對不可以。只有神才知道我們將來。這就是為甚麼我們必須保守在祂的話語裏。

「因為神賜給我們不是膽怯的心，乃是剛強、仁愛、謹守的心。」(提摩太多書1：7)

5. 我們過去的經驗

我們過去的經驗可能在我們認知不夠的情況下，繼續掌控並塑造我們的現在和將來。比如說我們可能曾經和某個男人有過惡劣的關係，導致我們因此害怕進入另一種新的關係，因為我們認為天下的男人都是烏鴉一般黑 (但這和事實相差很遠)。
我們也可能在工作時出了差錯，讓我們感到尷尬或丟臉。導致我們害怕再度出差錯，以至於只能受限於選擇我們所熟悉的。一旦我們選擇了安全的作法，就更不願在事業上作更進一步的嘗試。這樣我們便無法完全達到我們潛能的最高峯。

「弟兄們，我不是以為自己已經得着了，我只有一件事，就是忘記背後努力面前，向着標竿直跑，要得神在基督耶穌裏從上面召我來得的獎賞。」(腓立比書3：13、14)

這是我們必須記得的：
必須是**神的話語**改變我們的思想。
必須是**神的話語**影響我們每日的思想。

為甚麼我們需要改變我們的思想？

1. **我們必須這樣做，因為根據箴言23：7「因為我們心怎樣思量，我們為人就是怎樣。」**

   思量「失敗」，我們就失敗了。
   思量「生病」，我們就生病了。
   思量「沒錢」，我們就缺錢了。
   思量「問題」，我們就都有問題。
   思量「恐懼」「憂慮」，我們就沒有平安。
   而且可以繼續列表下去 ...

   我們要想成為勝利成功的男女基督徒，我們就必須改變我們的思想。我們要能夠興起並得勝。若要如此，我們必須思量「信心」和「勝利」。我們必須抓緊神的應許，就是我們靠着愛我們的主，在這一切的事上已經得勝有餘了。

2. **我們必須改變我們的思想，因為神的話語如此告訴我們。**

   「不要效法這個世界，只要心意更新而變化，叫你們察驗何為神的善良、純全、可喜悅的旨意。」(羅馬書12:2)

   原文裏的「變化」是「現在進行式」的動詞。意思就是我們必須不斷的改變及更新我們的心思意念。這是每日的過程。我們必須除去負面以及陳舊的思想並用神的話語來替代—那充滿信心的話語。

3. **我們必須改變我們的思想，這樣我們才能內心充滿生命和平安。**

   「體貼肉體的就是死；體貼聖靈的乃是生命平安。」(羅馬書8:6)

甚麼是體貼肉體？它的意思是我們不受聖靈也不透過神的話語影響；反而被我們所看到的、所聽見的、以及所感覺的影響。例如體貼肉體的人失業了，會這麼想：「我沒有錢，沒有安全感，沒有未來。」然而體貼聖靈的人則會問：「神的話語怎麼說？」；它說：「耶和華以勒是我的供應者。」

「所以我告訴你們：不要為生命憂慮吃甚麼，喝甚麼；為身體憂慮穿甚麼。生命不勝於飲食嗎?身體不勝於衣裳嗎?你們看那天上的飛鳥，也不種、也不收也不積蓄在倉裏，你們的天父尚且養活牠。你們不比飛鳥貴重得多嗎?」(馬太福音6：25-26)

我們晝夜思想神的話語，它改變我們的思想。透過神的話語我們可得到生命和平安。

4. **我們必須改變我們的思想，這樣我們才能影響他人。**

隨着我們讓神的話語改變我們的負面思想，我們的說話方式將會改變，我們的行為也將會改變。 那個「我」將會改變，而他人也將會看到那差別。

「你們作妻子的，要順服自己的丈夫。這樣，若有不信從道理的丈夫，他們雖然不聽道，也可以因妻子的品行被感化過來。這正是因看見你們有貞潔的品行和敬畏的心。你們不要以外面的辮頭髮，戴金飾，穿美衣為妝飾，只要以裏面存着長久溫柔，安靜的心為妝飾，這在神面前時極寶貴的。」(彼得前書3：1-4)

如果我們的思想和神的話語一致，我們將會有個溫柔和安靜的靈。

我們如何改變我們的思想？

1. **有「交託」的心意**
願意遵行神的旨意—住在基督裏。 每一日順服神，也就是將我們的心思意念交託於神。當我們將自己完全交給神，我們將會靠聖靈的大能擁有得勝的思想，並過得勝的生活。

「你們要常在我裡面,我也常在你們裡面。枝子若不常在葡萄樹上,自己就不能結果子你們若不常在我裡面,也是這樣。」(<u>約翰福音</u>15:4)

2. 有專注於神的心意

「你們要思念上面的事,不要思念地上的事。」(<u>歌羅西書</u>3:2)

愛慕屬天的事,並完全被它們吸引。不要埋頭在問題、問題、問題裏。

3. 有更新的心意

「不要效法這個世界,只要心意更新而變化,叫你們察驗何為神的善良、純全、可喜悅的旨意。」(<u>羅馬書</u>12:2)

我們如何更新我們的思想?讀經、默想、背誦和宣告神的話語。

「這律法書晝夜不可離開你的口,總要晝夜思念,好使你謹守遵行這書上所寫得一切話。 如此,你的道路就可以亨通,凡事順利。」(<u>約書亞記</u>1:8)

在聖靈裏禱告,使我們心裏的力量剛強起來,並破除我們所有的詛咒。在聖靈裏禱告也讓我們能更敏銳於神透過祂的話語對我們說話。

4. 有堅定的心志

「堅心倚賴你的,你必保守他十分平安,因為他倚靠你。你們當倚靠主直到永遠。因為主是永久的磐石。」(<u>以賽亞書</u>26:3、4)

耶和華(主)是萬世的**磐石**,永不被擊敗的那一位,永久堅固的那一位。祂保守我們在完全的平安裡;沒有憂慮、恐懼、或懷疑。

5. 有紀律的心志

「弟兄們,我還有未盡的話。凡事真實的、可敬的、公義的、清潔的、可愛的、有美名的、若有甚麼德行、若有甚麼稱讚,這些是你們都要思念。」(<u>腓立比書</u>4:8)

一個有紀律的心志擁有以下的特徵:

真實和誠實的思想
思想真實的事。聖經是真理，是真實的。晝夜思想祂的應許和充滿信心的話語。

公義的思想
不要對他人有不公平的論斷。首先要暸解所有的實情。凡事站在公義那邊。我們處理業務必須要公正，神必會祝福我們。

純潔/清潔的思想
不要聽髒笑話或黃色笑話。小心你所閱讀和眼所見的。

馬太福音15：18告訴我們，「惟獨出口的，是從心裏發出來的，這才污穢人。」

可愛的思想
抽空欣賞飛鳥、動物、花草 . . . 。我們現在住在吉隆坡 我也曾經住過群山環抱的台北，在那兒，我常引述詩篇121：1「我要向山舉目，我的幫助從何而來？」

美德的思想
不說流言蜚語和讒謗的話。不要總是把別人想得太壞，而要多想到他人的優點。

隨著我們堅持以上所提，我們將會發展成有紀律的心志，剛強的心意，這樣的結果我們的言語和行為就會正確。

你所思想的成為了你。讓我們的思想永遠和神的話語一致。讓祂的話語改變我們的心意，我們的想法，這樣我們面對我們生活中的每一景況都將得勝有餘。

第二章

更新心意

在 這末日，神要透過我們做特別的事!

以色列人在他們回去重建祭壇之前，經過七十年流放的日子。他們必須重建祭壇，因爲他們在迦南過得太舒適了。他們忽略了他們的生命，尤其是他們的靈修生活。

一旦屬靈生命被忽略，仇敵就來殺害、偷襲、毀壞。對仇敵要警惕! 牠用的策略是：
欺騙我們
支配我們
毀壞我們

撒旦會告訴我們：「當個基督徒不要太過委身，只要星期天去教會，星期一到星期六隨隨便便就好。」這是仇敵的謊言和騙局。

第二，仇敵要支配或掌控我們的思想、言語和行爲，把我們帶遠離神。

第三，他要毀壞我們的屬靈生命。

我們有三部分－靈、魂、和體。我們的靈和神必須有對的關係，要不然我們就聽信其它的聲音。我們必須顧及我們屬靈的需要，要不然仇敵會消耗我們屬靈的力量。要留意不要過度耽於舒適像以色列人那樣。在馬來西亞，我們享有太多了， 例如：食物、衣服、好工作。讓我們爲耶穌征服這地準備前進吧。我們不要過度習以爲常—我們必須改變我們的教會生活，每星期天不一定要固定坐在同樣的位子。不管在那裡，你都不要太過於享受舒適。

那時代在台灣，冬天暖氣設備不普遍，我講道時要圍著圍巾，並戴上手套。那些渴望聽神的話語的人們，也願意坐在又冷又硬的木板凳二、三個小時，唱歌、拍手和讚美主。若空調機沒運轉，你會來教會嗎?你會埋怨太冷太熱嗎?

神要激勵我們，興起我們有如一支強壯的軍隊去征服這地。 因此我們的靈要儆醒。激動我們裡面的恩賜， 我們每個人都有恩賜、才能與時間。 我們不該忽略建立我們的祭壇。不要每天工作到深夜，那會抹殺你靈命的。男士們，不要過度埋首在你的工作中，要不然就像那以色列人，你就必須重建那祭壇。家長們，你的孩子們是否與神同行? 他們是否見到你們禱告、讀經，而不是只聽見你抱怨他人，或主日禮拜不斷滴咕要早點結束。

你要謹慎不要忽略你靈裡的人、你的禱告生活、以及研讀神的話語。「不要效法這個世界。」(羅馬書12：2)

禱告和神的話語可以更新心意

亞當是神創造的第一個人。他是個完美的人(在墮落之前)。他的靈和神有良好的關係，他與神親密的交談。他的身體健康，而且心智上、他的想法和神的想法一致。墮落後，在屬靈上、人和神有了距離；有了疾病，而且他的想法也不一樣了，和神的話語不一致。

「 . . . 人有個腐敗的意念。」(羅馬書12：20)還沒有重生時我們每個人都有腐敗的意念，但感謝神藉著耶穌為我們流寶血，我們如今被寬恕、被洗淨，並被聖靈充滿。我們的意念和祂的一致。問題是「它們是否一致?」， 我們必須不斷的檢驗我們的思想。若我們和神有良好的關係，靠著聖靈賜給我們的大能來掌管，並拒絕那些不好的和負面的思想。

我們必須不再有個腐敗的心意，必須每天有經常更新的心思意念。希臘文裏「更新」的意思是革新；恢復成良好狀況。例如：整修房屋你要拿走老舊毀損的家具，放進新的家具。倘若那老舊的家具沒有完全挪走，幾個月後你會發現白蟻侵蝕進去，也蛀蝕了新的家具。所以必須是完完全全的取代或革新才行。神的東西也是一樣。我們拿開那腐敗的意念，透過禱告和神的話語更新我們的心意。很重要的是那些自私的想法，色情的想法，負面的思想，必須被正確的想法，乾淨的想法，和正面的想法替代。那負面的想法，來自世界和非信徒。這是那些沒被聖靈帶領的人的聲音，例如今早有些人可能會說負面的話，譬如，「Sandra牧師講道太長了！」他們抱怨講道的長短，或埋怨敬拜時沒有多選些他們喜歡的詩歌。其實他們不應該埋怨，而應敬拜神以及渴望得到神的觸摸。不要讓負面的東西侵入。

我們必須記得神要我們拒絕那些負面的想法。縱然你讀完整本聖經(從創世記及到啓示錄)，你也只有頭腦的知識。那只是更新了一半，因爲頭腦的知識和心裏的知識是不一樣的。頭腦裏的知識會害死我們，但心裏的知識是有啓示性和有生命的。

當我們每天讀神的話語，我們應該知道神所說的。我們應該聆聽神的聲音。禱告說：「主！打開我的心，透過祢聖靈的大能，幫助我更新我的心思意念。」

例証：
在台灣有個人，當他聽多了許多公司倒閉的負面消息後一直覺得提心吊膽。雖然他的公司經營得不錯，他卻老擔心他的公司會倒閉。這些負面的想法進入他心思，終究脫口而出。感謝神倒閉幸未發生，但他可得要更新他的心思才是。

又另一事件，有一次有一個人和我的丈夫同車。那人不斷的說出關於他自己、他教會、以及牧師們的負面消息。我丈夫問神：「爲甚麼祢把我和他一同放在這車裏？」主對他說：「這是要教導你忍耐。」但我所要提的重點是這些抱怨、負面、和無病呻吟的話會消耗你的靈。不要因此而貶低自己或他人。

神的話語說每個人都是獨特的。無論你是誰，你是獨特的。爲甚麼呢？答案就是神救贖了我們；我們因爲耶穌的寶血稱義，而我們裏面有了復活的大能，神選擇了我們，我們是屬於祂的。我們都是獨特的，因此不該說負面的話。我們凡事要正面，充滿信心和充滿神的話語。這不僅是以正面的想法或心思意念來勝過問題。乃是你的心思必須充滿神的話語，要說你凡事都能做—而並非你不能。哦！我主我神，在祢沒有難成的事。

如何更新意念？

頭腦的知識只是半途更新意念。我們也須要有神話語的啟示。你不須要一定要到神學院受造就。我曾經在那裏學習過，也看過某些教導可能抹殺頭腦和心靈。神學院可能是一些人的答案，但並非適合於每個人。事實上，我必須再學一些對我們的事奉並不實用的東西。我曾經禱告聖靈帶領我閱讀正確的書籍。如果你只是研討三一真神或討論耶穌第二次再來，但却看不到任何人透過聖靈得醫治、被釋放、或重生，你該知道有些事不太對。

我們多數人都會禱告求神改變我們的情況。例如：改變我們的丈夫，改變我們的妻子—離婚和再婚。這裏我們必須小心翼翼地—有些人離婚不一定是他們的錯，我們必須愛他們每一個人。整個家庭—父親、母親、和孩子們都必須透過聖靈更新他們的意念。我們必須除去負面的東西，例如：在台灣的家長常常叫他們的孩子「笨蛋」。這是不對的方式。我們必須愛他們。若我們的孩子做傻事，我們不要吼叫他們的化名，或說出負面的話，但要阻止並教訓他們。

我叫我的兒子們愛因斯坦I和愛因斯坦II。這不是因為他們以後會特別的聰明，而是我們必須給孩子們灌輸信心。我們的孩子是神奇妙、可畏的創造。我們必須說出正確的事。因此要有「**正確的宣告**」，宣告神的話語。

「與基督一同復活，就當求在上面的事。就當求在上面的事不是地上的事。」(歌羅西書3：1)

當求上面的事—我們必須操練我們的心思。「你們要先求祂的國和祂的義，這些東西都要加給你們了。」(馬太福音6：33)。地上的事是我們的工作、家庭問題、財務困難、所有的問題、和困難的景況。不要把你的心思放在這些事上。要站在神的應許上。每天更新你的意念。我們的心思意念不會完全被更新，必直等到我們和耶穌在一起，但不要放棄嘗試。

每天求天上的事。不要依靠五種感官感覺，那就是視覺、聽覺、嗅覺、味覺、和觸覺。這些是我們魂的部分。體貼肉體的基督徒，他們被這五個感官感覺和外在的狀況所控制。假若我今天有嚴重傷風，你們有些人可能會想「不要靠近她，要不然我們也會傷風。」(那是你的意念告訴你因為你這樣想；你說你會傷風，你就被感染了)。反之我宣告神的話語並說出：「奉耶穌的名，我不會得傷風。」因爲耶穌的鞭傷，使我得醫治。因爲耶穌的寶血，使我被救贖。這樣就能因神的話語成就了。要堅定地站在神的話語上。

定睛在天上，而不只是看我們的景況和感覺。 例如：你說你的婚姻無法維持。你就因你自己的話對你婚姻判了刑。你必須告訴自己，神會恢復你的婚姻，透過聖靈爲你創造奇蹟。要行在聖靈中； 你所說的、所想的、和所做的都要與聖靈有關。五、六年前，神啓示我必須每天來更新我的思想，以及停止負面的想法。說正面的事，你就不會有負面的行爲。你們有些人可能說 「你不知道我們的情況。」無論你的情況如何，要讚美神。無論你正經歷甚麼事，讚美祂。我雖不知道，但耶穌知道所有的事，也知道你內心的一切。你並不是單獨自己一人面對。

女士們，在你的婚姻裏─仰望神。神在你裏面， 與你同在，並幫助你。無論敵人說甚麼，神必不毀壞，祂會建造和恢復。你不是單獨一個人。你必須改變負面。

「至於我和我家，我們必定事奉耶和華。」(約書亞記24：15)

今天有許多妻子負擔工作養家的重擔，而她們的丈夫卻煙酒不離。神沒有忘記你。神要觸摸你的心。敞開你的心讓聖靈觸摸你。在這新的一年做新的事。這一年是新事發生的一年。

見證：
當我懷胎大衛時住在台灣。醫生說我年齡(36歲)太大了，還說了很多負面的話。若看外在的情況我似乎可能流產─我那時有出血現象而必須臥床。但有一天我閱讀舊約時，出埃及記第21、23、25、26章中，神的話語說：「你境內沒有墮胎的。」

憑著對神話語的信心，我拒絕了那些負面的話。 我禱告：「主，奉耶穌的名，我宣告你的話語，我不會流產。」感謝主我沒有流產。在我三十六歲、和三十八歲時，生了兩個兒子。現在我已經四十歲了，而我對年屆四十歲沒有任何負面的想法。若我們敬畏神和相信祂的話語，我們能夠活到八十歲。神的話語說七十歲，若我們強壯則八十歲。我常常對我丈夫說 ：「你無法太早擺脫我」。我們必須靠主和祂的大能強壯起來。我們需要靠祂的話語來更新自己。

我們如何能靠神的話語更新自己?

1. **閱讀神的話語**
   閱讀聖經—舊約和新約。聽神說話。聽聖靈說:「這是道路,你往這邊走。」聖靈您是我的師傅,帶領者,敞開我的雙眼去看那舊約和新約真理。讚美主,我因閱讀舊約而沒有流產。我們必須抓住神的話語。

   要每天閱讀。我們必須要有時間。現今在世界各地,人們都很努力的工作,花費很多的時間。他們工作到夜晚回家,吃晚餐、看報紙、看電視,但等到閱讀但時—只看了五分鐘就睡着了,他們卻能夠花好多時間看報紙和電視。到底那些事對我們較優先較重要?

2. **默想神的話語**
   不是快速的把聖經從創世記到啟示錄閱讀完,而是在我們心裏,一而再地思考神的話語。讓聖靈在我們內心作工。每天早上閱讀詩篇和箴言各一章,然後默想。大衛,雖然面對許多考驗和軟弱的時候,卻唱詩讚美神而走出那些困境。默想神的話語,將使我們從負面的情況裏起來。我們的思想會改變。

3. **熟記神的話語**
   不要說你老了不中用了這種話。你所想的和你所說的,都將會成就。不要說我不能,而要說:「靠著聖靈的大能和同樣復活的大能,我能夠恢復我的記憶。」(這是得勝的一個關鍵)。若壓力太多—釋放那壓力。

   有天早上,我第一次自己開車從蕉賴到芭達嶺寨椰的教會。大衛說:「媽咪,萬一我們迷路了,我們可以跟耶穌禱告。」我說:「我們不會迷路的!」。結果我只轉錯了一次方向,而且我也說了:「我沒迷路!」

   「你要專心仰賴耶和華,不可倚靠自己的聰明。」(箴言3:5)

4. **宣告神的話語**
   將神的話語放在腦海裏和心裏。我們所說的話語具有大能力。在創世時,神說:「要有光,就有光。」我們是照着神的形象造的,我們重生,也是以祂的的形象重生的。

「生死在舌頭的權下。」(箴言18：21)

我們說甚麼很重要。若一個人生病不要喊痛。要說：「我靠耶穌的寶血痊癒了。」，不要憑你的五官感覺。外在的感覺告訴你那是痛的，雖然所有的癥狀還在，但你要說我被醫治了，只要信靠神。我十九歲時，我得了風濕症，骨腫了起來。記得那是在我神學院畢業後，有一天聖靈告訴我：「你痊癒了。」我清楚的聽到那聲音，然後我轉身問我身旁的女人：「你說話了嗎?」，她回答說：「我甚麼都沒說。」。她以為我瘋了。當我回到家要吃藥時，我又聽到神的聲音說：「你已痊癒了。」我把那些藥物倒進馬桶裏沖掉，並且讚美耶和華。直到今天我風濕症沒了，我痊癒了。不過在此有個提醒，除非你自己聽到神的聲音，否則不要這樣做。

- 神的話語可以更新我們的意念。
- 禱告可以更新我們的意念。
- 神的聲音可以更新我們的意念。
- 準備傾聽和遵從祂的聲音。
- 我們的神是大有能力的。

5. 在聖靈裏禱告
- 用方言禱告。
- 重建我們的祭壇。
- 獻上燔祭就是我們禱告的生活。

當我們向神禱告時是否嘀咕埋怨?例如：「改變我的丈夫、改變我的妻子、改變我的孩子們、和改變我的牧師?」

我們應該禱告：
主啊，改變我。(這是突破的關鍵之一)。我們需要更新我們的意向。我們的禱告應該充滿神的話語、祂的應許、讚美祂，天上就會為我們而震動。

在靈裏禱告。 說方言不僅僅是一次的經驗而已—我們必須不斷的被聖靈充滿。使徒保羅他說方言比他們任何人還要多。我們要不斷的禱告和在靈裏禱告。禱告、禱告、禱告。 當我們在靈裏禱告我們的心靈會變得清晰，而我們會更加堅強，尤其是我們的靈、魂和五官感覺。

神要我們的心思意念被更新，因而我們就能積極成功，並充滿神的事。

神在我們每個人身上的工作還沒完成。祂在震動所有的東西。不要忽略重建我們的祭壇(我們的靈修生活)。唯有耶穌能夠醫治我們的心，使我們得到釋放。

第三章

當你說出就能成就

我們所說的話是如此的帶有能力。雅各書告訴我們，我們的舌頭是身體的一小部分，但它若不被聖靈控制，它能帶來如此多的破壞。同樣的我們的舌頭，當說正確的話，也能非常的有果效。因我們認知神是用說話來創造世界，因此我們可以透過宣告祂的話語，使我們生命裏的事成真。

1. 說出大有能力和創意的話

    在創世記1：1-3裏，我們注意到神的靈在水面上運行。水在那裏，黑暗在那裏，神的靈
    也在那裏。但任何事都沒發生，直到說出那話，直到神說「要有光」。神的話一說出，就有「光」了。過去和現在神的話都是祂創造的大能。

    根據創世記1：26，我們都是按照神的形像和樣式造的。因此若神的話語是有能力的，我們的話也是如此。

    今天許多人都認為說的話不重要。但「生死在舌頭的權下。喜愛他的，必吃他所結的果子。」(箴言18：21)

    從創世記1：2-3我們發現那話語創造的大能。而從箴言18：21我們學到話語有生與死的大能。當我們靠着神的靈重生，耶穌成為我們的救主和主。從此我們口而出的話應該和神的話是一致的。我們必須說神的話語，要不然我們就會說世界的話，那就是撒旦的話。

161

「這律法書不可離開你的口，總要晝夜思想，好使你謹守遵行這書上所寫的一切話。 如此你的道路就可以亨通，凡事順利。」(約書亞記1：8)

3. 晝夜思想包含喃喃私語，大聲對自己說或宣告某事。宣告神的話語能幫助在牢記心裡，當我們如此做我們就會成就。

2. 說出正面的而不是負面的話

「耶穌回答:你們當信服神。我實在告訴你們：無論何人對這座山說：你挪開此地，投在海裏!他若心裏不疑惑，只信他所說的必成，就必給他成了。所以我告訴你們：凡你們禱告祈求的，無論是甚麼，只要信是得着的，就必得着。你們站着禱告的時候，若想起有人得罪你們，就當饒恕他，好叫你們在天上的父也饒恕你們的過犯。」(馬可福音11：22-25)

我們該對「這座山」說。這裏「山」的意思是 「問題」。我們應該針對我們的問題說話，而不只說一些有關於它們的。

腓立比2：14「凡所行的，都不要發怨言，起爭論。」

所以我們要對我們生命裏的「高山」說出充滿信心的諾言。我們面對我們的問題沒有埋怨、悲歎、和苦惱。例如當我們的孩子有問題時，我們不該用「笨蛋」這樣的字眼來譴責他們!我們應該說：「你剛作了一樁蠢事，下次不要再犯了，因為你是個聰明的男/女孩。」

3. 說有生命而不是死亡的話

我們也不要對丈夫提出有關負面的說法。當我們有財務的問題，我們該說出神所應許的一「耶和華是我的供應者」—而不只是埋怨：「我似乎永遠都不夠用。」

咒詛、負面的話總是帶來死亡。我們可能在身體上沒謀殺人，但我們的話卻能殺人! 比如說； 若我們說「離婚」，那就會發生，但如果我們作相反的宣告，那婚姻就會成功。 同樣的，若我們說疾病一「我常常生病」—我們就會繼續生病。宣告健康，你就會健康。那些說「我的糖尿病」、「我的風濕病」、或「我的癌症」的人在使用「擁有詞」—「我的」和「有」。那疾病就成爲了他們所有物,除非他們放棄擁有那疾病,它就繼續停留在他們的體內!

我讀到一則有關一位醫生的故事,他不是基督徒,但他卻發現了言語能力的原則。他給病人開的藥方是:回家每天把這幾句話重複幾次—「我每一天會越來越好。」他的藥方擁有如此不可思議的果效,使得人們從世界各地不遠千里而來向他求助!

7. 這位醫生是非基督徒,而我們這些基督徒又當如何呢?我們有神的話語。我以自己的經歷當範例。我懷胎我的長子大衛時,我尿道感染。我去看醫生,她給我溫和的抗生素,因爲她不想傷害胎兒。一星期內那感染沒了,然而一星期後它又來了。我沒有再回去找那醫生,因爲我不想要吃太多藥物—每當我排尿,我宣告得醫治的經文,一個星期內我完全痊癒。神的話語是有生命而且能醫治身體。

4. 說祝福而不是詛咒的話

「污穢的言語,一句不可出口,只要隨事說造就人的好話,叫聽見的人得益處。」(以弗所書4：29)

身爲神的子民,我們該祝福他人,不是詛咒他們。如果我們找他們的麻煩,批評他們,我們就是在詛咒。我們的話語應該是讚美的話語、溫柔的話語、和鼓勵性的話語。

例如在聖經裏,巴拿巴和保羅帶馬可一起去旅行傳道,途中馬可離開了他們。所以當他們計畫下一次旅程時,巴拿巴仍要帶馬可,但保羅卻拒絕再帶他去,他和保羅之間發生了爭論。結果巴拿巴帶馬可,保羅帶西拉。然而,數年後保羅承認巴拿巴(他的名字的意思是「鼓勵之子」)是對的。因爲他在提摩太後書4:11說:「要把馬可帶來,因爲他在傳道的事上於我有益處。」

5. 說出那還沒成就的有如它已成就

如經上所記:「我已經立你作多國的父。」(羅馬書4:17) 在神的眼裏他是我們的父親,他所相信的神—那能使已死的得以復活的神,和宣稱那還沒成就的有如已成就的神。

例如：<u>亞伯拉罕</u>和<u>撒拉</u>超過了生育的年齡，但神使那些不可能的成爲可能，結果生了<u>以撒</u>。

一個不好的婚姻可以變好，當我們如此宣告它便成就。

叛逆的孩子將會順服神和他們的父母，當我們說出那還沒成就的，有如它已成就。

爲了使我們過得勝，聖靈充滿的生活，我們必須改變我們的用語措辭。我們必須非常注意我們每一次的發言。我們的心和我們語言必須有所轉變。它們必須從負面轉變成正面，從死亡轉變成生命，和從咒詛轉變成祝福。如此我們認爲不可能的變成可能。然後神的應許，以及爲我們計畫的神聖藍圖，將在我們的心裏和生命裏生根，我們所結的果子也將成爲我們裏面大能的見證。

第四章

靠神的話語而不憑感覺活

神創造我們的靈、魂、和體。我們的靈是和神有個人關係的領域；我們的魂是我們的思想、情感和意志；我們的身體是外體。我們的靈應該經常控制我們的魂與體，然而身為女人，我們太過於被我們的情緒—我們的感覺所支配。我今天不想烹調! 我今天不想禱告! 我今晚不想去婦女的聚會!有時候我們可能甚至說出「我不覺得我愛我的丈夫—尤其是他竟然又再一次的忘記我們的結婚週年紀念日?!」

但是神的話語在聖經裡怎麼說呢? 神的話語對我們每種情況均有個應許和答案，無論它是多麼的困難。那些話語深入我們的靈，使我們能超越我們的情感，征服我們的情感。聖經很清楚的指示我們要倚靠神的話語生活，而不是光靠我們的情感。

情感說：「全都失去了。」、「 沒有希望了。」、「多糟糕的一天!」
神的話語說：「我知道我的救贖主活着。」

讓我們研究約伯的生命並向他的反應學習。

約伯的考驗

他失去他的七個兒子、三個女兒、七千隻羊、 三千隻駱駝、五佰對牛，但約伯沒有一次責備神。

「約伯便起來，撕裂外袍，剃了頭伏在地下拜，說：我赤身出於母胎，也必赤身歸回。賞賜的是耶和華，收取的也是耶和華；耶和華的名是

165

應當稱頌的。在這一切的事上，約伯並不犯罪，也不以神為愚妄。」(約伯記1：20-22)

他可以依賴他的情感但他沒有。他將希望、信任、和信心放在神裏。

約伯當時承受全身從頭到腳起泡的瘡的痛苦。 他的妻子告訴他詛咒神。約伯的回應是甚麼?

「約伯卻對她說，你說話像愚頑的婦人一樣。嗳!難道我們從神手裏得福，不也受禍嗎?」(約伯記2：10)

注意在他面對考驗中，約伯沒有說有罪的話。 有時當我們心情不好，我們可能說不好的事，那可能是個罪。約伯肯定覺得很糟，但他沒有詛咒神。

然後約伯的朋友指控他犯罪，雖然他是沒罪的。 這是他對他們的回應:

「你們攪擾我的心，用我的言語壓碎我,要到幾時呢? 」(約伯記19：2)

對他朋友的指控，他情緒的回應可能是，「你是甚麼樣的朋友!」。他們的話壓碎了約伯，但他沒有情緒性的回應，無論他們怎麼說他依然當他們為朋友。

約伯的信心和勝利

「我知道我的救贖主活，末了必站立在地上。」(約伯記19：25)

九個月來撒旦帶給約伯煩惱，但因為約伯沒有依賴他的情緒感覺，他堅決不做錯或說不對的話，結果得勝。

「約伯為他的朋友祈禱，耶和華就使約伯從苦境轉回，並且耶和華賜給他比他從前所有的加倍。」(約伯記42：10)

「這樣 耶和華後來賜福給約伯比先前更多。他有一萬四千羊、六千駱駝、一千對牛、一千母驢。」(約伯記42：12)

在閱讀約伯的生命中，最首要的事變得晶瑩透澈。我們還有一些額外的東西是約伯當時他所沒有的。我們有這本寫下神話語的聖經。

「聖經都是默示的，於教訓、督責、使人歸正、教導人學義都是有益的，叫屬神的人得以完全，預備行各樣的善事。」(提摩太後書3：16、17)

謹記神的話語是大有能力的。他是生命和真理。 我們必須使用神的話語來克服我們的感覺。

情緒說：
「這問題太大了、太難了、沒有出路 ...。」

神的話語說：
「 ... 在半夜禱告和讚美神。」

接下來讓我們轉向保羅和西拉，找出他們對考驗的回應，和他們信靠神的結果。

保羅和西拉的考驗

有一段時間保羅和西拉在腓立比。他們曾經因為被指控引發擾亂被帶到判官面前。他們曾被逼迫、被赤身露體、和被劇烈鞭打、然後被關入監牢。 他們被關入機密的牢房，雙腳被扣住。

保羅和西拉的勝利

在這種似乎沒有出路的情況下，保羅和西拉怎麼做?

這是他們所做的事：

「約在半夜，保羅和西拉禱告唱詩讚美神，眾囚犯也側耳而聽。忽然地大震動，甚至監牢的地基都搖動了，監門立刻全開，眾囚犯的鎖鏈也都鬆開了。」(使徒行傳16：25-26)

在聖經裏「半夜」代表我們生命裏的一個危機，或多重危機的時刻。保羅和西拉他們的危機時刻做些甚麼? 他們讚美主。

他們的讚美，他們那不屈不饒的信心的結果是這樣：那監牢的門全開了，不但是保羅和西拉的鎖鏈，就連那綑綁眾囚犯的鎖鏈也都鬆開了。這就是神對他子民的禱告和讚美的回應。

謹記當我們讚美主，同樣的事會發生。我們將會從欺壓和沮喪裏被釋放。

有時候我們的問題或困難使我們感受到自己有如在監牢裏，因為我們「覺得」 我們的問題太大了，我們無法處理，但是聖經很清楚的指示我們不要依靠感覺。我們不該有負面的想法，我們不該說負面的話。

「死在舌頭的權下。喜愛他的必吃他所結的果子。」(箴言18：21)

「我們應當靠着耶穌，常常以頌讚為祭獻給神，這就是那承認主名之人嘴唇的果子。」(希伯來書13：15)

很明顯的是我們要常常以頌讚為祭獻給神。所謂的「獻祭」不都屬於好的時刻，當我們「心情」好的時候，讚美主是很容易的，不需要犧牲甚麼。 更確切地說「獻祭」是關係到考驗的時刻，或關係到我們讚美主時有困難的情況。當我們儘管在痛苦的情況下仍獻給祂讚美，那就是「獻祭」。聖經說：「常常以頌讚為祭獻給神。」 那「常常」的意思是我們每時每刻都在做。

情感說：
「主啊!為甚麼? 為甚麼是我? 」

神的話語說：
「照祢的話成就在我身上。」

最後讓我們研究馬利亞的回應，當天使向耶穌的母親顯現說：「妳要懷孕生子。」

馬利亞的回應

「天使回答說：聖靈要臨到你身上，至高者的能力要蔭庇妳，因此所要生的聖者必稱為神的兒子。況且妳的親戚以利沙伯，在年老的時候

也懷了男胎，就是那素來稱為不生育的，現在有孕六個月了。因為出於神的話，沒有一句不帶能力的。」(路加福音1：35-37)

當天使對她說的時候馬利亞是位處女。她已經許配了約瑟，還沒有迎娶。若她靠「感覺」回應那天使震驚的話，她可能會說，「主啊！為甚麼？為甚麼是我？」

馬利亞對那消息感到害怕和沮喪是很自然的事。在猶太人的文化裏，未婚生子將使她本身的名譽、她家人的名譽、約瑟的名譽受辱。她也可能被人用石頭打到死。

可想像她的感受。況且當時她還沒到二十多歲。 然而這是她對天使的消息的回應卻是：

「我是主的使女，情願照您的話成就在我身上。天使就離開她去了。」(路加福音1：38)

馬利亞的回應是個完全遵從神的旨意的回應。

我們必須問自己，當我們面對困難的時候，我們怎麼做？我們是否依着情感而說：「主啊！為甚麼，為甚麼是我？」或我們可以說：「我是主的使僕，情願照您的話成就在我身上。」因為出於神的話，沒有一句不帶有能力的。

我們必須讓神話語裡的應許在我們的信心裡激勵我們。無論我們的情況是如何─在家、 在辦公室、或在教會─在神裏面，沒有不可能的事。

我們不要依賴我們情感生活。我們必須站在神的應許上。祂已經賜給我們權柄，可以踐踏蛇和蠍子，並勝過仇敵一切的力量，斷沒有甚麼能害我們。我們要奉耶穌的名興起來，克服那負面的情緒。

第五章

治死老我

歷史上意義最深長的死亡是耶穌死在十字架上。 祂沒把自己放在首位。當祂成爲至高的獻祭，祂把我們放在首位。祂爲我們藉純愛的行動，治死罪和疾病，並且戰勝了死亡本身。耶穌配得我們所有的讚美。

「我的心哪，你要稱頌主，凡我裏面的，也要稱頌祂的聖名。我的心哪，你要稱頌主，不可忘記祂的一切恩惠! 祂赦免你的一切罪孽，醫治你的一切疾病。」(詩篇103：1-3)

耶穌爲我們而死，我們也應該回報治死我們的自我。自我是「我」在我們生命裏；我們的老我。使徒保羅說「我天天死」 注意保羅說「天天」不是只是在得救時一次、在受洗時一次、在聖靈充滿時一次，然後在成爲細胞小組組長、敬拜主領、長老、或牧師時各一次，而應該是「天天」。

要注意的是，我們天天捨己的最大的阻礙和障礙物就是我們的驕傲。無論我們是甚麼種族、社會地位、性別、或年齡，我們都是高傲的人。驕傲是不易見到的，它可能是難以捉摸的或被蒙蔽的。這是因爲身爲基督徒的我們，會很小心我們所說的所做的，尤其在我們牧師同工面前。

驕傲的定義

聖經對驕傲的定義和世界對驕傲的定義是不一樣的。當人們認爲自己把某些事做得頂好，或他們比別人更好時，世界就說這些人很驕傲。然而聖經的定義超越那定義。它說驕傲是一個遠離神獨立的態度，一個依靠自己的力量、自己的能力、和自己的智慧，而不是神超自然的力量、超自然的能力、和智慧。

「我是葡萄樹，你們是枝子;常在我們裏面的，我也常在他裏面，這人就多結果子。因爲離了我，你們就不能做甚麼。」(約翰福音15：5)

事實如此，離了祂，我們就不能做甚麼。離了祂，我不能帶領細胞小組。離了祂，我無法帶領任何人信主。離了祂，我也無法使任何人聖靈充滿。

爲甚麼? 因爲是神作的而不是我們。我們只是祂使用的器皿、工具。在我們自己裏面是空的。

驕傲遠離神的態度導致我們墮落

路西弗及其驕傲

「明亮之星，早晨之星! 你何竟從天墮落? 你這攻敗列國的，何竟被砍倒在地上?你心裏曾說:『我要升到天上! 我要高舉我的寶座在神眾星以上在北方的極處;我要升到高雲之上，我要與至上者同等。』然而你必墮落陰間，到坑中極深之處。凡看見你的，都要定眼看你，留意看你，說: 使大地戰抖，使列國震動。」(以賽亞書14：12-16)

注意那『我要』這字眼在以上的經文出現五次，但『神的旨意』的字眼卻完全沒出現。路西弗變得這麼多。

我們可能認爲我們不同，認爲我們的意志不會駕馭神的旨意。然而我們態度證實卻不是如此。 我們的態度可能如下:

- 我知道的比神還要好!
- 我知道我應該如何做。
- 我知道教會應該如何管理!

這些驕傲的話語會帶領我們墮落。

以賽亞書裏的經文清楚讓我們看到驕傲的開始改變了天使路西弗，由一個充滿愛神的天使變成一個邪惡和自私的撒旦。

我們看到路西弗停止依靠神的帶領與智慧，他的想法和行為開始變得好像他比神知道的更多。

當路西弗的態度變成驕傲、自滿，他不再愛神，不願更親密的來認識神。當我們有了驕傲和自滿的態度，我們將會失去對神起初的愛，還有我們曾經和祂有過的親密關係。

神要一個順服的心，一個謙卑的心，然後祂會使用我們和透過我們工作。

「你們年幼的也要順服年長的。就是你們眾人也要以謙卑束腰，彼此順服，因為神阻擋驕傲的人，賜恩給謙卑的人。」(彼得前書5：5)

彼得不是只在告訴一個人或幾個人謙卑，他用的字是你們眾人 . . . 」

彼得和他的驕傲

「主又說：西門！西門！撒旦想要的着你們，好篩你們像篩麥子一樣。但我已經為你祈求，叫你不至於失了信心。你回頭以後，要堅固你的弟兄。彼得說:主啊，我就是同祢下監，同你受死，也是甘心！耶穌說:彼得，我告訴你，今日雞還沒有叫，你要三次說不認得我。」(路加福音22：31-34)

為甚麼彼得否認耶穌三次？ 那是因為他充滿了極大的恐懼。彼得依靠他自己的力量，因此當他面對危機時，他自己的力量不足以去克服它。
之後當彼得的自我依賴減少，他變得比較依靠聖靈和神的超自然的能力。彼得能夠成就許多神蹟奇事，就連他的影子也能醫治人。

「我靠着那加給我的力量的，凡事都能做。」(腓立比書4：13)

尼布甲尼撒生命裏的驕傲

「王啊，求你悅納我的諫言，以施行公義斷絕罪過，以憐憫窮人除掉罪孽，或者你的平安可以延長。」(但以理書4：27)

這是但以理給尼布甲尼撒王的忠告，但是他的驕傲阻止他注意這忠告。我們知道如此是因為十二個月後，當尼布甲尼撒王遊行巴比倫王宮裡，他很驕傲的如此說：

「這大巴比倫不是我用大能大力建爲京都，要顯我威嚴的榮耀嗎？」
(但以理書4:30)

他口中尚未說完，他驕傲的回應已臨到他：

「這話在王口中尚未說完，有聲音從天降下，說：尼布甲尼撒王啊，有話對你說：你的國位離開你了。你必被趕出離開世人，與野地的獸同居，吃草如牛，且要經過七期。等你知道至高者在人的國中掌權，要將國賜與誰，就賜與誰。」(但以理書4：31-32)

在他生命中的某個階段，尼布甲尼撒曾經承認耶和華神是唯一的眞神。這是因爲但以理、沙的拉、米煞、亞伯尼歌，對他的影響。然而尼布甲尼撒讓驕傲控制了他的思想和言語。

驕傲是非常難以捉摸的。它先是影響我們的想法，然後我們的態度，再來是我們言語，最後我們的行爲。接下來的是榮耀自己，而不是榮耀神。我們所用的詞句和想法反映了這個狀態：

這不是我所建立的大細胞小組嗎？
這不是我所建立的大教會嗎？
這不是我所建立的大主日學校嗎？

沒有承認歸功於神所做的，神的超自然的能力和大能。

神對尼布甲尼撒的驕傲有甚麼反應？祂拿去他所有的東西，尼布甲尼撒變得瘋狂。

治死老我、治死驕傲

我們能夠如此行來治死老我：

承認我們自己裡面有驕傲

我們的驕傲使到我們不靠神的力量而靠自己的力量。我們可能缺乏天生的才能、技能、財物、權力、和社會地位，但卻還是有驕傲的態度。

也就是說，有財富和權力未必使一個人變得驕傲。有些人有財富和權力，但也很謙卑的在神面前。驕傲是非常難以捉摸的，所以我們必須學習認得它。

悔改

當我們承認我們的問題，我們必須謙卑在神的大能手下並悔改。真實的悔改不只是說「對不起」，而是完全棄絕我們驕傲的靈，行在謙卑中。

「我們若認自己的罪，神是信實的，是公義的，必要赦免我們的罪，洗淨我們一切的不義。」(約翰一書1:9)

穿戴謙卑，行走在謙卑中

真正的謙卑，是我們看到我們在祂和祂聖靈的大能之外甚麼都不是。

司提反是這很好的例子：
「 ... 就揀選了司提反，乃是大有信心，聖靈充滿的人 ... 」(使徒行傳6:5)

信心的定義是不疑惑的倚靠神，祂的話語和祂聖靈的力量與帶領。我們從使徒行傳6:3-15看到司提反讓他自己天生的才能、體能、人性的理由、普通常識、和人性的愛被聖靈充滿和掌控，並且依靠神的力量。

當司提反與那些宗教士們和世界的知識份子辯論，他依靠聖靈帶領他。即使當他們用石頭打他，他依然依靠聖靈。因為他說：「主啊！不要將這罪歸於他們!」(使徒行傳7:60)

使徒保羅使另一個信心的例子。他無法只靠自己的智慧或力量來成為一個神大能的使徒。惟有依靠神超自然的大能，才能講道以及運行神蹟奇事，保羅知道他必須憑信而行，而不是靠眼見。

「你們受苦如此之多，都是徒然的嗎？難道果真是徒然的嗎?那賜給你們聖靈，又再你們中間行異能的是因你們行律法呢？是因你們聽信福音呢?正如，<u>亞伯拉罕</u>信神，這就算為他的義。『所以你們要知道，那以信為本的人，就是<u>亞伯拉罕</u>的子孫，並且聖經既然預先看明，神要叫外邦人因信稱義，就早已傳福音給<u>亞伯拉罕</u>，說：『萬國都必因你得福。』可見那以信為本的人和有信心的<u>亞伯拉罕</u>一同得福。凡以行律法為本的，都是被咒詛的，因為經上記着：『凡不常照律法上所記一切之事去行的，就被咒詛。』沒有一個人靠着律法在神面前稱義。」(<u>加拉太書</u>3：4-11)

就像<u>保羅</u>和<u>可提反</u>，我們也必須治死老我，變成像<u>耶穌</u>。我們的驕傲必須除去，而且我們全都要治死老我。我們需要神的話語來更新我們的心思意念，且要有神的智慧，行在信、愛、和謙卑中。

天天捨己－這是我們每天的宣告和禱告。

第六章

靠信心而行不憑眼見

「**信**就是所望之事的實底，是未見之事的確據。」(希伯來書11：1)

「亞伯拉罕因着信，蒙召的時候，就遵命出去，往將來得爲業的地方去；出去的時候，還不知往哪裏去。他因着信，就在所應許之地作客，好像在異地居住帳棚，與那同蒙一個應許的以撒，雅各一樣。因爲他等候那座有根基的城，就是神所經營，所建造的。因着信，連撒拉自己，雖然過了生育的歲數還能懷孕，因她以爲那應許她的是可信的。」(希伯來書11：8-11)

因着信亞伯拉罕，雖然他已過了歲數—而撒拉自己也不孕—卻能夠成爲爸爸，因爲他認爲那應許他的神是信實的。

「亞伯拉罕因着信，被試驗的時候，就把以撒獻上；這便是那歡喜領受應許的，將自己獨子獻上。論到這兒子，曾有話說：『從以撒生的才要稱爲你得後裔。』他以爲神還能叫人從死裏復活，他也彷彿從死中得回他的兒子來。」(希伯來書11：17-19)

當神創造我們，他以三部分造人，就是靈、魂、和體。祂的話語說屬靈的人應主控一切。但假若體(肉體)主控，它也就操控了我們的魂(情感)和我們的靈(和神的正確關係)。就好像多數的男人，他們鍛練身體，作俯地挺身運動來強健他們的身體。當肉體主控，它掌控了魂(思想、情感和意志)，混亂感就會介入。肉體不該是主控者。

若由魂(思想、情感和意志)主控屬靈的人，(透過魂領域)則有許多恐懼會進入，我們就無法行在信中，因為是肉體和魂在操控。我們的思想、情感若帶有恐懼，我們靈就無法成長。

「...倚賴祂的大能大力，作剛強的人。」(以弗所書6:10)

若靈在主控，我們與神就有正確的關係。魂與體將順服靈。然後就會有愛、喜樂、平安、節制、和聖靈的果子顯明出來。當我們與神有堅固的關係，我們就行在信中，而不是靠眼見，因為我們不是倚賴自己的感覺、我們的思想、和我們固執的意志、而是倚靠神的信心。

信心或感覺

我們依靠甚麼?是我們的感覺或信心?

我們的感覺說:「哦，我今早必須去教會。」或是我們的信心說:「哇!又是星期天了!這是耶和華所定的日子，我要在其中高興歡喜。」

今早你起床時如何? 還有你有甚麼感覺?

你有沒有說:「哦不! 我必須起床上教會。我希望有停車的空位。我希望一切都安好。我希望敬拜會很好。」。我們全在希望、希望、希望之中。信就是未見之事的確據。

「信就是所望之事的實底，是未見之事的確據。」(希伯來書11:1)

感覺倚靠你所看到的去進行。若陽光普照，我們就會說今天是美好的一天。若陽光不普照，只因我們無法用我們天生的眼睛看到，我們就會說，哦! 今天真是個糟糕的一天。但神的話語說，有一次約書亞的確命令太陽停止。我們在耶穌基督裏有權柄，因此我們的信心必須被操練。

同樣的如果我們早上一起床時，因我們倚靠我們的感覺，所以我們靠我們的感覺就事先預測，還用我們的口說出來，說這一天將會是糟糕的一天。等這一天工作結束你從辦公室回家，當你的妻子在門口招呼你，或你們一起進門，她問你這一天如何啊? 你回答:「哦，糟的很!」「你呢?又如何?」她回答:「也是糟透了。」為甚麼呢? 因為你出門之前就預定如此了! 在英國他們常說:「憂鬱的星期一!」，因為我們必須在度過週末星期六和星期天之後，接著星期一就要工作。一般來說，整個辦公室就會籠罩著壓抑和鬱悶的氣氛，因為每個人都宣稱憂鬱星期一，因此你所說的便如此成就。

但神的話語說，信就是所望之事的實底。那意思是我們不可以依賴我們的感覺，來得到醫治。我們不可以來依賴我們的感覺，來使我們家人得救。我們不可以依賴我們的感覺，來謀得更好的工作。我們不可以依賴我們的感覺，獲得更好的教育。我們不可以依賴我們的感覺，來閱讀聖經和禱告。但是我們必須進入屬靈的境界，並因信過活。當我們因聖靈重生，我們每人都有一顆信的種子。但信就像自然界的種子一樣需要滋養。它需要灌溉，它在成長之前必須被照顧。這就是為甚麼我們有些人成為基督徒十多年，其他只是二至三年的基督徒，然而那二至三年的基督徒快速成長以及比那十多年的基督徒更前進。這是因為那二至三年的基督徒，他們的信的種子有滋養和灌溉多過那十多年的基督徒。這就是為甚麼兩者之間有差別。所以我們每一個人，需要滋養這信心的種子。

當我們從台灣搬到古晉，我們有個像叢林般的花園，我告訴我丈夫：「我們來種草坪吧。」他看着我說「甚麼? 在這裏?」我說：「沒錯，就在這裏。」他是位好丈夫，他為我除野草。然後他為我買了草籽，他說：「做你想要做的吧!」我依照肥料說明書指示：撒過肥料後，要在播種的草籽上面走動。所以在下午兩、三點的大太陽下，我就在草籽上走來走去，我邊走邊說，奉耶穌的名你會成長。是的，你會的，而且你將成為一片美麗的草地。我就這樣在炎熱的太陽下走上走下。我丈夫走下樓往窗外看，問我：「你在做甚麼? 」我說：「那說明書指示我要在那草籽上走走踏踏。我額外又多做了一點。我在為它禱告! 」

他是位信實的丈夫，他與我們的孩子大衛，每天早晚替我在種子上澆水。接著小小的綠苗開始長出，大衛要將它們拔起我就對他說：「不，不要拔那綠苗。 那是成長中的草。」。我們每天忠心的為它澆水，一到兩個星期後，我們開始見到一片美麗茂盛綠油油的草地開始成長了。為甚麼?我們照顧它，我們滋養它，還有當然是我們為它禱告。

神賜給我們每個人信心的種子都是一樣的。我們必須用神的話語灌溉它、用禱告和禁食、用讚美，和用出自我們的口充滿信心的話語。這樣種子會開花、繁茂成長為美麗的植物。我們的信心將會飛躍、超越，而此時此刻我們絕對能夠為任何事來相信神，因為我們不是光靠感覺而是靠信心。若我們不滋養我們得救贖時給我們的信心種子,我們屬靈的生命將會死亡,我們會變成軟弱的基督徒。但我們進一步從亞伯拉罕的生命裏找著如何擁有信心的確據,堅忍性的信心以及被考驗過的信心。

信心的確據

「亞伯拉罕因着信,蒙召的時候,就遵命出去,往將來得爲業的地方去;出去的時候,還不知往哪裏去。」(希伯來書11:8-11)

以我們的五種自然感官感覺,和我們肉體的想法來說,這簡直是不可思議的。爲什麼離開某個地方,而去一個你所不知道的地方。

此時亞伯拉罕得到一個應許,這是神的應許寫在神的話語裏,在我們裡面創造了信心。

「耶和華對亞伯蘭說:你要離開本地、本族、父家、往我所要指示的地去。你必叫他成爲大國。我必賜福給你,叫你的名爲大。你也要叫別人得福。爲你祝福的,我必賜福與他;那咒詛你的,我必詛咒他。地上的萬族都要因你得福。」(創世記12:1-3)

我們發現因爲神的應許所以亞伯拉罕才能夠離開。在希伯來書裏神的話語說,祂一直都是信實的,而我們必須認識我們的神是位信實的神。當我們從神的話語得到了我們一家得救的應許;或我們有了得醫治的應許;或我們有了對我們工作狀況或我們許多景況的應許,若神已經說了,那對亞伯拉罕信實的神,同樣的會對我們信實的。 祂會像祂祝福亞伯拉罕一樣的祝福我們。

是那應許給了我們信心,因爲那是神的話語,由神口所出的話決不徒然返回。或許神呼召你爲祂做一件事,但你就像亞伯拉罕一樣不知去向如何,但我們同亞伯拉罕一樣有了應許,而且我們要宣告那應許直到它實現。

你知道神呼召你全時間事奉祂,雖你不確知如何?在那裏?作甚麼?爲甚麼?但你知道那呼召就在那裏,就在你生命中—但你不能依靠五官感覺。我們必須相信我們的神,相信我們會到達迦南,相信神給了那應許之地。

當羅得(亞伯拉罕帶著他的姪子)一注意神沒有告訴他要帶羅得,但亞伯拉罕卻帶著羅得,神說:「你和你的家人 . . .」,而他的姪子不是他家中的一分子,但他卻帶著他的姪子。因此家裏開始有衝突和意見分歧。因為亞伯拉罕和羅得的供應增加,亞伯拉罕就對羅得說,「讓我們不要相爭, 讓我們不要爭吵因為我們知道這會咒詛我們。」你看 亞伯拉罕是一位很有智慧的人,與充滿信心的人。亞伯拉罕對羅得說,「眼前的地你做選擇。」然後羅得舉目望前,一邊是綠油油的地,另一邊是乾枯的沙漠。他依靠他的五官感覺—他看到某些是好的。

最後羅得決定選擇那綠油油的部分,而這地靠近所多瑪與俄摩拉。雖然羅得選了他認為好的,結果卻是最糟糕的!那裏的人活在犯罪裏,他在那城市過的很慘。讓我們了解到當我們看到有某些好的東西但它未必就是好的!

對亞伯拉罕來說,他舉目望外而那裏只是個沙漠——一個乾旱不毛之地。若他依靠他的五官感覺,他可能會對神說:「祢說祢會祝福我,我後裔將會極其繁多,我們會進入應許之地(迦南)。但看我所得到的卻是一曠野!沙漠!」。但是我們知道當亞伯拉罕深思懷疑之際,神提醒了祂對他的應許。

「 . . . 耶和華對亞伯蘭說:從你所在的地方,你舉目向東西南北觀看,凡你所看見的一切地,我都要賜給你和你的後裔如同地上的塵沙那樣多,人若能數算地上的塵沙,才能數算你的後裔。你起來,縱橫走遍這地,因為我必把這些賜給你。」(創世記13:14-17)

神叫亞伯拉罕起來,觀看周圍、舉目觀看,因此我們也要一樣做。我們必須舉目,而不要不斷的看我們的周遭的環境和情況。不要不斷的說,「哎呀!噎哦!啊唷!天哪!我為甚麼在這下面?為甚麼都是沙漠?為甚麼都是曠野?」然而神的話語卻說,要「舉目向上看」而且神還告訴我們不要看我們的環境情況。祂要我們舉目看祂這位信實的神。我們要仰望神大有能力的神。

我記得我們曾經唱一首主日學的兒歌:「我們的神是這麼大,這麼強又這麼有能力! 祂凡事都能做!」

當我們在困難或惡劣的情況下我們會忘了這些事。但神對我們說,我們該舉目觀看,祂對亞伯拉罕這樣說。祂說:「看北、 看南、看西、

看東 ，它都是你的。」祂對亞伯拉罕說走遍那地。同樣的，神在告訴
你走遍那地。你走入屋子裏每個房間(每個孩子的房間)，以及當他們
不在時，你按手在他們的床和東西禱告說：「奉耶穌的名，你這叛逆
的靈不順服的靈，你將離開我們的孩子們。」你進入屋子裏每個房
間，宣稱這些神的應許賜予你和你的家人。

你走遍這地，若你需要得醫治，你每走一步你就說：「因耶穌的鞭傷，
我得醫治。」我十九歲時，我的風濕病得醫治了，但有一次，它又回來
了，而且疼痛得很厲害。我真的痛到不行，痛到每一次我一動，我都以
為我要裂成兩半。但我站在神的話語上，斥責那仇敵必須離開。我宣
告「因耶穌的鞭傷，我得醫治。」

你必須走遍你的地並堅定你的立場。你必須宣告這地是合法屬於你
的，因為你在主耶穌基督裏擁有所有的權柄。阿們!

「我已經給你們權柄可以踐踏蛇和蠍子，又勝過仇敵一切的能力，斷
沒有甚麼能害你們。」(路加福音10：19)

魔鬼在你的心思意念裏說謊。他會挑撥那些情感向你說謊。但我們
的神是從不說謊的! 神的話語表明祂永不改變的。祂昨日、今日、直
到永遠是一樣的。哈利路亞! 我們必須站在神的應許上。神賜予亞伯
拉罕關於他本人、他的妻子撒拉將會生育一個孩子的應許。

「這事以後，耶和華在異象中有話對亞伯蘭說：『亞伯蘭，你不要懼
怕!我是你的盾牌，必大大地賞賜你。』亞伯蘭說：『主耶和華啊，我
既無子，你還賜我甚麼呢? 並且要稱受我家業的是大馬士革人以利
以謝。』亞伯蘭又說：『你沒給我兒子，那生在我家中的人就是我的後
嗣。』耶和華又有話對他說：『這人必不成為你的後嗣，你本身所生的
才成為你的後嗣。』 於是領他走到外邊，說：『你向天觀看，數算眾
星，能數得過來嗎? 』又對他說：『你的後裔將要如此。』亞伯蘭信耶
和華，耶和華就以此為他的義。」(創世記15：1-6)

神不斷的告訴亞伯拉罕舉目觀看。他要舉目觀看。 往上看數星星，
亞伯拉罕的信心每天在成長，因為神不斷地會來提醒他那些應許。
對我來說也是一樣的，我們應該停止往下看而該往上看，聖經說，「
我們得贖的日子近了。」神有能力成就他對你的應許。

堅持性的信心

但有一天，那五種感官知覺又來了。那魂的部份開始掌控制那屬靈的人。當<u>亞伯拉罕</u>與<u>撒拉</u>等了許多年，他們還沒有等到兒子甚或一個女兒，他們倆開始懷疑到底是怎麼一回事。<u>撒拉</u>對丈夫說：「看!耶和華使我不能生育，求你和我的使女同房，或者我可以因她得孩子。」<u>亞伯拉罕</u>聽從了他妻子的話。

<u>撒拉</u>確實認為她的方法很好；以人的頭腦來說是蠻合理的，也算是一種答案。但是神的道路高過我們的道路；祂的意念高過我們的意念，而且祂的道路永遠是最好的! 我們看到<u>撒拉</u>允許<u>夏甲</u>，她的使女，和她的丈夫同房。沒錯，他們有個名叫<u>以實瑪利</u>兒子，他們以為他們知道如何掌控那情況，但神的話語絕不徒然無返。最終他們發現讓<u>夏甲</u>懷孕和生子給他們帶來更多的麻煩。因為結果<u>撒拉</u>對<u>夏甲</u>與<u>以實瑪利</u>產生了更多的妒嫉和苦毒。後來她把母子倆趕出那家! 妒嫉和苦毒抓住了<u>撒拉</u>，結果她的情況比不孕更糟糕，因為她的心態也是錯誤的!

結果神必須處置他們。祂又來提醒他們，撒拉將會生育一個孩子。

「<u>亞伯蘭</u>年九十九歲的時候，耶和華向他顯現，對他說：『我是全能的神，你當在我面前作完全人，我就與你立約，使你的後裔極其繁多。』」(<u>創世記</u>17：1-2)

「然後神說，不然，你妻子<u>撒拉</u>要給你生一個兒子，你要給他起名叫<u>以撒</u>。我要與他堅定所立的約，作他後裔永遠的約。」(<u>創世記</u>17：19)

「到明年這時節，<u>撒拉</u>必給你生<u>以撒</u>，我要與他堅定所立的約。」(<u>創世記</u>17：21)

這個應許有了一個明確的確認，就是<u>亞伯拉罕</u>將會有個兒子。神明確的指出那時間。為甚麼? 我相信這是因為撒拉發笑，「哈!哈! 我怎能生育孩子? 我太老了又不孕。」然而，就在一年後，他們果真有了兒子名叫<u>以撒</u>。我們必須等候神的應許在我們生命裏成就。神的時間不會太慢，也不會太遲，剛好準時來到。

我們常常憑我們的五官感覺而行，說道：「必須現在，要不然就會太遲了。」 或「我現在想要有丈夫，不能太晚。」。我們需要明白神的話語裏的屬靈原理,神的時間不是我們的時間,但這不是說神的應許不會成就。只要我們站在神的話語上,並相信祂它就會成就。

被考驗的信心

爲甚麼神的話語成就在我們的生命裏需要花時間?

像亞伯拉罕,我們的信必須被考驗。神要使我們強壯。若凡事美好順利,那我們的信心多半不會成爲那麼強。我們必須運用和強化我們「信心的肌肉」!以色列人走遍曠野四十年,那路上的每一步,神來試驗他們看看他們心存甚麼。那四十年以及整個路程中,他們不斷的哼唉埋怨,這就是爲甚麼他們沒有進入迦南應許之地,而只有那些二十歲以下的人以及約書亞和迦勒進入。

我們發覺我們是如此的倚賴我們的感覺和情緒,以至於我們每時每刻總是七上八下忐忑不安。若我們心裏有神的話語,無論甚麼事迎面而來我們都不會放棄。我記得當我準備差派出去到亞洲當傳教士,我的差遣主任告訴我說:「Sandra,你去之前,必須募款$$$$ (某些金額)。」另外一位姊妹也是一起出去宣教的,她已經開始籌集她的募款並且預定四月份出發。那時已經一月份了,經過六個月的時間,我已跑過許多教會但幾乎沒有籌到任何款項。我對神說「主,不可能這樣的。祢呼召了我,祢對我有個計畫與目的, 祢將會供應我的。我感謝主!」

我的思想也告訴我,「許多人曾經走遍各地—有些人甚至兩年都無法籌足那款項。」但我拒絕倚靠我的思想和感覺,反而在每天早晨,還有我去過的每間教會,我都信實地宣告耶穌是我的供應者。非常突然地在一月底竟然達到了那筆金額,因爲有個教會說他們將資助我,而這筆金額在當時是相當大筆的。我興奮極了。我記得我遠從英國北部的布里斯本(Bristol)直接打電話回我的辦公室,告訴他們,我已得到了所需要的每一英鎊,我可以出發赴新加坡了。我的差遣主任竟不敢相信這是真的,要求我要寫封信來確定我所說的。因此我寫了封信,請求確認將要寄過來的金額。而那年四月,我和我的朋友就啓程赴新加坡了。

站在神的應許裏,我們的感覺會說,「這是不可能的。」但我們的信心會被考驗。我們必須將我們的信心靠交託神。我在台灣十年,我的信心也被考驗過。我沒錢,但我願相信神,財源將會來到。神是信實的,因這筆錢就進來了。記得我們所經過的每個考驗,必讓我們更堅強。不要相信你經過這考驗以後就不再有了。將會有更多的來臨。我們需要面對的越多,我們的信心就會越堅強。

亞伯拉罕曾被考驗過。如何呢?神要求他獻祭獻上他唯一的兒子以撒,他名字的意思是嘻笑。 但以撒出世時,亞伯拉罕與撒拉必定每天都歡笑而且非常開心,尤其是他是神所應許的兒子。你可想像到當神告訴亞伯拉罕獻上以撒時它們的感受是如何的?這是事實,不是個故事。

「這些事以後,神要試驗亞伯拉罕,就呼叫他說:亞伯拉罕!他說:我在這裏。神說:你帶着你的兒子,就是你獨生的兒子,你所愛的以撒,往摩利亞地去,在我所要指示你的山上,把他獻爲燔祭。亞伯拉罕清早起來,備上驢,帶着兩個僕人,也劈好了燔祭的柴,就起身往神所指示她的地方去了。」(創世記22:1-3)

亞伯拉罕不遲疑的遵從神的命令。他備上驢,劈好了燔祭的柴,就起身往神所指示她的地方去了。我可確定以撒會像我的四歲兒子大衛,不會遺漏任何東西會問他父親:「那燔祭的羊羔在那裏?」亞伯拉罕沒有擔憂或緊張或驚嘆,「我該怎麼對我兒子說呢?」他回答:「我兒,神必自己預備作燔祭的羊羔。」

「他們到了神說指示的地方,亞伯拉罕在那裏築壇,把柴擺好,綑綁他的兒子以撒,放在壇的柴上。亞伯拉罕就伸手拿刀,要殺他的兒子。耶和華的使者從天上呼叫他說:亞伯拉罕! 亞伯拉罕!他說: 我在這裏。天使說:你不可在這童子身上下手,一點不可害他!現在我知道你是敬畏神的了,因爲你沒有將你的兒子,就是你獨生的兒子,留下不給我。」(創世記22:9-12)
哈利路亞! 神的確供應了!

「亞伯拉罕舉目觀看,不料,有一隻公羊,兩角扣在稠密的小樹中,亞伯拉罕就取了那隻公羊來,獻爲燔祭,代替他的兒子。」(創世記22:13)

亞伯拉罕不需要追殺那隻公羊。那公羊爲他獻上,兩角扣在稠密的小樹中。神能在適當的時刻供應,亦即他的時間是完美的。在我們面對考驗或試驗時,記得神將會供應。祂是耶和華我的供應者。亞伯拉空最糟糕的時刻是他必須遵從神獻祭他的兒子<u>以撒</u>，但是他信任神以及相信神會供應。

信靠神並相信他會供應我們所有的需要，無論是身體的、情感的、醫治的、財務的、或屬靈的需要。在主裡及祂的大能大力裡剛強起來，以及讓我們行在信心中，而不是憑眼見。

第七章

過信心的生活

我們從神領受的每件事是來自信心。為甚麼是信心?甚麼是信心?又信心的動力是甚麼?聖經對信心的定義是:「信就是所望之事的實底,是未見之事的確據。」(希伯來書11:1)

1. 信心是現在。
2. 信心是實質。
3. 信心是持久忍耐。
4. 信心是和盼望有關。
5. 信心是未見之事。
6. 信心是傾聽神 (例如:彼得行走在水面上)。
7. 信心是超自然視覺—信看得見。(例如: 那漏血的女人、大衛看見勝利。)
8. 信心是從心裏知道。
9. 信心是說出神所說的並能看到成果,但並不是推測。(推測是基於一個好主意或意圖,但並不產生結果。)
10. 信心是個靈。
11. 信心的行動使魔鬼戰驚。
12. 信心是靈的眼。
13. 信心是屬靈爭戰必備的,而且我們必須穿上神的全副軍裝。
14. 信心是進入超自然和神蹟奇事的門。
15. 信心是必須的,能除去我們對神設定的限制。
16. 信心是得勝。憂慮是罪。
17. 信心是唯一能包含持續到永恆的愛與盼望。

每個人有一份信心，但不是每個人去發展它或使用它。使用你的信心，而不要說，「我沒有信心。」或「我信心不足。」為你的信心之戰而爭戰，神已為你爭戰。我們能在主裏堅強，也在信心裡與在靈裏的人。當我們聽到神說話，我們因信大膽的踏出而不懷疑或害怕。神在尋找有信心的男女。沒有信我們不能討神的喜悅。

學習釋放你對神的信心。當你如此做，憑着神所說的話語行動。相信它有如它已完成。相信你已經領受。(例如：你家人得救、醫治、...等等)。即使在你還沒看到任何證據前。(雅各書1：6-8)你能透過充滿信心的話來釋放你的信心，例如：大衛、保羅、與西拉；透過接觸點、和了解神聖的季節、與神的時間；透過神的同在、以及祂的恩膏與大能來釋放你的信心。

「我要歌唱你的慈愛和公平；主啊，我要向你歌頌...」(詩篇101：1)

「我的心哪，你要稱頌主，凡在我裏面的，也要稱頌祂的聖名。」(詩篇103：1)

「約在半夜，保羅和西拉禱告唱詩讚美神，眾囚犯也側耳而聽。忽然地大震動，甚至監牢的地基都搖動了，監門立刻全開，眾囚犯的鎖鏈也都鬆開了。」(使徒行傳16：25、26)

「他在無可指望的時候，因信仍有指望，就得以作多國的父，正如先前所說：你的後裔以後將要如此。他將近百歲的時候，雖然想到自己身體如同已死，撒拉的生育已經斷絕，他的信心還是不軟弱，並且仰望神的應許，總沒有因不信，心裏起疑惑，反倒因信，心裏的堅固，將榮耀歸給神。且滿心相信神所應許的必能作成。」(羅馬書4：18-21)

信心沒有行為是死的
「我們的祖宗亞伯拉罕把他的兒子以撒獻在壇上，豈不是因行為稱義嗎？可見信心是與他的行為並行，而且信心因着行為才得成全。」(雅各書2：21-22)

信心如何產生?

1. 透過異夢和異象。
2. 透過進入你心的神的話語。
3. 透過你心思意念的更新。

4. 透過與聖靈的交通和信靠—屬靈的成長與敬虔 。
5. 透過你的心而不是頭腦對神的知識—有個純潔的心和謙卑的靈。
6. 透過尋求並知道神的旨意—祂的計畫、時間、和地點。
7. 透過行在愛/寬恕中而不是活在恐懼或冒犯中。
8. 透過順服—我們全心來尋求神。

信心是根基於神的本性、神的同在、神的應許、和神的目的。

信心是尋獲你生命中神的旨意，同意神所說的而非魔鬼和世人的聲音。

信心是完全倚靠那不說謊的神。祂的話是真理。

你問，爲甚麼相信?要有智慧。它是值得的!

「但願使人有盼望的神，因信將諸般的喜樂平安充滿你們的心，使你們藉着生靈的能力大有盼望。」(羅馬書15：13)

信心使自然轉換變成超自然
使你翱翔如鷹且能看見並進入超自然。成爲一隻鷹。不要活得像雞或火雞。從神的視野看事情。

信心使魔鬼戰驚失敗而逃

信心的偉人雖然遇障礙與攔阻依然堅持到底。 他們克服那排山倒海而來的困境，以神的能力及信心取代他們的軟弱。信心使他們轉換成巨人來克服和勝過苦難與問題。聖經裏的故事，那些軟弱以及有極大問題的人，透過信心被改變了，這些人轉向神而大大得勝，征服了悲劇，試煉與災難，這完全得透過神的愛與大能。

信心的人堅持有如鬥犬般的信心，是不會停止或放棄的。例如：利斯特(Lister)儘管他人嘲笑，他發現了抗生素(carbolic)，因此改變了醫藥界的方向，這乃是因爲他的信心和恆心。他很有耐心的工作、研究、大膽的相信有個醫療方法。我們需要效法這些偉人生命中的信心。看他們如何在信心中操作，停止相信仇敵的謊言，就是：「你沒用、你不好、沒價值、你只不過是個無舉足輕重的一員、還有你是個無成就者、或說嘗試是沒用的。」停止負面性的行爲舉止。但你可能會說：「

你不明白我的情況、困境等等。」神知道我們所經歷的一切。要開始相信神在祂話語中所說關於你的種種。相信祂的應許是真的而且是給我們的。

「以色列人因着信，圍繞耶利哥城七日，城牆就倒塌了。」(希伯來書11：30)

「他們因着信，制伏了敵國，行了公義，得了應許；堵了獅子口，滅了烈火的猛勢，脫了刀劍的鋒刃；軟弱變為剛強，爭戰顯出勇敢，大退外邦的全軍。有婦人得自己的死人復活，又有人忍受嚴刑，不肯苟且得釋放，為要得着更美的復活。」

「存心忍耐奔跑那擺在我們前頭的路程，仰望為我們信心創始成終的耶穌 . . .」(希伯來書12：2)

神的話語說道耶穌是我們信心的來源，祂會使我們的信心成熟(意思是：成為「完全的成長」)。本於祂、倚靠祂，我們有個得勝的信心，去相信神在我們生命裏行神蹟奇事。

據說亞伯拉罕‧林肯七歲時，被迫離開家門去找工作來支助他的家庭。這樣的年齡找工作實在是太幼嫩了。更不幸的是，九歲時他又喪母。二十三歲時不但失業，他的生意夥伴還丟下一大筆債務跑了，他得獨自承擔全部債務負責償還。接著他希望結婚的對象拒絕嫁給他。他的甜心讓他的心整個破碎了，終於導致他精神崩潰。而在四十一歲時，又遭遇了喪子之痛。

他競選參議員失敗、被誤會、被鄙視、被嘲笑、被輕蔑、被忽視，然而他卻成為美國最偉大的政治家之一。這秘訣是甚麼?還有他又是如何克服沮喪? 他雖在五十六歲時被槍殺，然而他仍然被認為是美國總統中最偉大的一位。

有兩件事使他很自然的被紀念著：
1. 他從內戰中拯救國家，而且
2. 他為廢除奴隸制度擔負重責。

他如何克服憂鬱、精神崩潰、沮喪、和危機? 他向神禱告求智慧，並把信心交託給神，求神為他行神蹟。

約翰衛斯理在他的首度宣教之旅時看到了摩拉維亞(Moravian)弟兄的信心。那時約翰衛斯理還沒得救,他看到這兩兄弟的信心是真的,他們充滿熱心、愛心、和信心、奉獻、不怕風浪、並且充滿了喜樂。他們歌唱,不驚恐又鎮靜。他就問:「我要如何才能有這樣的信心?」他們的回答是:「口說你有了它,並行動出來,就如你已有了它,因爲神如此說,你已得勝。耶穌平定那風浪,因祂是風浪的主人。你相信嗎?如果相信,那爲甚麼要煩躁又大驚小怪?」

聖經說使徒保羅影響了世界,乃因爲福音書中他的信心得以救贖、得以醫治、又得以釋放。

「我已經與基督同釘十字架,現在活着的不再是我,乃是基督在我裏面活着;並且我如今在肉身活着,是因信神的兒子而活,祂是愛我,爲我捨己。」(加拉太書2:20)

真實的信心是經過考驗且是持久的!

「因爲神的義,正在這福音上顯明出來;這義是本於信,以至於信。如經上所記:『義人必因信得生。』」(羅馬書 1:17)

「但願使人有盼望的神,因信將諸般的喜樂平安充滿你們的心,使你們藉着聖靈的能力大有盼望。」(羅馬書15:13)

神在祂的話語裏應許我們,我們若有人因信相信就會有喜樂、平安、和盼望。

第八章

想像力的屬靈定律

「**我**實實在在地告訴你們：我所作的事，信我的人也要作；並且要作比這更大的事，因爲我往父那裏去。」(約翰福音14：12)

「你們既靠聖靈入門，如今還靠肉身成全嗎?你們是這樣的無知麼?你們是受苦如此之多，都是徒然的嗎? 難道果真是徒然的嗎? 那賜給你們聖靈，又在你們中間行異能的，是因你們行律法呢?是因你們聽信福音呢?正如『亞伯拉罕信神，這就算爲他的義。』」(加拉太書3：3-6)

神的工如何運作?

神的工作是個神蹟。神蹟又是如何運作的?

神一開始就說出結局。祂宣告結果(信心就是如此運作)。許多人卻因爲他們本身的禱告破壞了他們的信心。他們重覆他們的問題，禱告他們的問題，但是他們卻忘記爲結果禱告。(馬太福音11：23)

人們對他們問題的信心比他們的答案來得多。不要禱告問題本身。聖經教導我們要爲答案禱告。

舊約運用了這原則：

列王記下4：8-11， 14，18，19，23，26，32
在這故事中我們看到：
以利沙使死人復活的事奉。

191

神是生命的神。

不是神取走孩子的生命，乃是撒旦的作爲。

書念婦人甚至沒有告訴先知什麼是她的問題。她說出尚未完成的有如它已實現。她稱平安無事即使事實上並非如此。這書念婦人持守她信心的宣告。

耶穌在祂的服事中運用此原則：

1. 變水爲酒的奇蹟(約翰福音2：1-10)

耶穌對用人說：「把缸到滿了水」，「他們就倒滿了、直到缸口。」缸裡沒有酒，但耶穌稱它爲酒，當他們送了去時，它就變成了酒。

難道是耶穌在玩把戲使人相信？

這些人對它又指名又宣告的，難道他們被騙了？不，他們依據出口成真的屬靈原則運作，說出那不存在的成爲有。

2. 治好十個長大痲瘋的(路加福音17：12-19)

耶穌稱他們潔淨了當祂說，「你們去把身體給祭司察看。」，但醫治的彰顯只發生在當他們去的途中。

這是神的信心與奇蹟的方法和原則。

大部分信徒的問題是他們堅持要說，「我相信照實況說。」所以他們從沒領受他們的奇蹟，因爲他們總是宣告他們疾病的病徵。

你相信什麼，你就領受什麼。

做耶穌告訴你做的去做，你就會領受你的奇蹟，就說它已成就。

3. 池邊的醫治(約翰福音第5章)

耶穌問他：「你要痊癒嗎？」

耶穌並沒說：「你能嗎？」

接著這人談到他的問題。「水動的時候，沒有人把我放在池子裡。我正去的時候，就有別人比我先下去。」他不知道他在對誰說話。

耶穌對他說：「起來，拿你的褥子走罷。」

耶穌說出信心並操練權柄。

耶穌在做什麼：扮演造成相信－瘸腿的人能行走嗎?不,祂叫這人痊癒了。

第八節—耶穌說,「起來,你痊癒了。」在那人拿起褥子之前,耶穌就先叫出來痊癒了。

4. 耶穌醫治一位駝背的女人(路加福音 13：10-17)
耶穌對他說：「女人,你脫離這病了。」
耶穌在她得醫治之先就說了這話,其實
直到耶穌按手在她身上之前,她仍未見好 轉。但她相信按手。有些人靠話語釋放信
心,其他人則藉著按手。你相信什麼是很重
要。

想像力的屬靈定律與原則

耶穌給他們這答案：「我實實在在的告訴你們,子憑著自己不能作什麼,惟有看見父所作的,子才能作。父所作的事,子也照樣作。」(約翰福音5：19)

我們在創世記11：6看到想像力或**自我形象**的屬靈定律,主說：「如果他們成為一樣的人民,都是一樣的言語,如今既作起這事來,以後他們所要作的事,就沒有不成就的了。」

光是說話並不足以叫一些事情成真;首先它必須在你裡面形成一個形象。

甚麼是你的意識?它是失敗、懷疑、疾病、缺乏
信心、或是成功、醫治、和得勝。

「 ... 他若心裡不疑惑 ... 」(馬可福音11：23) 這意思就是在他屬靈的人裡面,他看見了。

我們不斷地在我們的想像力裡看事情,而且它在我們的信心裡也扮演一個很重要的部分。

撒旦透過想像力的定律操縱人的墮落。我們如何會墮入罪惡中? 乃撒旦玩弄人的心思意念。

「羅得舉目看見約旦河的全平原,直到瑣珥,都是滋潤的,同耶和華的園子,也像埃及地。」(創世記13:10)(這在主毀滅索多瑪和蛾摩拉以前)。羅得因他所看的惹麻煩。

約書亞記7:21是亞王的故事。他為偷禁物犯罪,導致以色列失敗。他如何挫敗?或是什麼使他犯罪?

「...當我看見...」

開始來看神說什麼。讓神的話語指出你內在的一幅圖畫。

在你希望你家人以你想要的方式團聚在一起之前,你必須在你裡面先看到它發生。這是一個屬靈的定律。想像力的定律。

你可以宣告、禱告、說出神的話直到你嘴都麻了,但除非你在你裡面看到它,不然你只不過是吹噓而已。

除非耶穌首先看到它,否則祂也不能做任何事,我們受限於這相同的律。

透過耶穌所有的生命和服事,耶穌在屬靈裡看事情,然後祂以祂看到的來行動—「主的靈在我身上,因為他用膏膏我,叫我傳福音給貧窮的人。差遣我報告被擄的得釋放,瞎眼的得看見,叫那受壓制的得自由。」(路加福音4:18)

你可以在神的話語裡看到的任何事,但你必須加添你的想像力或靈。

亞伯拉罕是一位信心的偉人,但他也必須去學習信心的原則。神試著要讓亞伯拉罕看見神的應許但他卻不能看見。「凡你都所看到的一切地,我都要賜給你和你的後裔...」(創世記13:14-16)

亞伯拉罕一直到創世記15:1-6才獲得啟示。

亞伯拉罕看見什麼?
他沒看見的後裔如同地上的塵沙那樣多。卻是「看我既無子。」。

依據神的話除非你先看到它，它才能成真。

神已經給他應許，但他裡面仍然沒看見或看不見圖畫。

4-5 節，神更進一步幫助他—「觀看，明白」，神給他一幅大自然的景象圖畫幫助他。

假如你在某件事上相信神，但它仍未發生過，你看到了什麼?
看到你身體得醫治。
看到你家人回來團聚。
看到你自己財務豐富。
看到你關係良好。
看到你自己的成功。

從起初創造迄今，這地上沒有一件事不是由一個形象開始。甚至當神創造天地時也運用了此原則。

「 . . . 我們要照著我們的形像，按照我們的樣式造人 . . . 」(創世記 1：26-27)

神在祂裡面已經有了人的形象，祂想創造出來，也將他所想要的宣告出來，這就是想像力的律。

第九章

認識神

「 . . . 惟獨認識神的子民必剛強行事。」(但以理書11：32)

我們信心最重要的根基之一就是認識神。但以理是位先知，他對我們的時代、我們的日子發預言。那些認識神的人們必定剛強並行大事。

我們如何認識神?

1. **透過祂的名認識神**

   我們透過祂的名認識神。祂的名揭示祂的本質與性情。但以理稱神，Elohim—至高至大、大有能力的神，掌管我們生命中的一切。

   看看約瑟的生命。他被排斥、受苦、煎熬；被自己的兄長們當奴隸般賣到埃及去，被出賣、被誤會、又被關進牢裏。約瑟是可以因此感到苦毒，但他認識 Elohim，大有能力、至高無上的神，無論他遭遇的處境與景況是多麼的艱難，神掌管一切。他認識他的神。

   神有祂的時間! 詩篇作者說，「約瑟—被賣作奴隸；他們用鏈鎖他的腳使他受傷 . . . 直到祂的話語成就的時間到來，神的話語考驗他。」(詩篇105:17-19) 約瑟認識他的神，相信神，而他對神話語的信心也被考驗。人們使他失望、拒絕他、傷害他，但他沒被他們影響。約瑟成功的要點是他認識神，而且他有對的靈。他知道至高至上的神，掌權在他生命中，沒有事可傷害他。他有對的靈，當時間到時，他被釋放、高舉並提升到法老的王宮。

在這末後的日子裏，神要一群認識祂並像祂的子民。神要一群心思意念已被更新的人；想法與祂一致，眼光與祂相同的人，一群被確認像祂兒子耶穌的人，如此我們能夠在這『豐盛滿溢擴張』的一年承受神的應許。除非我們變得像祂，不然我們無法得到祂的祝福。若我們要容納祂的祝福和擴張，我們必須先從內裡擴展！

我們不能靠自己的力量和智慧來完成神的計畫，就好像摩西或掃羅王！但當我們認識神並行在祂的路中，神會使祂的計畫成就在我們的生命中！

2. 透過祂的話語認識神

太初有道，道與神同在，道就是神。我們必須知道並認識神的話語。我們必須要有神話語的光，因為只有在祂的光中我們得看見光。神的話語活潑有能力，尖銳地剖開靈與魂。要認識神就要認識祂的話語。當你認識神的話語，那話語會與你說話。聖經告訴我們當我們躺臥，祂必保守我們；當我們睡醒，祂與我們談論。(箴言6:22)

3. 透過有信心的人的生命認識神

我們透過有信的人的經歷認識神。其中一件對我的基督徒生活有很大幫助的事是閱讀，如Martin Luther(馬丁路德)、 John G. Lake、(約翰雷克)、 Smith Wigglesworth(史密斯威格斯沃士、Alexander Dowi(亞歷山大杜威)，這些偉大人物的生平和傳記。他們的著作與卡帶那麼的有恩膏。 他們所領受的啟示和真理都是親身第一手經歷過的。他們所寫的都是從自己的經歷出來，不像我們所謂『扶手椅』的神學家 (那些只有理論的神學論者)。神話語裏的一切是能夠也應該在我們生命中經歷的！

4. 透過愛認識神

我們透過愛神而認識神。沒有愛心的，就不認識神，因為神就是愛(約翰一書4:8)。使徒保羅所說的是一條更棒的路—愛之路。在那最有名的一章『愛』篇的經文(哥林多前書13章)，我們有那愛的泉源、愛的力量、和愛的緣由。當你認識那愛的泉源，你就不會乾枯。當你認識那愛的力量，你就不會被嚇到，而願與神同行。當你認識那愛的緣由，你就能成為神要你成為的管道和工具。當你行在愛裏，你就認識你的神以及你可以行的大事。

197

5. 透過聖靈認識神

人是照神的形象造的而且像神。神是個靈，而人是個有靈的活人，這就是爲甚麼我們可以認識神。人用心靈和誠實拜祂。人用心靈事奉神 (羅馬書1:9)。神透過祂的靈向我們顯示祂自己和祂的旨意。「神爲愛祂的人所預備的，是眼睛未曾看見，耳朵未曾聽見，人心也未曾想到的。」(哥林多前書2:8、9)

「因聖靈所存的愛心」(歌羅西書1:8)，而且「那所賜給我們的聖靈，將神的愛澆灌在我們心裏。」(羅馬書5:5)。

先知瑪拉基說，「所以當謹守你們的心，不可以詭詐 . . . 」(瑪拉基書2:15)。在這末後的日子，其中一個靈在教會被釋放的是不忠誠的靈，造成許多紛爭分裂。不忠誠是屬靈的姦淫。

我們必須知道我們有甚麼樣靈。門徒們要像以利亞吩咐火從天降下，但耶穌責備他們說：「你們的心如何，你們並不知道。」(路加福音9:55) 他們引述正確的經文，但他們的靈不對!

你要知道爲甚麼參孫被殺？那不是因爲大利拉， 也不是因爲他剪了他的頭髮，而是因爲在他心裏有報復的靈。他所做的是爲了報復那非利士人。他擁有恩膏和恩賜，但他卻以不對的靈操作他的恩膏和恩賜，因此毀了他。在這末後的日子裏，神在尋找聖潔的人。你可能擁有恩膏與所有的恩賜，但你的靈若不對， 最終你將被毀了。但你若是聖潔又有對的靈，我們就不會犯與參孫同樣的錯誤，我們可以奪得那城，而非利士人只有低頭!

我們擁有對的靈是很重要的。「你要保守你心，勝過保守一切，因爲一生的果效，是由心發出。」(箴言4:23)

「我們既有這等應許，就當潔淨自己，除去身體、靈魂一切的污穢，敬畏神、得以成聖。」(哥林多後書7:1)

我們要潔淨自己，除去身體、靈魂一切的污穢。有許多方法能導致我們的靈魂被污染：

苦毒

「又要謹慎，恐怕有人失了神的恩；恐怕有毒根生出來擾亂你們，因此叫眾人沾染污穢。」(希伯來書12:15)

淫行

「你們要逃避淫行。」(哥林多前書6：18)

口舌

「惟獨出口的，是從心裏發出來的，這才污穢人。」(馬太福音15：18)

悲傷

「喜樂的心，乃是良藥，憂傷的靈，使骨枯乾...」(箴言17：22)
「...心靈憂傷，誰能承當。」(箴言18：14)

憤怒

「不輕易發怒的，勝過勇士；治服己心的，強如取城。」(箴言16：32)
一個愛挑剔、批評、論斷的靈。

行邪術

「不可偏向那些交鬼的和行巫術的；不可求問他們。以致被他們玷污了。」(利未記19：31)

更新我們靈的五種方法

i) **靈裏禱告**

「先知說:不然，主要藉異邦人的嘴唇和外邦人的舌頭...你們要使疲乏人得安息，這樣才得安息、得舒暢...」(以賽亞書28：11、12)

ii) **經歷神的美善與愛**

「耶和華所賜的福，使人富足，並不加上憂慮。」(箴言10：22)

iii) **和聖靈充滿的聖徒團契**

使徒保羅因他的朋友和支持者，靈得更新。「...他們叫我心裏都快活...」(哥林多前書16：18)

iv) **有恩膏的音樂**

「大衛就拿琴用手而彈，掃羅便舒暢爽快，惡魔離了他。」(撒母耳記上16：23)

v) 與神同在

　　「 ... 那安舒的日子就必從主面前來到。」(使徒行傳3：19)

6. 透過聖潔的生命認識神

　　「清心的人有福了，因為他們必得見神。」(馬太福音5：8)。 神以「使我們成聖的耶和華」(利未記20：8)顯示自己。祂是使我們聖潔的主。我們要獻上自己並成為聖潔。我們的心、靈、和魂必須被潔淨，這樣得以進入祂的產業，且進入豐盛滿溢擴張的一年。

　　那些認識他們的神的人將會做大事。像使徒保羅，讓我們的禱告是，「 ... 使我認識神 ... 」(腓立比書3：10)

第十章

帶有使命的金錢

我們都會很興奮聽到傳道人分享有關信心、醫治、讚美、敬拜、以及得釋放等等信息。但一旦有關**金錢**的信息被傳講，我們就開始嘀咕而且有負面的回應。在外面的世界提到錢不是問題，參加講習會及學習有關賺錢的方法也不是問題。然而在教會裏談它卻是個禁忌。我身爲一位牧師，很自然地會問道爲甚麼?

信任破裂—我們生活在一個非常沒有信任感的世代。在六十年代中期，每四位美國人中就有三位說他們相信聯邦政府，認爲政府大都時候多半會做對的事。十年前那數目卻掉落了44%。今年2004年，剩下只有19%對政府有信心。

人們也會警告你「只要相信你所聽到的一半，並且要確定是對的那一半!」

人與人之間的密切連接關係是基於互相的信任。但是信任感是那麼容易破裂—就算是我們基督徒之間也一樣—尤其是當有些傳道人濫用爲神募款」作藉口敲詐神子民的錢。
或有所謂的基督徒和你做生意，一旦交易失敗，他們藉機拿走你的錢逃跑，你的信心也跟著破滅!或許某位基督徒弟兄或姐妹說他們缺錢，而你相信了他們，也給了他們錢，但他們卻飛往瑞士渡假去!

你需要寬恕那人—並且求神進入你的心，醫治你那破裂的信心—並非每位牧師或基督徒都是如此惡劣—因此也要避免產生錯誤的反應—譬如在我身上曾經發生過一次，所以我就應防範每一位牧師或基督徒商人—認爲他們都是一樣的。其實他們並非都是如此!

201

但當你真正的記取,破裂的信任也未必是人們不喜歡他們牧師談論有關金錢的唯一理由。那 麼,人們爲甚麼不喜歡講道時談論金錢的主要原因,乃是觸及了一個心的問題—「因爲你的財寶在哪裏,你的心也在那裏。」(馬太福音6:21)

金錢能夠揭露一個人的真面目。只要看一眼就很容易從你的支票本認定你的過去、你的現在、和你的將來。它可以顯示你的生活方式、你的優先次序、你的價值觀、你和神的關係。因爲如果你要知道你的心在哪裏,你只須要找出你的寶藏在那裏。例如,若你花費很多錢買高爾夫球具及付當地高爾夫俱樂部會員費—你的心就在那裏。

若你開很多支票給電腦軟件店、服裝店、 書店、鞋店、或者我甚至敢說色情店,那麼你的心就是在那裏。

你的錢在哪裏,你的心就會在那裏!

金錢是在人們的生活中與神最大的敵手之一。 這就是爲甚麼你不喜歡講道提到它,因真理讓你扎心。所以寧願有個令人愉快的講道,使你聽得順耳,繼續停留在你的舒適地帶。

耶穌在路加福音16:13裏說,「一個僕人不能侍奉兩個主,不是惡這個愛那個,就是重這個輕那個。你們不能又事奉神,又事奉瑪門!」

注意:耶穌在兩個主之間作比較,祂稱它們兩位「主」—神是你的「主」,或瑪門(金錢)是你的「主」。我們對其中一個的忠誠,自然就代表我們對另一個不忠誠。我們不可以把我們的心同時給兩者。金錢有能力取代神在我們生命裏的地位。

你如何知道金錢是否是你的主人?問你自己這些問題:

你是否時常想到錢,或擔心錢的問題?

你是否爲了要賺更多錢,而放棄你應該做的,或你喜歡做的事?

你是否花費許多時間,照管你的所有物?

你捐錢時是否很爲難?

你是否有債務?

有錢是騙人靠不住的—我們想要舒適、權力、和操控、滿足自我、好面子,想在人前看起來很好。但錢的金額並不能提供我們健康、幸福、或永恆的生命。讓神成為你的主人才是最好的。

聖經不是說我們不可以有錢或富有,但你的心在哪裏? 金錢是你的奴僕,或者你是金錢的奴僕?

法利賽人是「貪愛錢財的人」(路加福音16:14)。當他們聽見耶穌在金錢上的教導,他們「譏笑祂」。當我們聽到有關金錢的講道,我們是否也會嘲笑?你現在外出午餐時,是否批評牧師在金錢上的講道,然後一點一點的將它撕碎?或你說「我再也不會去那教會。」因為你不喜歡聽真理,或者那真理刺痛了你?

我們生活在這以人們賺錢多少來衡量他們價值的世代。但無論你賺多或少錢—最重要的是你的心。你愛耶穌多過你的錢嗎?「因為你的財寶在哪裏,你的心也在那裏。」

第三個原因,我們為甚麼不喜歡聽到關乎錢,這是因為魔鬼的企圖。祂要教會貧窮,因而我們無法以福音來影響我們的世界。因此祂(撒旦)使基督徒相信在教會裏提及有關錢的事是不對的。他要我們對金錢有這錯誤的態度,因此教會將處於缺乏和不足的情況,以至於無法得到世界的注意。治理教會是需要經費的。舉辦神蹟佈道會也需要經費的。宣教之旅更需要經費。魔鬼若能夠讓教會和會友處於貧窮越久,教會就愈無法完成大使命到世界各國宣講福音的事工。

今天這世界上許多教會擁有很強的恩膏和有能力的信息,但它們的影響力卻非常小。為甚麼? 因為他們缺乏經濟資源來將他們的訊息傳出。

教會貧窮因為會友貧窮。會友貧窮因為他們沒有正面對付他們有關金錢的錯誤態度。他們有貧窮心態的靈,不要被魔鬼的手要弄—若你在奉獻上沒得到釋放,那就正中祂的下懷!

主內弟兄姐妹們,讓聖靈向你揭露你的心態—若你曾因為破裂的信任而被傷害,就讓神醫治你的心—不要留在苦毒和不饒恕裏—並且開始再度釋放那些財務。

你若錯認金錢是你的主,向神悔改、道歉,求祂成爲你生命的主,並要求釋放那些財務。

不要給魔鬼有了立足點來掌控你的生命,讓你因爲錯誤的想法而繼續陷於貧窮─摧毀貧窮心態的堅固營壘,興起釋放你的財務。
神要祝福你嗎?是的,沒錯。神的旨意是要你興旺富足。

第十一章

神釋放的鑰點

為甚麼我捐獻了卻沒事發生?
「各人要隨本心所酌定的,不要作難,不要勉強,因為捐得樂意的人是神所喜愛的。」(哥林多後書9：7)

你是否帶著喜樂的心捐獻?
有些人說要捐獻到痛心為止。但其實我們應該繼續捐獻到不再覺得心疼,而當我們的奉獻滿了喜樂,就必蒙福;若我們捐得心疼,那表示我們的老我還沒死透。

在馬可福音 4章 和 馬太福音13章裏我們看到神擔保我們投入的錢、時間、精力、愛、仁慈、和禱告,將有30倍、60倍、或100倍的回報。

為何沒有回報?
你的捐獻是路旁的捐獻嗎?
淺土或石地代表錯誤的動機或企圖、競爭、控制、名譽、自尊、內疚感、責任、失去面子等等。這類的奉獻是不會帶來收成和回報的。

荊棘和蒺藜象徵世界的壓力。它也代表屬肉體的。

我們必須明白神的時間以及栽種與收穫的律。

若你手上所擁有的不夠,那就表示它是你所該栽種的種子,因此不要吃了它,要不然就將沒有收穫。

任何的傷痛和不饒恕若沒被釋放，將會阻礙你的收成。帶著慷慨喜樂的靈自由捐獻，不要心懷恐懼、義務、或傷痛。像乃縵的女僕—放棄自己傷痛的權利，釋放他人。

不信、懷疑、和心懷二意，將會耽擱我們的收成。
難道你不期望回報嗎? 你期望甚麼?

儘快回應。不要失去栽種和收成的機會及特權。

你是否憑信心栽種撒種?
誰是你的源頭? 你是否行在聖靈中?
如果你要收穫你的莊稼你就必須憑信心捐出，而不是憑懷疑或不信的心。

「萬軍之耶和華說：你們要將當納的十分之一全然送入倉庫，使我家有糧，以此試試我是否為你們敞開天上的窗戶，傾福與你們，甚至無處可容。萬軍之耶和華說：我必為你們斥責蝗蟲，不容牠毀壞你們的土產。你們田間的葡萄樹在未熟之先，也不掉果子。」(瑪拉基書3：10-11)

跟隨神的帶領，聽從和順服神的聲音是有效捐獻的鑰點。是撒旦或是神叫你捐獻?撒旦不希望你因捐獻而得到神的祝福。

杜魯門(Le Truream)是挖土牽引機的原創者，因為他的承諾；神給了他主意、慨念、和有創意的發明。你怎麼知道那是神的?他停止奉獻的那一刻，那些創意的主意也停止湧現。

我們必須活在神的祝福下，而不是詛咒下。當你確認那向你偷竊的賊後，牠必須還你七倍。若你被搶竊、欺騙，就索回。

你在說甚麼?
心裏所充滿的，口裏就說出來。

祂是慷慨的耶和華(El Shaddai)，不是價廉的耶和華(El Cheapo)!
祂超越你所需要的，而不是個缺乏的神。

是否你的毒舌，或你的負面導致你的種子死亡，或者你用讚美神來栽種祝福和感恩?

不在於你捐獻的金額，而是因你捐獻的靈，決定從神而來的流露(釋放)。

我們在**路加福音第五章**看到**末日先知性教會的八個特徵**是：

1. 對神的話語有極大的饑渴並看重神的話語。
2. 人們具有不放棄的性格而像法勒斯子孫般的的突破。
3. 人們會全心的跟隨神或委身於神。
4. 人們會有膽量、勇敢、且有堅持的信心。
5. 人們會很快的悔改並且聖潔。
6. 人們會有神蹟奇事大突破。在這末日將有很大的恩膏和聖靈澆灌下來，神蹟奇事將盛行，大收割亦隨之來臨。
7. 一個在愛裏分享與合一的教會。
8. 一個豐盛又樂於分享且給予他人的教會。

那鑰點是甚麼?

我們在經文裏看到許多人都有船，但<u>彼得讓耶穌使用他的船</u>；他答應了耶穌。
捐獻釋放出神蹟奇事的鑰點，也釋放末日先知性教會特質的神聖啓示。

我如何捐獻的心態，無可避免的將會影響我如何過活，和我對他人的看法和關係。這是個應該用慷慨和心甘情願的心捐獻的時刻，不是帶着絕望或放棄的心態，而是交出自己的意志與自以為義。讓我們放棄埋怨、論斷、負面，而給予信心、讚美、和感恩。

這是饒恕、釋放怨恨、憤怒、傷痛、創傷的時刻；放棄真的或察覺到的不公正。

這是交托於神的手裏，也只有祂才能處理的時刻。

這是給與他人、供應他人需要的時刻。我們不該背離神相互給予的律，因為給予是神的律，得以釋放神的靈並啟開天窗。

第十二章

克服懼怕

有五個希伯來字能被翻譯成一個英文字，這字的意思是「懼怕」。從創世記到啓示錄裏提到六百次「懼怕」。例如：亞伯拉罕、摩西、基甸、大衛、但以理、耶穌的母親馬利亞、彼得、和約翰，當他在拔摩的海島時，他們全被命令「不要怕」。一年裏有三百六十五天，因此每一天有一個不要怕的應許。其實，每天有兩個!

我們若不克服懼怕，懼怕就會征服了我們。因此我們必須辨別懼怕的情緒和懼怕的靈。一個會幫助我們，另一個會傷害我們。例如，當我們聽到槍聲我們會跳、跑、藏。在這當下，恐懼感會幫助我們，是神爲我們的安妥而設的。但若懼怕侵入我們的思想，模糊了我們的理智和感受，也偷走了我們的平安—那就是個懼怕的靈，而它是不健康的，也會傷害我們。

懼怕是從那裏來的呢?它是在當亞當和夏娃犯罪時進入了伊甸園裏。然後在整個聖經裏我們都可看到許多偉大神的僕人都被懼怕影響。以利亞因爲耶洗別王后威脅要殺他而害怕地逃跑。大衛因爲害怕他的兒子押沙龍而逃跑。掃羅王因爲害怕人們而失去他的事奉恩膏。彼得因爲害怕而說謊否認了耶穌，加略人猶太因爲害怕他個人計畫被破壞而出賣耶穌。

懼怕是具感染性的。有一個故事，一個美國中西部的一個市鎮裏有個男人跑到街道上高喊：「水壩破了!水壩破了!」。在超市場裏採購的女人放下她們所有的購物，加入街道上的人群。他們奔跑過那理髮店，接着理髮店的人也來加入他們。他們又奔跑過警察局，警察也出來和他們一起奔跑。在這時候，一群混亂的群眾往那出市鎮的橋狂奔。在橋上有個跛子，拄了支拐杖慢慢的站起來，向空中高舉他的拐杖。群眾停了下來，當他向他們說：「你們為甚麼逃跑?這市鎮並沒有水壩阿!」。懼怕展開它懷疑的翅膀，而且有如瘟疫般的擴散。當懼怕敲門，我們應該送信心到門口對付它。

懼怕也可以是個自我實現的預言。有位名叫尼克的人，他做冷凍貨櫃的工作。他是位好人，但他卻懷有深深的懼怕，唯恐有一天他會被關在冷凍貨櫃裡死亡。有一天，他竟意外地被關在裏面。他敲打門但沒有人聽到他。尼克相信那貨櫃裏的溫度是零度，而且他肯定會死。因此他想辦法找了一片厚紙板，寫了遺言給他的家人，他寫說若他無法出去肯定會凍死。隔一天，他果然被發現凍死，驗屍報告說他是被凍死的。然而那是個損壞的冷凍貨櫃。因此那冷凍貨櫃真正的溫度是六十一度，而不是零度。他的意念讓他自己相信那過去曾經深植於內心深處的懼怕。那懼怕變成了一個自我實現的預言，一語成讖。

懼怕的靈會搶走了我們的產業，在民數記十三章裏，以色列人看到巨大亞衲族人但他們也看自己有如蚱蜢，因此他們拒絕進入迦南，那流奶和蜜之地。懼怕阻擋他們接受主的祝福。

啟示錄21:8告訴我們「惟有膽怯的、不信的、可憎的、殺人的、淫亂的、行邪術的、拜偶像的和一切說謊話的，他們的分就在燒着硫磺的火湖裏，這是第二次的死。」

懼怕有不同的種類。有不知的恐懼、死亡的恐懼、疾病的恐懼、失敗的恐懼、被拒絕的恐懼、匱乏的恐懼、懼怕人的恐懼、被出賣的恐懼等等。讓我們研究死亡的恐懼感。死亡不分假日也不分任何人。只有那些預備妥面對死亡的人才能真正的活。希伯來書 9：27 告訴我們「按着定命，人人都有一死，死後且有審判。」 生命不是永久的，它是過渡性的。死亡不是終止或休止，而是過渡，從一度到另一度空間的一個改變。

雅各形容死亡為蒸氣，而生命為草。傳道書說：「生有時，死有時。」當靈魂離開身體是就是死亡。 詩篇23篇中死亡是叫陰影。那獅子和劍的陰影是不會傷到我。耶穌握有生和死的鑰匙。

啟示錄1：17、18 說，「 ... 不要懼怕! 我是首先的，我是末後的，又是那存活的；我曾死過，現在又活了，直活到永永遠遠，並且拿着死亡和陰間的鑰匙。」

懼怕可以打倒我們，但不能打敗我們。耶穌被猶太出賣，大衛被押沙龍出賣，保羅被底馬出賣，但那些被出賣的反變得更好而不是苦毒。他們拒絕讓一個不好的經驗成為他們生命裏的懼怕。

我們有個選擇， 讓懼怕征服我們，或相信耶穌幫助我們克服我們的懼怕。當我們將生命交託給祂，順服祂的話語過活，我們就能夠得勝的。

路加福音1：74 說，「叫我們既從仇敵手中被救出來，就可以終身在祂面前，坦然無懼地用聖潔，公義事奉祂。」

得勝的基督徒生活

Alfred Ee&Sandra Ee 牧師著

目 錄

第十三章

如何在屬靈爭戰中得勝?

當我們藉神的靈重生，我們每人立即進入屬靈戰爭。在我們生命裏有四個策略的戰地;我們的意念、心、口、和身體。在聖經裏，我們看到四個人有過和撒旦面對面相遇的經驗。他們是亞當和夏娃、約伯、尼布甲尼撒、和大衛。他們在以上所提的四個領域爭戰，我們能夠從這些人身上學習如何在屬靈戰爭裏得勝。

四個人			
	亞當和夏娃	約伯	尼布甲尼撒	大衛
撒旦的目標	意念	身體	口	心
撒旦的武器	謊言 欺騙	受苦	驕傲	控告 混亂 後悔 自責 壓制
撒旦的意圖	對神的旨意 無知	對神的旨意 沒耐心	不倚靠 神的旨意	不倚靠 神的旨意
你的 防衛武器	神的話語	神賜的恩典	順從內住的 聖靈	神的兒子 耶穌的代禱

心思意念

進入我們心思意念的每一想法可能有四個來源: 自我、 撒旦、世界的人們、或神。

215

根據約翰福音8:44,撒旦是謊言之父,他的武器是欺騙、壓力、壓迫、擔心、和憂慮。因此我們必須保護我們的心思意念不被撒旦的謊言侵入,一個沒有更新的心思意念是很危險的,我們的心思意念是神形象的一部分,是神與我們交通和顯明祂自己之處。

例如,撒旦問夏娃:「神豈是真說嗎?」,所以 牠懷疑神的話語。然後牠否認神的話語而對她說:「你們不一定死?」, 最後牠替代神的話語說:「你們便如神?」,這全都是謊言和欺騙。

撒旦透過迷惑、懊惱、困擾、隱瞞、壓制、和沮喪。再次提醒我們需要辨別我們思想的真正來源; 它是否狡辯的、自我榮耀、批評領袖、負面的、吹毛求疵、貪心、自私、控告、 猜疑、不信、懼怕、或常常擔憂?

「他心怎樣思量,他為人就是怎樣。」(箴言23:7)

身體

撒旦攻擊約伯透過他周遭的景況、他的孩子、他的財產、他失去的朋友、他的妻子、他的鄰居,接著他的身體得到可怕的疾病。這個苦難不是從神而來,但祂允許它發生來試煉約伯,煉如精金(約伯記23:10)。

撒旦要攻擊和毀滅我們的身體,因為那是聖靈的殿。神要使用我們的身體當作器皿,向這失落的世界顯示祂自己,撒旦知道牠能夠透過攻擊神的僕人,摧毀他們的使命來阻礙神的工作。我們的肢體是聖靈手中的工具,用來幫助建造地上教會。

「豈不知你們的身子就是聖靈的殿嗎 ...」(哥林多前書6:19)

撒旦攻擊我們的身體,因為那是神的試煉場所。身為神的子民,我們必須為榮耀神來照顧身體。

口舌

「生死在舌頭的權下,喜愛它的,必吃它所結的果子。」(箴言18:21)

我們的口因為責怪,和說負面的話而污損我們。它若充滿驕傲,也能導致我們墮落就好像尼布甲尼撒王的例子。

「他說：這大巴比倫不是我用大能大力建爲京都，要顯我威嚴的榮耀嗎?這話在王口中尚未說完，有聲音從天降下，說:尼布甲尼撒王啊，有話對你說:你的國位離開你了。你必被趕出離開世人，與野地的獸同居，吃草如牛，且要經過七期。等你知道至高者在人的國中掌權，要將國賜與誰，就賜與誰。當時這話就應驗在尼布甲尼撒的身上，他被趕出離開世人，吃草如牛，身被天露滴濕，頭髮長長，好像鷹毛，指甲長長，如同鳥爪。」(但以理書4:30-33)

既使在他身上發生一切事，約伯他從不用他的口犯罪(約伯記 2:10)。我們又如何呢? 若我們在約伯的情況中，會有甚麼話從我們的口中出來?

「惟獨舌頭沒有人能制伏，是不止息的惡物，滿了害死人的毒氣，我們用舌頭頌讚那爲主，爲父的，又用舌頭咒詛那照着神形像被造的人。頌讚和咒詛從一個口裏出來，我的弟兄們，這是不應當的。」(雅各3:8-10)

心

撒旦的目標是要得到我們的心來掌控它，因爲心是我們的情感的溫床。

在歷代志上21章裏，大衛的心思意念不受欺騙，但他內心的動機竟被攻擊。他自己本身沒遭苦難，他的王國也強盛，他贏取了許多光榮的勝利，也享受了功成名就。然而卻犯了自以爲是，榮耀自己的罪，結果是喪失70,000條人命。

心思、身體、口舌、和內心經常受撒旦攻擊，那我們如何克服他? 魔鬼是個被擊敗的敵人，但是我們許多人因爲沒有認清自己在基督裏的權柄， 在神話語裏的權柄，及穿著神軍裝的重要性，而仍然過着挫敗的生活。

戰勝仇敵

我們在基督裏的身份

生爲重生的基督徒，我們必須認識我們在基督裏是誰以及祂爲我們所完成的。第一、我們已蒙祂揀選(以弗所書1:4)。第二、我們藉著祂寶血已蒙救贖(以弗所書1:7)。祂已赦免並塗抹我們的罪，我們在祂裏面是一個新造的人。第三、我們屬於神而且有聖靈爲印記。因此撒旦來時，牠看到我們有印記，我們屬於神的牠不能傷害我們。(以弗所書1:13)

我們有基督的權柄

神給我們權柄踐踏仇敵的力量，當我們行在聖靈中並順服祂的話語，就沒有什麼可以傷害我們。
「我已經給你們權柄可以踐踏蛇和蠍子，又勝過仇敵一切的能力，斷沒有甚麼能害你們。」
(路加福音10:19)

神的話語

每次耶穌在曠野裏被試探，祂對撒旦說：「經上記着說 ... 」

我們必須認識神的話語，這樣我們能夠防止撒旦的攻擊。我們需要熟記神的話語，默想神的話語和應用神的話語，意思就是順從它遵行它。 神的話語更新我們的心思意念，保守我們靈裡的人剛強。

神的軍裝

「你們既聽見真理的道，就是那叫你們得救的福音，也信了基督，既然信他，就受了你應許的聖靈爲印記。」(以弗所書1:13)

真理的帶子—耶穌是真理，所以我們必須相信真理，並說出真理。

公義的護心鏡遮胸—所以我們能夠做對的事。
平安的福音當作預備走路的鞋穿在腳上—耶穌是我們的平安。我們當如此告訴他人，又當我們周圍有騷亂發生，讓我們做個使人和睦的人。

信德當作藤牌，可滅盡那惡者一切的火箭。

戴上救恩的頭盔，來保護心思意念。

聖靈的寶劍就是神的道，用來戰勝撒旦的欺騙和謊言。

禱告和禁食

禱告和禁食應該是每位基督徒一項定期的操練。從舊約到新約，信徒都會定期的禱告和禁食。根據以賽亞書58：6-9，它會鬆開兇惡的繩，解下軛上的索，使被欺壓的得自由，折斷一切的軛和醫治速速來臨。

靠着聖靈禱告

「靠着聖靈禱告，隨時多方禱告祈求，並要在此警醒不倦，為眾聖徒祈求。」(以弗所書1：18)

「當用各樣的智慧，把基督的道理豐豐富富地存在心裏，用詩章、頌詞、靈歌、彼此教導，互相勸戒，心被恩感，歌頌神。」(歌羅西書3：16)用方言禱告會增強我們裡面的人，在屬靈禱告爭戰中加添給我們更多屬靈的能力。在台灣，在我居住的城市，在教會裏，我知道每當有強烈的屬靈爭戰時，靠聖靈禱告是戰勝個人營壘的鑰點。

讚美

「我們應當靠着耶穌，常常以頌讚為祭獻給神，這就是那承認主名之人嘴唇的果子。」(希伯來書13：15)

保羅和西拉在被嚴厲的鞭打之後，半夜在牢裏向神禱告和唱詩。地震發生，牢門打開。當我們在困難的情況時讚美神，祂會打開我們的牢門，我們會戰勝仇敵。有一讚美的祭能夠幫助我們戰勝。

亞當和夏娃、約伯、尼布甲尼撒、大衛的心思意念、身體、口舌、和內心被攻擊。讓我們從他們的錯誤中學習，如同羅馬書8:37 說：「然而靠着愛我們的，在這一切的事上已經得勝有餘了。」

第十四章

聖潔的生命

聖潔並非是外在的裝飾，而是內在的道德態度和內心的情況。「因此，祂已經將寶貴，又極大的應許賜給我們，叫我們既脫離世上從情慾來的敗壞，就得與神的性情有分。」(彼得後書1：4)

我們有些人發覺很難相信神要我們聖潔。他們以為只有當他們死後上了天堂，才會也才能夠聖潔。神所想要的是你**現在**就**聖潔**。基督徒若他不想成為聖潔，就會錯失神的心意，以及神為他而定的目的。如果你真想要神的聖潔，你必須要準備面對你的不聖潔，雖然可能因此痛苦。

「那召你們的既是聖潔，你們在一切所行的事上也要聖潔。因為經上記着說『你們要聖潔，因為我是聖潔的。』」(彼得前書1：15、16)

神呼召我們要聖潔：
揀選—多麼榮幸!
王者—王權、治理、得勝。
聖潔—神子民的性格。
特定的—獨特、 特殊。
以賽亞書8：18，馬可福音16：18

為讚美神—榮耀神是神給人最高的榮譽。

你選擇做什麼樣的器皿? 榮耀的器皿或不榮耀的器皿?(希伯來書10：10)。提摩太後書2：21說：「人若自潔，脫離卑賤的事，就必作貴重的器皿，成為聖潔，合乎主用，預備行各樣的善事 ...」。

保羅在希伯來書12：10裏說我們「在祂的聖潔上有分 ...」，但罪、不信、叛逆、妥協、說謊、欺詐、懷疑、埋怨、或恐懼，會阻止我們看到神的榮耀或聖潔。

承認神的聖潔帶來真正的敬拜和讚美，因為聖潔和神的榮耀、祂的同在、祂的大能、和祂的美善有關聯的。(出埃及記15：11)。因此我們必須追求聖潔，得以看見神的榮耀，和體驗祂的美善、祝福、和能力。神的旨意是使我們全然成聖(帖撒羅尼迦前書5：23)

神是位聖潔的神

「因為耶和華我們的神本為聖。」(詩篇99：9) 神是聖潔的，若我們不聖潔，又怎能敬拜祂? 不只是祂大能能證實耶穌是神的兒子，而祂聖潔的生命也是一大特徵。

為甚麼要聖潔?

「你們豈不知不義的人不能承受神的國嗎? 不要自欺!無論是淫亂的、拜偶像的、姦淫的、作變童的、親男色的、偷竊的、貪婪的、醉酒的、辱罵的、勒索的，都不能承受神的國。你們中間也有人從前是這樣；但如今你們奉主耶穌基督的名，並藉着我們神的靈，已經洗淨、成聖、稱義了。」(哥林多前書6：9-11)

神的旨意是要我們成為聖潔：
帖撒羅尼迦前書4：1-4

我們屬於神的； 我們在祂聖靈裏重生過聖潔的生活，將像我們的父神：創世記1：26、約翰一書4：17、 彼得後書1：4、以弗所書1：4、希伯來書2：11。

我們是聖靈的殿或神的居所：以弗所書2：22、 哥林多前書3：16、17；6：9-11。

沒有聖潔，我們無法有神的啓示： 希伯來書12：14 耶穌說：「非聖潔沒有人能見神。」

神正尋找聖潔的教會並爲它而來：以弗所書5：26、27。

聖潔的生命是一個有能力的生命： 羅馬書1：4。

承認神的聖潔帶來真正的敬拜和讚美。聖潔和神的榮耀是有關聯的：出埃及記15：11，啓示錄15：4。

透過聖潔的生命我們得以向世界顯示神。
「豈不知你們是神的殿，神的靈住在你們裏頭嗎?若有人毀壞神的殿，神必要毀壞那人，因爲神的殿是聖的，這殿就是你們。」(哥林多前書3：16-17)

當我們讀聖經時，我們明白神期望我們的生命是聖潔的，除非像基督，沒有生命是純潔和聖潔的。我相信神呼召我們、祂的子民，成爲聖潔。

穿上新人

「但現在你們要棄絕這一切的事，以及惱恨、憤怒、惡毒、毀謗、並口中污穢的言語、不要彼此說謊，因你們已經脫去舊人和舊人的行爲，穿上了新人，這新人在知識上漸漸更新，正如造他主的形像。」(歌羅西書3：8-10)

哥林多前書6：9-11告訴我們曾經是甚麼和我們現在是甚麼。

哥林多前書1：30，帖撒羅尼迦後書2：13、14， 希伯來書2：11， 以弗所書4：22。我們被呼召穿上新人，歌羅西書3：8-10。

羅馬書第六章說到聖潔的榮耀。聖經提及公義的榮耀和聖靈服事的榮耀。它也說到關於聖潔的榮耀。

我們可以從兩個角度或觀點看聖潔

1.地位性的，就是合法的、給予的、歸於我們的。

2.進行性的，就是外勤的工作且需要我們的決定、意志、參與、合作、試驗和考驗。

聖潔的定義

聖潔真正的意思是肉體爲神分別爲聖，或着爲了神聖或屬靈的目的，或爲了行在聖靈裏。例如，在亞伯拉空、約伯、和約瑟的生活裏。

當一個人接受基督時，成聖不但是立即性的，它也是進行式的： 羅馬書1：11， 腓立比書2：12。

我們是如何成聖又如何有聖潔的生命？

「親愛的弟兄啊，我們既有這等應許，就當潔淨自己，除去身體、靈魂一切的污穢，敬畏神、得以成聖。」(哥林多後書7：1)這經文說敬畏神使我們的愛完全或聖潔。

甚麼是敬畏神？
彼得前書1：17，箴言8：13，9：10
敬畏神的定義是：爲祂而活，照祂旨意去行，遠離罪與那些不討祂喜悅的事。

以弗所書4：23，穿上新人。那是一個深思熟慮行動的選擇。求神使我們聖潔，希伯來書2：11

行在聖靈裏或愛裏：羅馬書8，加拉太書5：6-16， 22-25

知道與基督合一，與祂同行同活，將自己獻給神，羅馬書6章。

靠神的話語更新我們的心思意念並降服於神，羅馬書12：1。

「 ...將自己的身體獻上，當作活祭，是聖潔的，是神所喜悅的，你們如此事奉，乃是理所當然的。」(羅馬書12：1)

「 ... 你們當順着聖靈而行，就不放縱肉體的情慾了。因爲情慾和聖靈相爭，聖靈和情慾爭，這兩個彼此相敵，使你們不能做所願意做的。」(加拉太書5：16-17)

「聖靈所結的果子，就是仁愛、喜樂、和平、忍耐、恩慈、良善、信實、溫柔、節制。這樣的事，沒有律法禁止。」(加拉太書5：22-23)

進行式的成聖是脫下舊人，穿上新人：以弗所書4：17-32。

聖潔是「像基督」性情的發展。甚麼是成聖?它是歸向光明，同得我們的基業。(使徒行傳26：18)

「但現今你們既從罪裏得了釋放，作了神的奴僕，就有成聖的果子，那結局就是永生!」(羅馬書6：22)

神僕人的果子是聖潔的。我們從罪裏得了釋放過聖潔的生活，而無酵節指向我們聖潔的生命。

「要用水藉着道把教會洗淨，成爲聖潔，可以獻給自己，作個榮耀的教會，毫無玷污、皺紋等類的病，乃是聖潔沒有瑕疵的。」(以弗所書5：26-27)

讚美神，耶穌的寶血救贖了我們。我們的信心和希望是在神裏。我們是在聖靈裏重生並憑信進入神的大能裡，使我們能夠勝過罪惡，過聖潔與得勝的基督徒生活。依據神的目的和計畫，神照祂的形象創造我們來反射祂的公義和聖潔。

「主啊，誰敢不敬畏祢，不將榮耀歸於你的名呢?因爲獨有祢是聖的，萬民都要來再祢面前敬拜，因祢公義的作爲已經顯出來了。」(啓示錄15：4)

第十五章

禱告得勝

除了禱告和信心外，我們在各個領域都有各類的教導和輔導。因著基督是禱告的學校。神要我們成功，只能透過禱告來成就。屬靈的事必須源自禱告。

「...神答應我們祂聽見我們和祂給予的肯定事祂會回應我們的禱告和祂要我們成功...」(詩篇34：17-19)

「耶穌說：我就是生命的糧，到我這裏來的，必定不餓；信我的，永遠不渴。」(約翰福音6：35)

神要滿足我們所有的需要!

耶穌是我們的榜樣。 例子：耶穌過禱告的生活。

神呼召教會去做甚麼? 暫停來聆聽、禱告、宣告、等候神。

為甚麼當神要我們成功，而我們卻失敗呢? 鑰點在於我們的禱告生活。

「眾百姓都受了洗，耶穌也受了洗。正禱告時，天就開了。」(路加福音3：21)

耶穌以禱告開始祂的服事。(馬太福音3：13-17)

當耶穌正禱告時，天就開了，聖靈恩膏祂，這樣，禱告打開了天窗，神將祂的福傾倒在我們身上。

耶穌大能的秘密是甚麼?

「但耶穌的名聲越發傳揚出去，有極多的人聚集來聽道也指望醫治他們的病。耶穌卻退到曠野去禱告。」(路加福音5：15-16)

「那時耶穌出去上山禱告，整夜禱告神。到了天亮，叫祂的門徒來，就從他們中間挑選十二個人，稱他們為使徒。」祂繼續整夜地向神禱告。」(路加福音 6：12-13)

這揭露耶穌大能和神蹟奇事背後的秘密。祂在盛大的聚會後也禱告，沒有因此輕鬆下來或自滿。初代教會有一小時的禱告，而神國的事都是透過禱告而生。。

每位神的傳道人要學習的一課，就是所有承擔神話語的傳道人，命定會招來仇敵最強烈的戰火。我們被呼召進入屬靈戰爭，不是憑血氣肉體。每位神所呼召的人，若在未進入事奉工作前，先準備自己，分別一段時間特別等候在神面前，他就會做得很好。初期的教會在差遣他們第一個傳道士前先禱告。(使徒行傳13：2-4)。耶穌在開始踏入積極服事奉前先禱告。祂獨自退去曠野禱告，自己做最後的充電來與撒旦對決。(使徒行傳4：1-2)

耶穌每日以禱告開始。

「次日早晨，天未亮的時候，耶穌起來，到曠野地方去，在哪裏禱告。西門和同伴追了他去。遇見了就對他說：眾人都找你。」(馬可福音1：35-37)

無論我們的恩膏多有能力，也須要每日以禱告來使恩膏持續。

耶穌以禱告開始這一天。
「耶穌卻退到曠野去禱告 . . . 」(路加福音5：16)

讚美和感恩是禱告的重要的一環。耶穌在祂的禱告中有一時段讚美和感謝神。

「那時,耶穌說:父啊! 天地的主,我感謝祢!因爲祢將這些事向聰明通達人就藏起來,向嬰孩就顯出來。」(馬太福音11:25)

「耶穌餵食了4,000人,拿着這七個餅和幾條魚,祝謝了、擘開、 遞給門徒,門徒又遞給眾人。」(馬太福音15:36)

耶穌行使拉撒路復活的神蹟奇事之前向父神禱告。

「 . . . 父啊!我感謝你已經聽我;我也知道你常聽我。但我說這話,是爲周圍站着的眾人叫他們信是你差了我來。說了這話,就大聲呼叫說:『拉撒路出來!』那死人就出來了,手腳裹著布,臉上包著手巾。耶穌對他們說:『解開,叫他走! 』」(約翰福音11:41-44)

耶穌認識父神的聲音,與父神有親密的關係,以及祂與父神的交通團契(禱告的生活),釋放出神聖的大能,也彰顯了神蹟奇事。

許多時候不幸和困難驅使人們跪下禱告。歷史顯示領導者常陷入群眾的言論裏。但耶穌不被那些今天封祂爲王,明天要釘死祂的眾人所蒙蔽。 反之祂察覺前面的危險,爲了避免它,祂必須逃離去禱告。 祂看到那逼祂成王的計劃。

「散了眾人以後,祂就獨自上山去禱告。到了晚上,只有祂一人在那裏。」(馬太福音14:23)

「耶穌說:我不是揀選了你們十二個門徒嗎? 但你們中間有一個是魔鬼。耶穌這話是指着加略人西門的兒子猶太說的,他本是十二個門徒裏的一個,後來要賣耶穌的。」(約翰福音6:70-71)

耶穌察覺眾人沒有真心改變。他們要封祂爲王因爲祂餵他們食物,(約翰福音6:26-31,66)

若眾人強封祂爲王,那將完全挫敗神救贖的計劃。

我們必須在做重要的決定之前先禱告。

「他們就滿心大怒,彼此商議怎樣處治耶穌,那時耶穌出去上山禱告整夜禱告神。」(路加福音6:11-12)

每個緊要關頭的決定之前,耶穌都在禱告中尋求父神的面。讓我們以基督的例子學習,那就是當我們有重要的決定,我們應該先禱告。

「耶穌自己禱告的時候,門徒也同祂在那裏。耶穌問他們說:眾人說我是誰?他們說:有人說是施洗的約翰,有人說是以利亞,還有人說是古時的一個先知又活了。耶穌說:你們說我是誰?彼得回答說:是神所立的基督。耶穌切切地囑咐他們,不可將這事告訴人。」(路加福音9:18-21)

在使徒行傳9:17裏,神因爲掃羅的禱告而差遣亞拿尼亞,結果是神以聖靈醫治他並爲他受洗。

禱告的結果在啓示和引導。

禱告可使他人從神那裏得到啓示。

保羅透過他的禱告改變那教會,以弗所書1:18-23。

「說了這話以後約有八天,耶穌帶着彼得、約翰、雅各上山去禱告。正禱告的時候,祂的面貌就改變了,衣服潔白放光。」(路加福音9:28-29)

禱告改變生命中的事 。

「我們既然敞着臉得以看見主的榮光,好像從鏡子裏返照,就變成主的形狀,榮上加榮,如同從主的靈變成的。」(哥林多後書3:18)

禱告帶來神的榮耀和從神來的啓示。

我們以敞開的臉(透明的),好像從鏡子裏返照,就變成主的形狀,榮上加榮,如同從主的靈變成的。

禱告為神來影響人們。

有時我們雙膝跪下禱告，能完成的事比用口說話來的多!

「耶穌在一個地方禱告。禱告完了，有個門徒對祂說：求主教導我們禱告，像約翰教導他的門徒。」(路加福音11：1)

禱告是贏得靈魂的鑰點：

約翰福音6：44，馬可福音16：10、17。彼得得到了耶穌是基督的啟示，但在彼得宣告前，耶穌獨自禱告神向彼得和其他人顯示祂的身份和使命。

禱告預備你面對將來。

「我不求祢叫他們離開世界，只求祢保守他們脫離那惡者。」(約翰福音17：15)

「西門，西門!撒旦想要得着你們，好篩你們像篩麥子一樣;但我已經為你祈求，叫你不至於失了信心。你回頭以後，要堅固你得弟兄。」(路加福音22：31-32)

真正的領導者必須做榜樣。

你有禱告嗎? 我們花費多少時間禱告? 我們的優先順序是甚麼?

方法可以不同改變，但禱告的原則須保持優先。

禱告最要緊的是堅持。

「耶穌設一個比喻，是要人常常禱告，不可灰心。」(路加福音18：1)

「我告訴你們：要快快地給他們伸冤了。然而人子來的時候，得見世上有信德嗎?」(路加福音18：8)

這樣的信心從不放棄禱告。若一個人不禱告，他會沉淪於沮喪氣餒而消沉下去。

「約翰的門徒來，把屍首領去埋葬了，就去告訴耶穌。耶穌聽見了，就上船從那裏獨自退到野地裏去。眾人聽見，就從各城裏步行跟隨他。耶穌出來，有許多的人，就憐憫他們，治好了他們的病人。」(馬太福音14：12-14)

禱告是個超自然的活動且釋放超自然的能力。

釋放、神蹟奇事、醫治、神的引導、和啓示來自禱告。得勝是透過禱告而來的。聖經告訴我們如此：

以利亞爲那寡婦停止呼吸的兒子禱告。耶和華聽見以利亞的求告，那男孩的靈魂仍入祂的身體，他就活了。(列王紀上17：20-23)。

．．．仇敵因禱告而被勝過了．．．(出埃及記14：15-16)

復興和恢復來自禱告。(列王紀上18)

希西家的禱告導致一個瘟疫，撲滅了185,000名敵人。(列王紀下19：15-35)。

耶穌在危機時做什麼? 他如何回應?

馬太福音14：32、39、42「．．．他們上船，風就住了。」

耶穌已經爲擺在前面的景況禱告，並且爲他們要面對的試煉有了準備。

禱告不是逃避，而是加強攻擊撒旦的工作。

耶穌在受苦時禱告。耶穌爲對抗邪惡和誘惑而禱告。耶穌禱告神的旨意完成。禱告是爭戰的屬靈力量。例如我們在馬太福音26章裏看到沉睡的靈。

耶穌不斷的在禱告中求聖靈的引導。祂的神蹟奇事是來自祂的禱告。祂的禱告改變世界的命運。祂的禱告預言性的影響我們。

不同型態的禱告：

按手禱告
按手禱告的教義是根據經文的：馬太福音19：13-15，馬可福音16：18。

醫治禱告
對於每位委身的禱告勇士，通常多少會遭遇個人的客西馬尼時刻。經歷此時刻可能帶來極度的痛苦，然而雖經此境遇仍如耶穌般禱告的人肯定會得勝的。

「耶穌同門徒來到一個地方，名叫客西馬尼，就對他們說：你們坐在這裏，等我到那邊去禱告 . . . 祂就稍往前走，俯伏在地禱告說：我父啊，倘若可行，求你叫這杯離開我；然而，不要照我的意思，只要照你的意思。」(馬太福音26：36、39)

爲神在我們生命中的旨意禱告
「第二次又去禱告說：我父啊，這杯若不能離開我，必要我喝，就願祢得旨意成全。」(馬太福音26：42)

饒恕的禱告
「當下耶穌說：父啊，赦免他們！因爲他們所做的，他們不曉得。兵丁就拈鬮分祂的衣服。」(路加福音23：34)─耶穌最後的禱告

同心合一的禱告
「 . . . 有兩三個人奉我的名聚會，那裏就有我在他們中間。」(馬太福音18：20)

聖靈裡的禱告
「 . . . 靠着聖靈，隨時多方禱告祈求 . . . 」(以弗所書6：18)

爲衆聖徒的禱告和代禱
「 . . . 並要在此警醒不倦，爲衆聖徒祈求。」(以弗所書6:18)

耶穌爲自己禱告(約翰福音17：1-5)
耶穌爲祂的門徒禱告(約翰福音17：6-19)
耶穌爲衆信徒禱告(約翰福音17：20-26)

神的同在和禱告

「你們存心不可貪愛錢財，要以自己所有的為足，因為主曾說：我總不撇下你，也不丟棄你。」(希伯來書13：5)

「凡我所吩咐你們的，都教訓他們遵守，我就常與你們同在，直到世界的末了。」(馬太福音28：20)

「我往哪裏去躲避你的靈?我往哪裏逃躲避祢的面？」(詩篇139：7)

「摩西說：你若不親自和我同去，就不要把我們從這裏領上去。」(出埃及記33：15)

耶穌如何與我們同在?

「我要求父，父就另外賜給你們一位保惠師，叫祂永遠與你們同在，就是真理的聖靈，乃世人不能接受的，因為不見祂；你們卻認識祂，因祂常與你們同在，也要在你們裏面。」(約翰福音14：16-17)

新約中有名的三件事：神為我們成就，神與我們同在，神在我們裏面。那就是說神是多麼的接近－祂就在這裏：約翰福音14：23，出埃及記33：14。

你和神成為多數，詩篇46：1。神是我們的避難所，是我們的力量，是我們患難中隨時的幫助。

「等我進入了神的聖所，思想他們的結局。」(詩篇73：17)

當大衛進入神的同在，他開始看透一切事情。

雖然我們可能沒有意識到祂的同在，事實上神的同在總是與我們在一起。藉著信在祂話語中，祂永遠與我們同在。祂說祂不撇下我們或丟棄我們。

「你們禱告的時候，不可像那假冒為善的人，愛站在會堂裏和十字路口上禱告，故意叫人看見我實在告訴你們：他們已經得了他們的賞賜。你禱告的時候，要進你們內屋，關上門，禱告你在暗中的父，你父在暗中察看，必然報答你。」(馬太福音6：5-6)

為甚麼人必須獨自禱告? 禱告的舉動是他們進入神的同在。

神是無所不在。祂沒來也沒去。認識神的同在使禱告更容易且有信心。

雅各書5:16 告訴我們:「 . . . 義人祈禱所發的力量是大有功效的。」

讓我們相信神在我們的禱告生活裏大有功效,跟隨耶穌的榜樣,透過我們為自己的禱告和為他人的代禱,帶來神蹟奇事與釋放。

第十六章

不住的禱告

如果我們期待像新約的信徒般委身於不間斷的禱告，禱告就應該是很享受又滿有果效的。而我們若把禱告當作只是沒話可說或無事可做之時，極爲無聊又無效的差事，這樣的想法則完全是錯誤的。我要提出三項信心的聲明，當你明白這些聲明將會激勵你去相信並幫助你，使禱告成爲你基督徒生命中一個又重要又享受且不止息的部份。

當我們禱告時，美好的事會發生或事情會改變。 (雅各書5:16)

在聖經RSV版裏「fervent」(熱情的)這字含有連續的意思。所以我相信雅各書5：16的禱告是一位敬虔的男人或女人，迫切地、由衷地、不斷地禱告，大有果效的釋放大能。禱告導致事情發生在你的婚姻、你的教會、或你的牧者或平信徒主領的講道。主日的早晨會不一樣，只因你或你的太太不斷的、由衷的禱告。(路加福音18：7-8， 使徒行傳10：3)

我們呼召去影響我們的孩子、我們的婚姻、我們的教會、和我們的國家的命定。你可以影響國家。並不是莫斯科統治這世界乃是神。教會將透過代禱來治理這世界，而不是透過統治。

在歌羅西書4：12-13介紹我們一個人叫以巴弗，他肯定不比保羅、提摩太、或提多有名。但爲甚麼他的名被提及?保羅提到他乃是因爲他竭力的祈求，因爲他不斷的禱告使信徒們在神一切的旨意上得以完全、信心充足、能站立得穩。以巴弗委身自己不斷地爲他人禱告。神喜悅那些委身自己不住的禱告的人。我們在使徒行傳裏找到「委身」這個字好幾次。禱告包括委身—爲某事經常不間斷的去做，並且持續的做。使徒行傳1：14的成果是在五旬節。一個禱告聚會成立了第一個五旬節(使徒行傳2：42)。初期教會在四方面建造了它自己：

i)   委身於聖經
ii)   團契
iii) 聖餐
iv)   禱告

我們往往想要得到神的大能卻不尋求祂。使徒行傳4：23-24，31 是在禱告中尋求神的結果。初期的教會委身於禱告，每次他們禱告聖靈就開始運行。他們的禱告是持續不斷的、迫切的、由衷的，以至於極有果效的且釋放出神的大能。我們也能如此。

恩典的寶座為我們大開

保羅給提多的信特別地告訴我們神將為我們做的恩典。提多書2：11-15，希伯來書12：15 這段經文有關聖潔。神給的恩典不是一張可以供犯罪的執照，而是表明我們如何脫離罪惡，能得勝有餘地去饒恕人，有仁慈，有純潔和聖潔的心思意念，心存對的動機成為一位正直的人。難道恩典教導我們離世時才去棄絕不敬虔和世俗的情慾嗎？不，它說我們必須在現今的日子裏認真的、公義的、和敬虔的過活。

當我們談論恩典和禱告，我們是在談論得勝。我們談論不斷禱告透過生活中的問題，直到它們不再存在。神的恩典帶來救贖和釋放，教導我們棄絕不敬虔和世界的情慾。神給我們恩典去饒恕，但恩典藉禱告將理論移入我們的心。人們缺乏神的恩典，乃因他們寧願保留苦毒，卻不向耶穌禱告求祂挪去苦毒。我們透過跪地禱告來領受恩典(撒迦利亞書4：6-7)。你生活中有沒有一座你想要挪開的山(一座憂鬱、懼怕、憤怒、不潔淨的思想、和壞習慣的山)？你必須向那山呼求恩典。大山可藉神的恩典被征服剷平。神是站在你這一邊，若你持續在禱告中，祂的恩典或能力是足以夠用的。(希伯來書4：16，以賽亞書30：18，33：2，哥林多後書12：9)

透過不斷的禱告，神的旨意得以成就，祂的國度得以建立。

馬可福音1：40-41—我們在這裏看到神的恩典觸摸到一位痲瘋患者，因為這是神的旨意要他被潔淨、被釋放。今天耶穌也要觸摸你，就在此時、此刻、此地，祂要治理你在地生活中屬於祂的國度。

你絕對不會因太老、太忙、或太過罪惡而不能改變；你可以改變，而禱告帶來改觀。就算你已經禱告過，還是要繼續禱告，直到你禱告透了，你尚未得勝不是因爲神不願意，而是有攔阻。(例如：抽煙多年的一個人，他雖禱告了卻無法勝過菸癮，爲甚麼?是甚麼攔阻勝利? 若是他對父母的叛逆導致他吸煙。他須先處理那叛逆的心，接著才來戒煙，這樣問題就能解決了。)

沒有代禱或不住的禱告無一事能成就。你所關心的人不會上天堂，除非耶穌透過你或某人來觸摸他。醉酒或毒癮者不會得到釋放，除非耶穌透過某人或你來觸摸他。沒有代禱就沒有醫治發生。(以賽亞書66：7-9)。 雖然整個堂會每個星期天都有敬拜和神蹟，但只有部份的人被耶穌觸摸。透過不住的禱告，耶穌觸摸我們。(馬可福音5：27-20，列王紀上18：41-46)

讓我們禱告而不疲倦，成爲英勇的男女，不住的禱告直到我們突破，並且看到神的國度臨到地上，祂的旨意行在祂子民的身上。以利亞在下雨之前禱告了七次(雅各書5：17-18)。讓我們像以利亞一樣，因信迫切地求告神，爲你所須要的勝利及突破禱告。禱告直到你知道勝利已來臨。

第十七章

神的聲音

因有評論家爭辯著今日神已不再透過聖經向我們說話，所以讓我們先翻閱聖經看看有甚麼有關神的聲音。這樣做立即就會讓人聯想到爲甚麼會有人排斥，神用許多方式向人類顯示祂自己─包括直接向一個人或一群人說話。從有歷史開始，神已經且仍然還在透過至少七種方式說話：

1. **創造**
   神如此清楚地透過創造的榮耀、藝術、和尊貴說話，聖經甚至說全人類都要單單基於這些來相信那創造的主，看詩篇19：1-6；羅馬書1：20。

2. **人類的良心**
   神透過存於人類良心的道德感說話。基本的對錯感與生俱來，神可能基於這基礎實行審判，看羅馬書2：14、15。

3. **屬天的供應**
   神透過屬天供應的證據來說話。這些證據影響我們的生活，向我們的心靈說話，經常導致人們發出驚異、智慧、感恩、或悔改的回應。看創世記28：10-17，使徒行傳1：7。

4. **神蹟奇事和預言**
   神說話透過聖靈運行的神蹟、奇事、預言、以及方言和翻方言，藉這些方式來造就信徒，並讓非信徒信服於祂的大能與同在，看列王紀下2：15，使徒行傳13：12，哥林多前書14：5，22-26。

5. 安靜微小的聲音

神說話透過祂「安靜、微小的聲音」，祂藉祂自己選擇的表達方式向人們的內心傳話，使他們產生個人的確信、改正、內省、或指引，看以賽亞書30：21，使徒行傳10：9-12。

6. 聖經

神說話透過祂有權柄的話語，啓示性的和無誤的經文，看提摩太後書3：14-17，就是在舊約和新約裏，祂藉聖靈透過祂的先知和使徒所賜下的，看彼得後書1：19-21。

神話語的憑據就是祂總是在傳揚和述說，經常尋求去觸摸和擁抱，以及教導和糾正。然而看到這些方式，再度提醒我們聖經的權柄可在我們這爭辯中作各個方面的判斷：

第一，我們只知道我們可以相信神透過這些方法向人們說話，並且和他們在屬靈上確實是有根據的，因爲聖經如此說。

第二， 我們只能藉著聖經完整的教導和權柄來衡量，讓我們覺察神是透過這些方式說話。

換句話說，神藉著任何方式所說的，都必須被檢驗—乃是在光中以絕對的方法來檢驗—這絕對的，當然就是整本聖經。

這些原則應該可解決這爭辯。那些過度害怕「神對我說話」這樣相對重要性的話，或是害怕因任何話語或靈而落入騙局，已被用來教導信徒絕對要去避免，甚至要去拒絕「繼續的啓示」(continuing revelation)的理念。這樣的話表明了錯誤的想法，就是有關神的旨意與真理，聖經不是最終的權威。

聖經確實是所有生命的基礎，與重大事情的最終權威。任何的反對意見都應被忽視；所有反對意見的基督徒領袖都應被質問。

但從這些要點可知，聖經裡面沒有支持某些人所認爲，今日神不再對人講話的立場，也沒有支持任何人宣稱，神對我們講話就是涵蓋錯誤。

兩位知名的反靈恩的作者(兩位都稱我爲朋友，爲此我很感激)。把每一位說「神對我說話」的人，歸列爲「繼續啓示論」或 「聖經外加(extra Biblical)啟示」謬論的人。(他們也說我是其中之一)。當然他們誤解了我，也對我所知道大多數的靈恩派有了錯誤的判斷。

當我們談及「聖經外加論」可以聲明的就是主張「聖經外加論」在教導今日神不向祂的百姓說話，因為聖經裡充滿神對祂的百姓講話的例子。

並且，我們必須清楚明白，聖經用「啟示」這個字有雙重意思。讓我們停止挑剔使用啟示這字眼。在以弗所書1：17-18裏，使徒禱告祈求「智慧和啟示的靈」來光照信徒的心，這表明神今日仍在向他的孩子啟示。

這種啟示絕不等同於聖經正典結束的經文，我們清楚明白聖經是一本關閉了，已完成的書。但是，當聖靈帶著神話語的真理，為我們活化並點燃信心，去擁抱父神對我們的命定時，這種啟示應該是受歡迎的。

但以理書11：32談到認識神就是與神親密。你生命中最深的渴望的是甚麼呢？

所有那些你服事中所完成和所成就的，都與你有多認識祂，或與祂有多親密有關。成功得須靠它。你生命中的渴望是什麼？成功、恩寵、顯要或認識神，甚麼是你所追求的？

約翰福音15：5 你在靈裏的程度有多深是依據你渴望的程度。你認識神的渴望與花時間在祂的同在中，決定你與神的關係有多深。

若你看那些屬神的偉人生命，他們和別人不同的一個因素，不在於他們有口才、有名氣、有魅力、有學歷、有能力，而是他們有一個很深的飢渴，不斷的渴望認識神與神親密，因此神就大大地使用他們。此乃外在的宗教形式與現實和團契的對比。

申命記6：5，馬可福音12：30，若我們用我們全人來愛神這樣我們就不容易去犯罪、或憂愁、懷疑、懼怕、有錯誤的態度、和不順服神。我們不該看重服事多於神本身。例如馬大相較於馬利亞，把職位、儀式、日常工作置於「認識」神之上，甚麼是教會？它是帶領我們認識神的工具。

啓示錄2：1形容以弗所的教會的光景。服事可以讓生活變得非常忙碌，導致我們只能花很少的時間與神有密切的團契和交通。若我們對神的渴望變軟弱，對其它事物就會轉強，如此就會給我們帶來麻煩。(約翰一書2：15)

我們的喜好和渴望將會引領我們這一生，或決定我們生命的命定方向。詩篇27：4是大衞的呼求。他非常的專注。「有一件事，我曾求耶和華，我仍要尋求：就是一生一世住在耶和華的殿中。」那最好的節目也無法取代神自己和祂的同在。詩篇91篇得到滿足感的關鍵是在祂的同在中(第1、9、14節)。大衞所做的是來自他對神的渴慕。詩篇34：10「那些尋求神的什麼好事都不缺。」

爲甚麼我們應該認識神? 只要我們認識神，我們所有的問題如有關醫治、信心、禱告、聖靈、家庭、或其他等等的問題就不會如此這般。現在我們親近神，將來也必如我們選擇這樣。 當你靠近神，祂就會靠近你。

舊約中親近神的四層次

1. **外圈**

    出埃及記19：11-12 . . . 神告訴摩西祂的希望及意圖。

    出埃及記20：18-21 . . . 那人民遠遠地站立因爲懼怕。 當神降臨甚麼事發生? 他們保持距離 (第21節)

    他們不要與神說話。神在考驗他們的心。但他們站得遠遠地。只有摩西靠近。我們能站立在人面前而我們的心可以不受審判，但在神面前卻無法如此，有些人就是喜歡這種方式。

2. **第二圈**

    出埃及記24：9-12，15 . . . 這裏摩西和長老們與神共享自助餐。我們看摩西和長老們走上山往前去與神說話。這就是領導力，我們必須更往前去領受指示。像那樣的經歷一定會改變你的生命。與神吃喝。然而摩西和約書亞甚至要更往前上去。第12節是表明好領袖的特質。取悅他人是否讓你覺得比等候神、渴望神感覺到更舒適?出埃及記32章，神向他說話之前，摩西等守了六天。

3. **第三圈**

   出埃及記24：14-18 ... 我們看到摩西和約書亞比其他人走得更遠登上西奈山上。約書亞被選爲領導者因爲他親近神。在這末後的日子神尋找那些選擇與祂同在的人。摩西和約書亞待在山上四十晝夜。那些長老應該也在那裏，但他們無法等候。

4. **內圈**

   出埃及記33：11 ... 我們看到摩西與神有親密的關係，他與神好像人與朋友面對面說話一般。這也是神對我們的期望。摩西的臉反射神的榮耀，因爲他花時間與神同在。

新約裏親近神的五層次

我們看到在新約裏與耶穌親近的五層次。

1. **群衆**

   最大的一群人(靈性相較於教會的大小)經常在那裏領受、受教、但卻極少付出。 一個成熟的基督徒生命只能來自付出與領受，我們必須從人群裏走出來。

2. **七十人**

   路加福音10：17 那七十人從群衆中出來，他們付出，餵養，並教導。他們比群衆更接近耶穌。

3. **十二人－比那七十人更接近耶穌。馬可福音3：14**

   他們的目的是要與耶穌在一起。

   許多時候耶耶穌教導祂的們門徒但他們卻不明白，但之後祂會在與他們單獨時向他們解釋。

4. **那三人－彼得、 雅各和約翰.**

   路加福音8：51 耶穌到管會堂的家，只有三人與耶穌進入這家裏。

   馬太福音17：1耶穌在變像山上與摩西和以利亞說話，只有這三人與祂在一起。馬可福音13：3耶穌在橄欖山與安得烈說有關末世的預兆。馬太福音26：36祂帶那三人更往前去，把那九人留在客西馬尼園的入口。

彼得、 雅各、和約翰更靠近耶穌，因爲他們渴望如此，不是因爲他們是超級聖人或是完美。 彼得不斷說出被人糾正的話。

選擇權是我們的。追求神是你的渴望嗎?若你做了選擇，神會使用並祝福你。領導能力來自那些與神同行的人。若我們不花時間與神同在，我們就無法帶領教會走在它該行的方向。你在人前得力完全倚靠你與神在一起的時間。

5. **被愛的約翰**

約翰福音18：15—耶穌已被出賣。每個人都逃跑了，只剩彼得和約翰。

約翰福音13：22，只有約翰知道誰是出賣者的秘密，其他人則沒聽見。

若你要從神知道和聽到，親近神是一大關鍵。你將會剛強、大有作爲、成爲有信心的人、有勇氣、敏銳聖靈的帶領並能成功。

第十八章

奉獻

聖殿是供奉給上帝的，所羅門和眾人爲敬拜祂而預備的。
奉獻的意思是爲了特定目的分別一個地方、 一個物件、或一個人。

奉獻聖殿的目的是分別一個神殿，或一個地方用來敬拜神。

但是你我知道，有個地方一起敬拜祂是好的—但教會是你和我—其實聖經告訴我們今天我們的身體是神的殿—「因爲我們是永生神的殿，就如神曾說：我要在他們中間居住，在他們中間來往；我要作他們的神，他們要作我的子民。」（哥林多後書6：16）

我們必須獻上自己

我們爲神分別我們自己。哥林多前書6：19說 「豈不知你們的身子就是聖靈的殿嗎?這聖靈是從神而來，住在你們裏頭的；並且你們不是自己的人。」

所以當我們獻上自己，神對我們會有甚麼期待?

獻身於敬拜

這是神與你。敬拜不只是合唱和向神唱詩歌，而是我們與神每日的關係，馬可福音12：30「你要盡心、盡性、盡意、盡力、愛主你的神。」

神不只是要我們生命的一部分。祂要我們心的全部－但我們被家庭、工作、朋友、和金錢，拉扯到如此多的方向。

但神對三心兩意的委身、部份的順服、或只獻出我們剩餘時間和金錢，並不感興趣。祂渴望的是我們完全的委身。

羅馬書6：13 (TEV) 說「將自己獻給神，並將肢體作義的器具獻給上帝。」

敬拜的心是降服，而降服是個不受歡迎的字－在今日英語裏「我降服」 的意思，含有鬆懈、或在戰役中承認失敗、或在遊戲裏棄權、或退讓給更強的對手。

我們寧願談贏家、成功、得勝、和征服，而不願說退讓、服從、順從、降服。

　　但降服神的意思單單只是意味獻身，讓耶穌成為你的主，拿起你的十字架、 捨己、順服聖靈。

　　神要我們生命的全部而不是95%－有兩件事阻礙我們完全降服神；懼怕和驕傲。

　　懼怕阻止我們降服，但愛驅除所有的懼怕。我們越是發覺神對我們的愛，降服祂就變得更容易。神是那麼的愛我們，祂關心我們生命的每一細節，而且祂對我們的生命有着美好的計劃。

　　當我們完全降服自己給耶穌，我們發覺祂不是暴君，而是救主；不是老闆，而是個兄弟；不是獨裁者，而是朋友。

　　第二個攔阻我們完全降服的是我們的驕傲。我們不喜歡承認我們只是個被造的，而且無法主宰一切事。世界上最古老的慾望是「擁有完全的掌控」，那個慾望的意思是「我們要成為我們生活中所有一切的神。」

　　但是我們不是神而且我們永遠都不是。我們只是人。

　　降服神簡單的意思，是過順從和信任的生活。

我們如何知道我們是否真正的順服祂? 因為我們信賴神成就萬事,就不再企圖要掌控他人,或強制我們的計畫和控制情況。放棄我們強求的方式而讓神工作。

一個降服的心也會有更多的信任,來取代更努力的嘗試—例如我們不會對論斷過度反應,想衝動的自我防衛。

和其他人有關係,我們不排擠外人或要求自我的權利,我們也不自我服務,只願降服。

獻身於敬拜的意思是完全降服的心。

救世軍的創辦人布斯威廉(William Booth)說:「一個人偉大的力量是在於他降服的程度。」

降服的人是神所用的人。神選擇了馬利亞, 耶穌的母親,那不是因為她有才能、有錢、或美麗,而是因為她完全降服於祂。那就是為甚麼她能夠說:「照你的話成就在我身上。」 (路加福音1:38)

奉獻我們自己,不只是以完全降服的心敬拜,也是獻身於服事。

1. 獻身於服事—你和教會

你會唉唉叫 「哦不啦,牧師。」—讓我來教會,享受敬拜讚美,享受講道信息,就回家吧! 等下個星期天再來。「但服事呀!不、不、不,太忙啦! 工作、工作、工作,又有家庭的需要 ... 還有我有朋友呢? 」

另外還有其他想要服事的人—但他們不做「骯髒」的工作,讓其他人做罷。扮演僕人的角色不是個受歡迎的主意。

偉大的世界定義為權力、財富、聲望、和地位。若你有能力要求他人為你服務,這代表你功成名就了。

然而耶穌以服事,而不以地位來衡量一個人的偉大。

神以我們服事多少人,而不是多少人服事我們,來決定我們有多偉大。

我們如何知道自己是獻身於服事，並且是個真正的僕人?

i) **真正的僕人當被召時隨時準備好。**
若我們只是自己方便時才服事，我們不是真正的僕人。

ii) **真正的僕人注意他人的需要。**
僕人經常尋找幫助他人的方法。

iii) **真正的僕人盡其所有盡其所能的去服事**
僕人不找藉口、拖延、或等候更好的時機。僕人從來不說，「某一天」或「當對的時機」。他們只是去作需要完成的事。

若我們要等到完美情況，我們永遠不會完成任何事。

iv) **真正的僕人以同等的心態做每件事工**
不管什麼工，僕人「盡全心去做」。事工的大小是不相干的。神是不會免除我們從事世俗、低賤的事工。那是我們性格訓練重要的一部分。

偉大的使徒保羅，在船毀後，揀木材、起火取暖每一個人。他像其他人一樣的精疲力竭，但他先滿足每一個人的需要。當我們有顆僕人的心，沒有任何工作是太低賤的。

v) **真正的僕人忠心於他們的事工**
僕人完成他們的工作，盡他們的責任，遵守他們的承諾並完成他們所委身之事。 他們不會半途而廢而離開，也不會因爲遭遇挫折而放棄。真正的僕人是值得信賴和可倚靠的。

忠誠一向是很難得的特質，因爲多數人不明白委身的意思。他們輕易的作承諾就委身，然後只因小小的理由，就毫無猶豫、毫無悔意、無情的毀約。

你是否有許多承諾須要你去遵守，許多誓約須要你去完成，或委身須要你去尊重?

這是個考驗而神正在測試你的忠誠度。

vi) 僕人保持低調

他們不宣傳自己或把注意力放在自己身上。自我宣傳和僕人性格不要混爲一談。真正的僕人不會爲了得到他人的認同或掌聲而服事。他們活著唯一的觀眾是一大有能力的神。

當你的服事不被注意，或被視爲理所當然，不要沮喪一繼續服事神。

聽聽這個故事一獻身於服事的意思是，盡你的全心，而且是一顆僕人的心。

> 有一位偉大又有智慧的人，對他的工人說：「你到鄉下爲我建一棟房子。所有關於一切企劃和建築工程的事都由你來做決定，但記住，你完工後，我會爲了我一個非常特殊的朋友前來接收。」

> 因此這名工人帶著輕率的心離開，來到他的工地。那兒有一大堆各種建材，但那工人有他自己的想法。「當然」他想，「我很內行，我可以用劣質的建材，神不知鬼不覺的偷工減料一番，完工後看起來還是完好的。只有我才會知道我建造的缺陷。」

> 因此，最後工程完畢，工人向那偉大有智慧的人報告。「很好」，他說：「記得嗎?我要你用最好的建材和最巧妙的手藝來建造這房屋，因爲我之前說過，我想要把它當做禮物。我的朋友，你就是那位，我專爲你建造這房子的那人。它完全屬於你。」

神要我們的全都是最好的。

獻身於敬拜的意思是降服。
獻身於事奉的意思是僕人心。

2. 獻身於宣教—你和非信徒

「所以，你們要去，使萬民作我的門徒，奉父、子、聖靈的名給他們施洗。」(馬太福音28:19)

我們必須圖謀大事!不只是地方性,而是國際性。我們必須是有宣教胸懷的教會。

想到他人而不只是自我中心。
想到全球而不只是本地。
想到以創意的方式去完成大使命,和轉換藉口的想法:

例如,「我只說英語。」—可能要學英語,或本地方言。你得學習另一種語言。

「我沒有任何東西可以奉獻。」—有的,你有一我們都有能力和才幹。

「我太老。」 或「我太年輕。」—胡說! 我有一位許多年前到台灣當宣教士的朋友,她四十多歲時嫁給一位五十多歲的英國人—他隨她回到台灣住了二十年,也學會了流利的華語。

獻身於宣教(傳福音)—是的,我們要為它付上代價—是的,那是苦差事—但完成大使命是我們生命中最偉大和最滿足的事。

耶穌說「去 」—首先進去你的家人和朋友中間,你的社區、你的國家、然後世界各地。但並不是我們每一個人都要到海外去—神會在你所在的地方使用你,只要你願讓祂作。

十名小基督徒

十名小基督徒無時無刻常來教會;
一名與傳道人鬧翻離開,剩下九名

九名小基督徒夜貓子熬夜;
一名在星期天睡過頭,剩下八名。

八名小基督徒行走天路;
一名選擇走低路,剩下七名。

七名小基督徒,唱歌像雞叫;
一名不喜歡這樣唱,剩下六名。

六名小基督徒似乎生氣勃勃；
一個渡假去，剩下五名，

五名小基督徒來到天堂岸邊；
一個停下來休息，剩下四名，

四名小基督徒忙碌像蜜蜂；
一名感覺被傷害，剩下三名。

三名小基督徒無法決定做甚麼；
一名無法隨心所欲，剩下兩名

兩個小基督徒各要多一個；
難道你沒看到，二加二等於四。

四名小基督徒早晚工作不休；
每人各帶領一名，現在有八名。

八名小基督徒他們若如前雙倍成長；
只要七星期內，我們就有了一千零二十四名。

這順口溜有個真功課；
我們若不屬於建造的，就成了破壞的一員。

作者不詳

你是否願傳揚或破壞?

結論

讓我們全然獻上，不只是建築物而已乃是我們自己獻給主：

獻身於敬拜－降服
獻身於服事－僕人心態
獻身於宣教－傳揚福音

第十九章

恩膏(上)

撒 <u>母耳記上</u>10：1，16：1，<u>列王紀上</u>1：29，<u>以賽亞書</u>61：4，<u>使徒行傳</u>4：27，10：38。

恩膏深深的根植於舊約裏。

祭司要恩膏列王、祭司、和先知，用油倒滿他們的頭。

那不只是個儀式，乃是一個人爲服事神，自己分別爲聖，並賜予他神聖的能力來完成使命。

高價甜的及苦的香料，與油混合一起，象徵著神的跟隨者，歷經甜與苦的經歷，領受聖靈真實的能力。

那膏油是神聖的，不可以倒在任何不潔淨之人及物上。非給陌生人或任何尚未分別出來服事神的人。若任何人想取代或模仿恩膏(聖油)，他將會從祭司職份和以色列的領導層中被開除。

恩膏給予你神聖的能力(力量)去壓制仇敵。恩膏授能給你操練權柄，建立神的治理。恩膏使你面對挑戰和機會，超越你的才能、訓練、技術、和教育。恩膏分賜給你力量去完成任務。

恩膏的希伯來字：

Balal─意思是膏油滿流。
Dasher─意思是被餵養。─象徵的健康的，滿足的。

yistar—油的一個名詞用來產生光(光照，啓示)或恩膏爲奴的眼睛。
mimshach—意思是去應用或用油擦，特別是醫藥的塗抹(治療特性)。
masah—意思是倒灌油或塗抹油。
aleipho—字義上是在身體上塗油。
Chrisma—比喻爲油本身和分賜的塗抹。
Greek word chrio—意思是特別的約定去安置分別出來一個人。

恩膏是，聖靈的能力和影響，使人充滿、並浸泡其中。恩膏使服事更有效。

膏油的特質是什麼?

1. 它柔軟。
2. 治療瘀傷等。
3. 太陽下不會乾燥。
4. 它可復元更新。
5. 芬香。
6. 用作光(啓示、引導)。
7. 潤滑(有果效)。
8. 具商業價值、且比水輕(浮起)；浮水面上。

路加福音 3：21 及 4：1，14，18 是耶穌恩膏以及服事基礎和根基的一個記錄。(使徒行傳2：39)

恩膏的十個要點及觀點—路加福音 3：21、22

1. 順服/ 悔改/耶穌降服於父神的旨意。
2. 謙卑
3. 純潔/分別/聖潔
4. 降服治死老我
5. 禱告生活
6. 公義
7. 父神的肯定/同意
8. 信/愛
9. 打開天
10. 經歷考驗/預備 (曠野經歷)

耶穌的受洗是位低的替位高的施洗，約翰有一耶穌的啓示，而且約翰的施洗是一個悔改的洗。

鴿子象徵聖靈 (約翰福音 1：32，33)
鴿子言及三件事：
1. 純潔/柔順/溫和
2. 恩典/愛
3. 專注－信 (信實)

耶穌分享祂的順從，藉透過道成肉身以及緘默的二十年，順服於祂地上的父母，等待顯明祂自己的時機。耶穌活躍的服事始於加利利。祂的試探發生在靠近約旦河處。仇敵企圖要基督服事萌芽期出差錯。

曠野的經歷或考驗，總是帶來新鮮的恩膏。

當你經過試探/試煉、或考驗，從神來的新的恩膏將臨到我們的生活和服事。考驗和試探臨到最聖潔的聖人。(哥林多前書10：13)。

我們談的是什麼樣的能力？　是智力、社交、政治、經濟或是靠著神聖的能力/恩賜，藉著膏抹的運作使我們的身心強壯/有活力，去贏得靈魂及 行神蹟(悔罪，改變)。那是神的智慧、泉源、力量與大能的得勝、豐富、豐盛的恩賜(禮物)。例如，路加福音1：7及 路加福音1：41。這恩膏不是一時的情緒，不是任性的衝動，也不是興奮，而是用一個安靜、持續、穩固的確信或膏抹，形成了耶穌的性格，反射在器皿上，不僅僅是才幹、或自然能力、宗教知識(清楚)、訓練、或個人情緒(個性，魅力)等等。

靈恩並沒給予任何人勝過撒旦或勝過罪的能力，神蹟的能力和釋放的能力等等。當真的恩膏果真帶來釋放並擴展神的國度，我們看到也不至於沾沾自喜。

恩膏的四項影響與證明

撒母耳記上10：1-7，約翰福音14：12，路加福音16：10，歌羅西書 1： 27。
罪是敵擋恩膏的，約翰一書2：15-17

1. 恢復。
2. 超自然進展—往前。
3. 從神得恩寵—神聖的神爲你安排事情。
4. 身分改變；變化；你不能保持原樣。

驕傲造成以事物或地位去定義一個人的身分。
房屋的大小、學位的高低、職業薪水、經歷、著作多少、教會的大小、都能造成驕傲。自我中心生活、人的喝采、對神和生命的獨立見解均是驕傲的根源。驕傲即敵擋恩膏，以及血氣的工作或倚靠自己多於神。

「小子們哪、如今是末時了。你們曾聽見說，那敵基督的要來，現在已經有好些敵基督的出來了。從此我們就知道如今是末時了。他們從我們中間出去，卻不是屬我們的。若是屬我們的，就必仍舊與我們同在。他們出去、顯明都不是屬我們的。」(約翰一書2：18、19)

約翰一書2：20-26「你們從那聖者受了恩膏、並且知道這一切的事。我寫信給你們、不是因你們不知道真理、正是因你們知道、並且知道沒有虛謊是從真理出來的。誰是說謊話的呢。不是那不認耶穌爲基督的麼。不認父與子的、這就是敵基督的。凡不認子的就沒有父。認子的連父也有了。論到你們、務要將那從起初所聽見的常存在心裏。若將從起初所聽見的存在心裏、你們就必住在子裏面、也必住在父裏面。主所應許我們的就是永生。我將這些話寫給你們、是指著那引誘你們的人說的。」(約翰一書2：20-26)

敵基督，爲什麼?牠是敵擋恩膏、或是假冒、或是反對恩膏。

我們如何知道和辨別牠?
不倚靠神、驕傲的態度、不願倚靠神。諾斯底主義者宣稱有知識至上的啟示。恩膏使我們喜愛真理。真理是單純而不複雜的。

「上帝叫孤獨的有家，使被囚的出來享福，唯有抒逆的住在乾燥之地。」(詩篇68：6)

上帝叫孤獨的有家。使被囚的出來享福，唯有抒逆的住在乾燥之地。神的靈教導信徒，幫助他從錯誤中區分真理。一個人若頑固、叛逆、反動、或不順服神的話語，則不住在且不行在神的恩膏裡。恩膏使人樂意受教、願接受指正、不驕傲，(約翰一書3：16-5：8)。

一個人有恩膏就有火熱、熱誠、熱情、熱心。例如耶穌在<u>以賽亞書</u>59：1
及<u>約翰福音</u>2：17

火熱是強烈的熱情，與冷淡、或血氣、漠不關心、自大、懶散、不情願
犧牲、無負擔、無熱情、不在乎超自然的事，成了對比。(<u>啓示錄</u>3：16)

主的恩膏鼓勵為了神的家、神的事、及神的子民火熱等等：

1. 火熱的愛神的家。(<u>詩篇</u> 28：6 & 132：13-18，<u>哥林多後書</u> 4：7-12 &
    6：1-10，<u>以所弗書</u> 5：25)

2. 火熱的奉獻給神的家。(<u>詩篇</u>4：24， 55：14， 122:1， 12& 127：4，
    <u>以賽亞</u>2：1-4，<u>希伯來書</u>10：25)

3. 火熱的建造而非拆毀神的家。(<u>詩篇</u>127：1，12，<u>箴言</u>4：1 & 24：3，
    <u>哥林多後書</u>11：1-4)

4. 火熱的在神的家中找到滿足。(<u>詩篇</u>36：8， 42：1-2 & 87：7，<u>以西結
    書</u>47：3-6)

5. 火熱的受栽培並根植於神的家。(<u>詩篇</u>1：1-3， 84：10 & 92：10、13，
    <u>以弗所書</u>2：20-22)

6. 火熱的維護神家中的合一。(<u>詩篇</u>133：1-3， <u>使徒行傳</u> 1：14、21， 2
    ：46， 4：32 & 5：12)

負面的想法和說法抹殺了火熱，而且削弱在一個缺乏委身於耶穌基
督的教會，又不倚靠神的靈之下。任何人若不服事或犧牲就不能用基
督的恩膏來膏抹。(<u>馬可福音</u>10：35，<u>腓利比書</u> 2：3)

<u>希臘</u>人教導：
　　要聰明，認識你自己。
<u>羅馬</u>人說道：
　　要強壯，訓練你自己。
享樂主義者說：
　　要放縱，享受你自己。
今日教育說道：
　　要機智，擴展你自己。

心理學說道：
　　要有信心，表現你自己。
唯物主義說道：
　　要滿足，取悅你自己。
人道主義說道：
　　要有能，相信你自己。

但耶穌說：
當一個僕人，奉獻你自己，否定你自己，
不要為自己活，捨棄你的生命：(腓立比書2：21，馬太福音16：24)

十字架談到治死我們自己意志以及選擇神的目的。如果你想行在並住在恩膏裡，你需要重視這些教導。你有多想要神?

一名領袖犧牲他的形像，所以他就能穿戴基督來服事而不是被服事的形像(馬太福音20:28)。他犧牲他的時間、金錢、資源成為神聖資源的接收者。

例如：大衛在撒母耳記下24：24對亞勞拿說，「不然。我必要按著價值向你買，我不肯用白得之物作燔祭，獻給耶和華我的上帝。大衛就用五十舍客勒銀子、買了那禾場與牛。」

神的恩膏住在那些住在基督裡，而且容許服事和犧牲成為他們生活方式的人。神不會恩膏一位自私、自我、罪中的領袖。讓我們來尋求這真正的恩膏。

如何領受聖靈雙倍的恩膏

以利沙的呼召
列王記上 19：19-21以利沙的呼召顯示，當他一離開他富裕的家，(六頭牛是一個富裕的表徵)神的呼召就來臨。

他極其尊敬他的父母(20節)而且他燒掉了一切 (21節)。燒掉一切表示完全離開他舊有的生活。不再回頭，看腓利比書3：13。這是完全的委身。

他願意成為先知的僕人。他能從以利亞學習，跟從他、聽從他、並觀摩。他洗了以利亞十年的手。聖經有一節說，「他倒水在以利亞手上。」(列王記下3：11)。字義上的意思是他是以利亞私人的僕人。

偉大的要點是謙卑和順服。

領受聖靈雙倍恩膏的四個步驟，看列王記下 2：1-14。

1. **吉甲 (約書亞記 5：6-9)**
   約書亞帶領以色列第二代，渡過約旦河來到一地稱吉甲─就是「輥」的意思。他們在此受割禮。吉甲是進入迦南地的起點。

   以利沙和以利亞在吉甲。吉甲代表一個遺忘了的舊生活。這地我們稱之為「在耶穌基督裡，我是個新造的人。」─重生、水裡受洗、聖靈的浸。這是一處我們感覺舒適之地，但還有更多。雙倍恩膏能成為我們的，但我們必須向前邁進。

2. **伯特利(列王記下 2：2，創世記 28：10-22)**
   伯特利意思是神的居所，這是約瑟在創世記28章作異夢後說神在這裡。

   當神同在之地能再次成為如此舒服的地方。所以我們必須作一決定，保持或繼續前進。

   對以利沙而言，伯特利是一決定之地。以利亞對他說，停留在此，等候主差遣我去耶利哥。但以利沙不論如何決定要前往。

3. **耶利哥**
   這是爭戰之地。耶利哥附近就是耶穌面對撒旦四十天試探之處。

   在耶利哥，約書亞遇見主部隊的元帥，告訴他要做什麼以及如何征服這城。

   耶利哥乃是一得勝之地，因也是城牆倒塌之處。

   當我們從過去治死老我之地邁入決定之地，撒但將會壓制我們的呼召、我們的家庭、我們的財務、我們的身體、我們的心思意念，牠將試著來攔阻我們。但記住我們是在爭戰之中，這意味著奇蹟近了。勝利是我們的。城牆將倒塌。但這仍不是得雙倍恩膏之地。

4. 約旦

這是施洗約翰看見聖靈如鴿子降臨在耶穌身上。

在約旦，以利沙開始看見超自然的事(列王記下 2：6-11)， 而且他領受了雙倍恩膏。

讓我們禱告我們的眼睛將打開看見超自然，讓我們定睛在神身上，而不是這世界或人的事。

這些地的每一處都有恩膏，但我們是否願意為雙倍恩膏而付出代價。那意味著要離開舒適之地並治死老我，離開決定之地並作了決定往前去。離開爭戰之地，因我們已得勝且邁入約旦之地，那就是超自然與雙倍恩膏之處。

以利沙當了十三年以利亞的僕人後，他才領受雙倍的恩膏。以利亞行七個神蹟，以利沙行了十四個神蹟。這不是在競爭，而是一種渴望想要更多。渴望更多的恩膏，並前進邁入在神裡那偉大又美好的事。

第二十章

恩膏 (下)

約瑟的恩膏

約瑟是基督的代表。他是一位從受苦和逆境試煉中得勝並興旺的人。他是一位在他生命中有神的目的與預言性命定的人。他是一位擁有一份不尋常恩膏的人。神也想在末日釋放約瑟的恩膏給我們。

約瑟的生命裡有遮蓋。
遮蓋是神賜給你屬靈權柄的程度。

1. **不成熟的遮蓋**
   約瑟是爹地的寶貝/最寵愛的兒子。他有件彩衣。在約瑟的時代從文化上來說，它是權柄的象徵。這恩寵的權柄理應屬於長子流便。但因雅各知道約瑟身上有神恩膏的權柄 所以給了約瑟。

   約瑟話太多，犯了錯(大嘴巴)。創世記37：2告訴我們，當他還是十七歲小童時，因他向他爸爸報告哥哥的惡行而遭兄弟懷恨。但他並沒有從他播放他第一個異夢時學到教訓，又因他的不成熟再度洩露了第二個夢。在此有一重要原則。我們生命中皆有時，當神顯露事情給我們，並不希望我們不成熟的馬上顯露出來，祂會引導直等到曝光的時候來到。舉個例：瑪麗亞—當天使向她顯現，告訴她有關她的使命，她存記在心裡(有智慧)。

   約瑟被丟在坑中(先知訓練期)。

『坑』(PIT)的意思是「先知仍在訓練中」 (Prophet *still* In Training)。

我們生命中的坑,的確是神的訓練場,對我們的成熟度與成長極其重要。

2. **恩寵的遮蓋 (創世記37:36)/人的權柄**

不管我們生活景況如何,我們必須為神的事占滿(忙碌、辛苦工作)。有人發現當神想要完成某些事情,祂通常會尋找忙碌的人。舉例來說,當以利亞找到以利沙時,他和十二頭牛正在耕種。

彼得正忙著捕魚,當耶穌找到他時。
(容許神不時地改變你的計畫,除非祂說不)

我們看到神的恩寵在約瑟生命中(遭難)的結果,約瑟被任命為法老的護衛長或管家。

約瑟的恩膏是神放置於你生命中的一個恩膏,在困難的時候加能力使你興旺有成就。

我們看到法老的房子因著約瑟而被祝福。

約瑟的恩膏引來了撒旦的兩種攻擊:性試探(創世記39章)及逼迫(馬可福音10:30)。

當神把約瑟的恩膏加給你,保證仇敵會攻擊你的生活,造成流產並拖延而否認你的產業。 約瑟的兄弟嘲弄他乃因著恩膏:「作夢的來了!」

3. **尊崇的遮蓋 (創世記 41:40)/神聖的恩寵**

當你有約瑟的恩膏,你將獲得政治的恩寵。
那就是你將在王面前大膽的站立,你將興旺並發預言服事王及王子。

一天之內,約瑟的情況從囚犯轉換成法老身旁的宰相。(宮殿之前是監牢和土坑,這是神提升的方法)。 不管你在那個位置,神能在一天之內提升你到一個位置如屬靈大臣。

約瑟恩膏的幾個特徵：

4. **神的恩寵在他身上。(創世記 39：44)**

5. **約瑟有良好的行政才能(創世記 39：4)，和一預言性的遮蓋。**
   他預言性的事先預見七年的豐年和荒年，如此能為國家的未來有
   充分的準備。他也是一名機敏的生意人，創世記47：13-26。末日福
   音的傳揚需要上百萬人去收割，而我們須要去準備。

6. **約瑟作大異夢**
   神的夢總是比我們的大，而且我們不能單靠我們自己的力量去做
   或完成，所以神獨得所有的榮耀。

7. **約瑟有能力/堅忍的性向**
   Woodrow Wilson 的名言：「絕不，絕不放棄」。不論如何受苦約瑟
   仍堅忍著。這夢花了十七年才完成(「十七」在聖經中代表勝利的
   數字)，你命定要得勝不被打敗，但約瑟也因他的不成熟，他的
   勝利仍舊是在他的血氣中。十五年之後他的年齡已屆三十二，約
   瑟與他爸爸團圓。(「十五」在聖經中代表休息的數字)，其它的信
   心也被開展過。在他與爸爸團聚前他被苦待過。當我們為某個目
   的受苦，我們的受苦就變得有意義。 (創世記 45：5)不論此刻你
   正經歷什麼，要了解神在你生命中的目的。那麼它就可以幫助你
   忍耐你目前的經歷。目的是終點，也是創造了另一起點。如果我
   們是預言性的一群人，我們應有先見之明作好足夠的準備， 所
   以當不預期的情況發生，我們可以有信心地存活，因我們內心清
   楚的知道神有特定的目的。

8. **約瑟有謙卑**
   當他還是年輕小男孩，他是自大傲慢的。但當他站立在法老面前，
   他的謙卑則是顯而易見的。約瑟謙卑的告訴法老，「我不能解夢，
   但神會給你解答。」我們看到他在主裡信心的倚靠與成熟。 (創
   世記 37：5-9， 41：16)他在自己受苦中仍然去服事酒政與膳長，即
   使他本身也沒得什麼好處，尚且他自身也仍處於極大的需要。

   神正尋找像約瑟的人，雖然他們本身經歷困難。舉個例，那寡婦
   只剩一瓶油和餅，仍然能服事他人。這樣的人終將獲得突破。

9. **約瑟有個燃燒的願望去供應他的兄弟和家人。**
神使用約瑟最終乃爲整個國家而預備。(創世記50：20)撒旦原爲惡，但神將牠轉爲善。有約瑟恩膏的人將締造成功的商機，並足以供應他人。

10. **約瑟有一顆偉大的心去饒恕人。 每當饒恕發生，供應就能釋放。爲什麼約瑟能原諒他的兄弟，即使他們的行爲如此的醜陋?**

   答案伏筆在他爲兩個兒子取的名：
   「瑪拉西」的意思是「主使我忘了。」
   「以法蓮」的意思是「主回報了。」

   約瑟與主往前走，且在生命中拒絕回頭看他過去的經歷、悲劇、自憐、自責、失望、憤怒、傷害、怨恨、忌妒、猜忌。

   如果我們內心深藏積怨，祝福的通道就被阻斷；但當你饒恕，你就將在你生命中經歷神蹟。

   有約瑟恩膏的人們，表面上大都容易被誤解並引起他人的忌妒和猜忌。但我們自己必須作決定繼續釋放饒恕和謙卑，(彼得前書5：6)。

   神想要在祂的教會中有這些約瑟恩膏的七大特徵(箴言13：22)。

第二十一章

讚美的衣裳

在舊約時代，人們並不直接接近神。祭司扮演神與人中間的媒介角色。

因著耶穌在十字架上的得勝，形態因此改變。現在我們得以毫無懼怕的直接進入神的同在(希伯來書4：16)，而且我們被賦予責任來帶領他人到祂面前。(哥林多後書5：18-21)。

所以我們一旦重生，我們就在基督裡。而根據彼得前書2：1-10，我們是蒙神揀選的，而且是寶貴的。

所以像舊約的祭司，我們須要穿上我們服事的聖衣去接觸他人。出埃及記39：1說，「...用藍色、紫色、朱紅色線、作精緻的衣服、在聖所用以供職。」每一種顏色各有一個意義，而且代表我們在服事中所應有的什麼樣的特徵。

這服事不只是這使徒、先知、傳福音的、牧師和教師五重職事，而且還有平信徒的服事(職場的人/教會中非全職者)。你們全都有一個為耶穌去接觸失喪者的服事。我們都有責任作見證為耶穌贏得他人。

我們來瞧一瞧這三種顏色—藍色、紫色、和朱紅色，並看一看我們能學到什麼。

藍色

藍色是天空的顏色，且代表天。藍色也言及某人有屬天的心志。

我們從我們主耶穌基督的生命看到了美麗的藍色。祂不只本源於天，而且祂的真性情及樣式 也是屬天的。

藍色言及屬天的心志。
假若我們有屬天的心志，它將影響我們的思想、態度、言談、和行動。

耶穌有有屬天的心志，祂總是敏銳於父神的聲音及父神的道。

「子憑著自己不能作什麼，唯有看見父所作的，子才能作；父所作的，子也能照樣作。」(約翰福音5：19)

「祂說，我憑著自己不能作什麼。我怎麼聽見、就怎麼審判。我的審判也是公平的。因為我不求自己的意思、只求那差我來者的意思。」(約翰福音5：30)「 . . . 我所講的話、正是照著父對我所說的。」(約翰福音12：50)

我們在耶穌基督裡，而且因為我們與祂的認同 ，我們必須尊榮祂，並活出祂要我們活出的樣式。

為了如此行，我們必須常常問我們自己兩個問題，來幫助我們擁有屬天的心志：
耶穌會怎麼做?
耶穌要我怎麼做?

當我們問這些問題，它們將影響我們的想法、態度、言談、和行動。我以前已談過聖靈洗的經歷，不只是讓人感覺良好，還對每個人宣稱人人都能說方言。聖靈也期待我們活出或行在祂的路上，而不在肉體裡，那是指血氣之路。例如，怨恨、自滿、憤恨猜忌、暴怒、自我野心、忌妒等等。

以屬天的心志來服事他人，意思是我們若要有果效，首先要對付我們自我的的生命。這得要從我們的思想和態度開始。

我們許多人說生命是不公平的。我們常問：「為什麼這些事發生在我身上?」 然而生命的百分之十是：「我發生了什麼事?」，而卻有百分之九十是在於 「我對它如何反應?」。 我們的態度決定我們所看到的，以及我們如何處理我們的感覺。這兩個因素大大的決定了我們生命中的成功與否。

Norman Vincent Peale在他的書 *"Power of the Plus Factor"* 中敘述這故事：

有一次我在香港九龍，穿梭過一條彎曲的小街巷，來到一間刺青工作室。櫥窗裡展示現成的刺青樣本。你可以在臂上或胸前刺上錨、或旗、或美人魚、或什麼都可。但讓我當頭棒喝的是『生來失喪』(*Born to lose*) 四個字竟能刺青在一個人的身體上。我極訝異地進了這店，指著這些字，問這位中國的刺青藝術家：「真有人會把這句『生來失喪』這麼可怕的字眼，要求刺青在他的身上嗎? 他答道：「是的，有時候。」只要我們的心思意念以負面的想法來「刺青」，我們長期成功的機會就會消失。我們無法繼續運作在一種我們無法真正相信我們自己的態度。我常看到人們因錯誤的想法而自暴自棄，毀了自己。

憎恨和憤怒負面的想法／思想，並非屬天的心思意念思想，而且它們會從我們的言談及行動中流露出來。

耶穌的性情與祂的行事也是屬天的。(加拉太書5：22、23)。

在服事他人中，不論見證、協談、或探訪，我們都必須去學習仁愛、喜樂、和平、忍耐、恩慈、良慈、信實、溫柔、和節制。

耶穌從不論斷。我們可從祂在井邊遇見那婦人、與馬利亞和馬大的例子。他總是在愛裡服事—愛並非是漫不經心的或是柔弱的，而能在堅定中去做且不傷害他人的。

如何擁有屬天的心志?

首先認同你有問題的思想、感覺、行為，然後悔改。

別一直斷定你自己是對的，而其他每一個人都是錯的。與神和好，而且如果有需要也與他人和好。

羅馬書12：2 告訴我們要「心意更新而變化。」每日在禱告中用話語更新你的心思意念。

希臘字「更新」意思是修理恢復。例如：整修房屋你必須拿走所有全部舊的家具，放進全新的家具。假若那舊的家具沒有完全挪走而有白蟻，最後連新的家具也被蛀毀了。

所以它應隨著我們的思想生活一拿掉我們老舊的、肉體的、屬世的思想方式，有如自私、性思想或負面的思想而代之以正確的、清潔的、和正面的想法。

「少年人用什麼潔淨他的行為呢，是要遵行你的你話。」
「我將你的話藏在心裡，免得我得罪你。」(詩篇 119：9、11)

「你們若真與基督一同復活，就當求在上面的事。那裏有基督坐在上帝的右邊。你們要思念上面的事、不要思念地上的事。」(歌羅西書 3：1、2)

「當求在上面的事，要思念上面的事。」一雙重強調的意思就是神試著要得到我們的注意。這是每日的操練與訓練。

成為行道的人，不單是聽道的人。

朱紅色

它言及犧牲。在聖經時代，朱紅色源自一種東方的蟲會群襲某種樹。把它們收集起來、壓碎、乾燥、磨粉製造成亮麗鮮紅色顏料。

耶穌是我們的犧牲

為了離開天上來到地上，他的犧牲很大。神的兒子成為人的兒子。因此我們在服事中必須為別人犧牲自己。為什麼呢? 那是因耶穌是如此行，而且祂是我們服事他人的典範。

亞當和夏娃的故事顯明自我意識、自我關心、和自私的根源；強調我、是我、我的、我自己，(創世記3：9-10)。

當神更深入探討，亞當與夏娃變得更防衛，他們彼此互擲矛頭控訴，接著指向神。

「這女人 ...！」
「你給我的這女人 ...！」

「這蛇 . . . 」

這模式並沒改變，有嗎?因爲這源頭的一幕下傳歷經了數世紀，人性的歷史被這自私的醜惡記號抹黑。

如何活出爲他人犧牲的生活?

1. **爲自私悔改。**

2. **與世界分別。**
「凡事不可結黨、不可貪圖虛浮的榮耀。只要存心謙卑、各人看別人比自己強。個人不要單顧自己的事，也要顧別人的事。你們當以基督耶穌的心爲心。」(腓利比書2:3-5)

這世界的態度是完全不同:

快樂是推銷者，因他們在世界發跡出頭天。

快樂是不動感情的人，因他們從不讓生活傷害他們。

快樂是過度享樂的人，因他們從不爲他們的罪憂傷。

快樂是嚴厲的主人，因他們一切爲得果效。

快樂是世界的聰明人，因他們精通要領。

快樂是惹麻煩的人，因他們要人們禮遇他們。

3. **穿上服事的衣裳與犧牲的衣裳。**
爲服事他人，必須穿上服事的衣裳和犧牲的衣裳。
我們要成爲給予者，而非接收者。
我們要成爲饒恕者，而非積怨者。
要成爲僕人，而非超級巨星。

紫色

它來自藍色與紅色的混合。它是皇家的顏色。

我們的王權是在耶穌基督裡。

耶穌是萬王之王、萬主之主。是的，耶穌是人的兒子。是的，祂順服於父神且有屬天的心。是的，祂活出犧牲的生命。但是，祂知道祂是誰。我們知道我們在耶穌基督裡是誰嗎?我們是否行走在那權柄下，或是游走於挫敗的生命?

祂是一位得勝者，所以我們也都是得勝者。祂活出得勝的生命，所以我們也能活出得勝的生命。祂有權柄，所以我們能活出有權柄的生命。耶穌是我們生命中的王嗎?

服事他人時我們須要穿上王者的衣裳和權柄的衣裳。

耶穌說話帶有權柄。例如，祂平定風暴，甚至 風與浪也聽從了祂。耶穌行動帶有權柄 ，在那地有許多神蹟可見。祂教導帶有權柄—甚至當他十二歲時，聖殿裡的人們也驚訝他竟懂這麼多。

這全與話語有關—「生死在舌頭得權下。」(箴言 18：21)

耶穌為何有如此的權柄?

你可能說祂是神的兒子。但記住，祂捨棄祂的神聖成為人的兒子，他是完全的人類就像你與我。

你可能說祂是神的兒子。但記住，他放棄祂的神性成為人的兒子，祂完全是人如你和我。

藍和紅產生紫—祂屬天的心志與樣式混合著犧牲，或因祂是受苦的僕人使祂能活出權炳。

當我們照樣作—我們的想法、態度、言談、和行動帶有屬天的心志，加上活出為他人犧牲的僕人樣式，我們將能有像耶穌這樣的權柄，來統管治理神的國度，而神蹟奇事亦將從我們的生命中流露出來，當我們:

說話帶有權柄
行動帶有權柄
教導帶有權柄

朋友們，這對所有的信徒皆可行，因你是君尊的祭司，所以靠神賜給你的權柄起來，起來成為得勝者而非受害者。

服事的衣裳屬於你

藍—屬天的心志
紅—犧牲的僕人樣式
紫—生活中的權柄

它是屬於你的，但你卻不曾有，只因你不求。

有一個人，買了一張船票上船去旅遊。旅途中他每晚只是吃他自己帶來的食物，而別人卻每餐在餐廳裡享用了五道菜。有人問他為什麼他不願加入他們，他回答說：「我沒有錢所以我自帶食物來。」，那人說：「難道你不知道這些餐飲費全包括在你的船票錢內?」他吃了那次好的。

我們許多基督徒並未認清這些服事的衣裳是針對所有人的—它全包括在你的救恩票中，宣告什麼是你所有的。

但總要記住，在謙卑裡服事與行動，則所有的權柄都屬於你。

第二十二章

爲教會超自然的授能

我們來思考爲教會超自然賦能的聖經基礎。

教會增長對某些人來說似乎是一個嗡嗡慌忙的字眼，就是那些企圖找出教會如何成長，以及甚麼是最新進的方法、節目、計劃、策略，或者一些可以用來教導使教會成長的新方法的人。

難道我們忘記在我們追求和獻身之際，耶穌承諾祂是唯一建造教會的那一位？那麼我們就不須本末倒置的以方法、模式、和市場策略取而代之，換言之，這樣反倒失去了最重要的因素。

神超自然的授能已經被沒有神聖超自然膏抹的節目所取代。我們必須設立正確的基礎，那就是，我們必須先建造教會的特性。如果我們先依靠方法使我們教會成長，我們就冒險製造了一個教會成長方法的偶像，並且擺明了了這樣我們就能夠成長。

在某些場合，教會成長已墮落到我們只能軟弱得企圖以機械性的方法，去執行神要以超自然的方式，並僅透過神聖的授能、或能量、和力量去做的原意。

肉體的罪，莫大於我們以人爲的努力，透過人爲的能力去做超自然的工作。

如果只有節目和方案是唯一的答案可以產生成長，那我們就寧願依賴它們，並且自我滿足的往前走，而不願全然的依賴和信靠超自然的全能神—就是那一位如我們在聖經裡所看到的；唯獨祂能造成成長。許多次我們看到人們試著要幫神做祂的工，然而人的努力與肉體的工作並非神聖授能的替代品。

我們有亞伯拉罕的例子，就如在創世記15-16 章所見，他找尋憑血氣的方法，藉著收養他的僕人，和透過撒拉的使女夏里生子產生後代，來幫助神完成超自然的承諾。我們看到企圖去幫助神完成承諾，寧願透過血氣的人為努力與方法、策略和計畫、而捨棄神聖的授能，其悲慘的後果是可預期的。在大衛王的生命中我們也看到如此，在那兒有兩個場合以色列人被數點。

第一個例子記錄在民數記第一章，這普查是在神直接的指令下為了照顧和保護人們。然而，在第二個例子，這計畫乃是大衛的主意，源發自他的驕傲和欲望，或計劃以展示以色列的軍隊 (歷代志上12章)。這第二個行動數點以色列被神責難，因神想要以色列記住只有唯獨祂為勝利負責，而不是一個計畫、人、節目或人為的工作。

教會成長應來自聖靈超自然的工作，而榮耀總歸於基督，而不是人；不管他是主教或牧師，更不是方法，唯是神祂自己。

為什麼教會成長的方法與模式，雖然對某些教會成功，然而對大多數的教會卻無效？

我相信我們把次要主題變為主要。我們必須聚焦在超自然的授權。事實上方法與模式有某些限制的，我願意提出教會似乎忽略的五件事。(摘錄自Hemphill)

1. **我們必須了解不同的背景。**
   我們不能轉換背景。在西海岸所做的，與農村或城市少有關聯。當我們去找尋轉換一個外表看來是成功的模式，而不去查看背景，它將證實會有高度的失敗。

2. **你不能轉移恩賜和個性。**
   對一個領袖有效的，對你不見得會做得好。這並不意味著你恩賜較少，而只是表明你是不一樣的。如果你打算模仿領袖樣式，就像有些人模仿貓王艾維斯，你可以一兩首歌娛樂一下，但很難有艾維斯真正的味道出現。

3. **你不能轉換靈性。**

   只有神能做而且得花時間，因品格發展和靈性包涵成長。

   只企圖去模仿某一事工模式或一節目，會很輕易的忽略更重要的屬靈性格和屬靈授能的主題。這是神對你神聖的承諾和教會的屬靈發展。

   屬靈的發展或成熟，是每次與神的相遇，必須個人或會眾他們自己去發展和經歷來的。它不是透過方法或節目，而是來自神的一個神聖觸摸。

4. **你不能轉換一個有多樣恩賜的獨特堂會。**

   不只是我們找尋仿效的教會牧師是獨特的，而教會堂會也是獨特的。每一牧師必須發現他特定教會的獨特恩賜。

   啟示錄有七個教會。每一教會領受從神而來為這特定教會的神聖承諾、神聖授權、和神聖的呼召。

5. **我們不能轉換時間和成熟的程度。**

   我們必須認清的是，典範教會在殷勤找尋以及節目發展上歷經了許多年，為的是它要興起我們今日所看到的有效事工。若你想要隔夜就可複製成功，那完全是自以為是，而且也是極其愚蠢的想法。

屬靈的授能是與神相遇及超自然的事件。

我們必須小心，不要假設我們無須超自然能力就能使一間教會成長。我並沒建議，我們不需要研究學習教會成長有效的模式，或有效的宣教策略。神不是一位混亂的神。祂通常選擇透過結構和組織，但我說的是教會成長是超自然事件，以及與神超自然的相遇。第一優先是發展與神更深的關係。教會成長並不是我們靠人力所作的一些事，卻是與神有正確的關係的副產品，而教會的頭就是基督。當教會深深愛慕基督，它就進入神的大能中。而且因著這深深的愛的關係，自動自發的、自然而然的、興起這份熱情和意願去贏得失喪者，服事他人並且親切的分享。然而，任何時候我們尋求教會成長的方法勉強加在人們身上，我們將認清結果是屬血氣的。

許多牧師當他們從屬靈成長特會或退修會回來非常的興奮,而通常要面對不預期的敵意或直接的反對。

爲領受屬靈的授能付代價

我們愛甚麼超過一切?
(約翰 福音21:15-19)

如果我們不管如何,想看到成長成爲超自然的授能,我們願意付代價去改變嗎?

每一成長的教會,有一神聖的異象、神聖的授能,而且當神指示並進一步引導他們時,願意去改變。 要談論教會的成長,而不先考慮到教會的創始者耶穌所說的話,那是很奇怪的事。

在馬太福音第十六章中,我們被導引入這重要性的時刻,進入主的服事。如果我們看上下 文,你將看到耶穌已經在擴展他的使命,其間有許多神蹟發生。有關祂的身分被置疑。法利賽人接近耶穌,要考驗祂並找尋天上的徵兆。

門徒們自己在這時候仍掙扎著相信耶穌能滿足他們的需要。(馬太福音16:5-12)在這時候他們屬靈的發展並沒有留下令人深刻的印象。耶穌曾問過祂的門徒有關目前對祂身分的推測。有人說是施洗約翰;有人說是以利亞;又有人說是耶利米,或是先知裡的一位。彼得,一向是這十二人的發言人,領受了神聖的啓示,分賜了授能,當他說:「你是基督、是永生神的兒子。」 (馬太福音16:16) 。這很容易習以爲常認爲彼得只不過發聲而已,而漠不關心彼得所宣告的重要本質。

這宣告對許多人似乎是褻瀆的。當彼得說,「你是基督—彌賽亞,給世界帶來救贖的、是恩膏的、是永生神的兒子。」,他到底說了什麼? 基督,意思是超自然的賦能者,是神所膏抹的 要藉著恩膏去建立教會。假如我們真的相信,教會將超自然的授能、被恩膏,那麼我們對教會特質的想法,必須永遠被超自然的授能所掌控。短短的幾年後,一些人真正地爲這宣告而死。這不是一個人的宣告或觀點,而是耶穌,創建者的教導,就是教會應以神超自然的授能以及恩膏來建造成長。耶穌誇讚彼得領受神聖的啓示。耶穌說他要建立教會在這啓示上。彼得使徒性的宣告就是,耶穌是基督,是建造教會的盤石,而地獄之門不能勝過他。 真實的教會成長是一個蒙應允的神聖活動,來自教會與基督有正確的關係(神聖的授能與恩膏)。

所有教會成長的第一步是超自然的授能。活在聖潔和順服是我們的特權,如此我們乃是器皿,祂的能力流至正確認識建造的教會。它的特質將增加真正教會的成長。教會成長是同時有超自然和自然。神設計教會要成長。祂渴望它成長並且祂授能去成長。因這非常的理由,教會成長是自然的。它是超自然的,因為只有神使它成長,而非方法。所以,當我們看到真正的教會成長,祂就得到榮耀。因著祂的恩典,我們有特權在這些活動中與祂一同參與。人不能發動真正的成長;它是神掌權的活動。

我們現在要思考使徒行傳的一個例子,我們試著去發現安提阿教會領受的超自然授能。在使徒行傳11:21告訴我們主的手與他們同在。這句話清楚的指出領受超自然的授能,結果是大數量的人信而歸主。整本聖經經文中提到,無論何時只要神的手在誰的身上,誰的活動就會成功;而當主挪開祂的手或移開祂的手在其他人身上,則結果會是很悲慘的。舉個例,如掃羅王。當神挪開祂的手和恩膏及賦能,結果災難馬上臨到他和以色列。我們必須問的問題是神的手是否在我們的教會與服事上?甚麼證據引導我們作這結論?
沒有主超自然的授能,除了從人的好主意產生出來的血氣工作外,則一事無成。知道這些是很有趣的,就是安提阿教會是由因遭逼迫而四散的平信徒所建立,(使徒行傳第八章)。沒有主教、牧師、和使徒在他們中間。

他們(平信徒)被拔根逐出他們的家鄉開始講道;而神超自然授能臨到,克服了它們的軟弱,因他們在對的順服裡,和他們的頭(神)有了正確的關係。安提阿教會是由平信徒建立;他們第一優先是行在順服神中 (基督膏抹了神聖的授能)。從順服當中,興起了教會,見證和拯救失喪者的熱情。

現在讓我們看使徒行傳11:23第二個有意義的句子。聖經說當巴拿巴看見神所賜的恩。我們知道我們能經歷神的恩典,但如何看見它?巴拿巴看見了神恩典的怎樣的證據來使得他信服?

「恩典」這字有若干意義。在希臘文,「恩典」這字意思是超自然的賦能和有能力。當我們讀此經文,有些事馬上湧現心中。

<u>巴拿巴</u>看見**許多**人歸服了主。神的神聖超自然能力在教會成長中造成數字的增加。

<u>使徒行傳</u>13：1-3，他看到獻身於虔誠的**禱告**和**禁食**。當神的子民真正與祂相遇，他們透過禱告和禁食，發展出一個飢渴想與神有密切和規律的交通。每一教會經歷了超自然授能，就是一個已發展出有了親密胃口喜愛禱告和禁食的教會。

<u>巴拿巴</u>見證了**犧牲和自動自發的奉獻**。 一間教會的擴張、成長或增長乃根據它的慷慨。使徒行傳11：27-30，我們看到<u>安提阿</u>教會立即回應了使徒<u>亞迦布</u>有關將影響<u>猶太</u>地大饑荒的消息。 他們就定意照個人的力量，慷慨大方捐錢不受限的人。

神恩典最明顯可見的見證，就是在<u>安提阿</u>教會成立的，介於<u>猶太</u>人和外邦人之間的**契團**，(<u>加拉太</u>2：11-12)。這可能對我們沒甚重大的印象，但在猶太人和外邦人間很少聽到。他們之間有許多阻礙分隔他們，不只文化上、種族上或傳統上、還有他們的信仰。很明顯的從經文的推論，他們一起領聖餐。這意味在猶太人和外邦人之間的隔閡，在神恩典裡的那一刻即已消失。

<u>巴拿巴</u>看見**神**的**恩典**在<u>安提阿</u>教會，因它有世界的異象和使命。<u>安提阿</u>教會是一間無牆的教會。它的傳揚超越邊界，並支持全球宣教使命。<u>保羅</u>就是在<u>安提阿</u>教會開始他的宣教。它是一間不往內看而向外發展異象的教會。他們相信一位很大的神，又對全球異象懷抱一顆很大的心。

你將看到關係的醫治、愛、合一、分享、喜樂、和平、和超自然國度生活、或共存。神的恩典融化了所有的驕傲和競爭。 我們應看看就像在<u>安提阿</u>的教會神恩典的證明。如果宇宙的神與人們同住，則在我們生活中應有恩典的顯明與果實。如果我們在我們的家、教會、家人和與他人的關係關係上沒看到此，我們須要問為什麼沒有，還有我們是否被主環繞，又神聖的授能是否來自祂的恩典？

現在我們最後在這經節裡做個結論，成為一間超自然授能的教會的意義何在？找到<u>使徒行傳</u>11：26來看，說道門徒是在<u>安提阿</u>首度被稱為基督徒。基督徒這字在<u>安提阿</u>這裡第一次被提到，雖然它是一些世俗社區用來罵門徒的一個字眼；「基督徒」實際的意義是「小基督」或「效法基督」。

我禱告這世俗的世界和我們的朋友控告我們就像基督。祂是建造教會，授能教會的這一位，而且祂說你的教會得以成長，乃因神祂自己應許了它，以及祂渴望他的子民因此而成長。

依據馬太福音第十六章，一次與復活的主超自然的相遇(啓示、授能、恩典)必須先於方法論的實施。當我們有恩典與超自然的授能，我們將被聖潔的神喚醒。祂的恩膏將帶領我們進入深深的悔改，與人類罪惡的覺醒；使我們有熱情去向失喪者作見證，並活得像耶穌。

有五件事發生就如同它發生在安提阿，成了我們生命中屬靈覺醒的一憑證：

1. 一個想要認真的禱告和禁食的新渴望

2. 一份更新的熱情去贏得失喪者。沒有渴望神的的心我們無法遇見聖潔的神。

3. 如果我們經歷神的恩典，它將產生關係間的醫治。

4. 當教會經歷神的恩典，它將創造出一種自動自發的奉獻和犧牲態度與氛圍，這些對所有教會的成長是很重要的。

5. 當教會經歷神的恩典，它將帶領發展神的神聖策略或方法，到全世界去完成大使命，以及派遣宣教士的全球宣教。

    你要明白我並不反對方法，但如果我們企圖介紹方法給一未預備好的教會，或一尚未復興的教會(未發展特性)，你將面臨肉體世俗的混亂。教會發展是超自然的。禱告是所有教會真正成長的鑰點，和一個教會神聖的授能。如果我們想要看到我們教會成長，影響我們的社會，你和我必須謙卑我們自己，成爲一位禁食禱告者，深深的愛慕耶穌，如此祂能力可以膏抹我們，使我們能經歷祂的恩典。(哥林多後書7:14)

教會改變或發展的三層次：

1. 小改變

2. **主要的改變**

    人們發展一個新的觀點，並以新的方法行動。新來者被當尊貴的客人對待，而不只是過渡訪客；專注於外來的失喪者，而非只往內看。

6. **轉換性的改變**

    在一群會眾的生活中均有時機，當唯一的開口來臨，要容許轉換性的改變發生(加拉太書6：10)。我們必須抓住它，不然若我們沒行動，它就可能擦身而過。

五種改變的機會：

1. **危機的時機**

    這是某些事必須完成的時刻。危機擴大一個堂會改變的開口。

2. **牧者改變的時機**

    這是一位新的牧師提出教會未來問題的時刻。它對有目的的異象、使命和目標的教會打開門。

3. **預備預算的時機**

    我們再度思考優先次序和方向。

4. **復興的時機**

    這是更新的特別時刻，新的機會和新的宣教接觸之門打開。

5. **計畫的時機**

    為將來長程計劃的發展。它也是更新與展望一個更好未來的時刻。我們教會的目的是榮耀神，藉著接觸失喪者、訓練和建立人們。(福音化、同質化和成熟化)。

轉換過程的七步驟：

1. 生命中的機會和可教導的時刻。
2. 教會更美好的未來展望。
3. 異象與目的一一個教會的存在乃基於聖經的理由。
4. 異象的擁有和如何實現異象—短程、中程和 長程。
5. 在看法上更換標準。
6. 動員。

7. 改變的開始—評估結果。

仇敵利用的五件事造成道德的低落：

1. 當領導者遭失敗，領導者乃爲失敗設立教會。
2. 我們因有負面的思想不去慶祝勝利而犯下錯誤。
3. 領導者因誤解失去對會眾的信任。
4. 以低道德的偏差決定來操縱教會。
5. 諾言不能實現。

自尊的十項正面表徵：

1. 會友向他人談論他們教會的好處。
2. 會友想要他人去經歷他們所經歷的。
3. 會友主動活躍參與。
4. 會友瞻望未來，不看過去。
5. 會友願意去冒險。
6. 會友以維護器材引以爲傲。
7. 會友顧及每一人都是特別的。
8. 會友經常肯定他們的領導者，反之領導者亦如是。
9. 會友有高水準追求卓越。
10. 會友對未來有異象，敢憑信心邁出。